the art of JUST SITTING

ESSENTIAL WRITINGS ON
THE ZEN PRACTICE
OF SHIKANTAZA

Edited by

John Daido Loori

with an introduction by
Taigen Dan Leighton

Second Edition

Wisdom

Wisdom Publications
199 Elm Street
Somerville, MA 02144 USA
wisdomexperience.org

Library of Congress Cataloging-in-Publication Data
   The art of just sitting : essential writings on the Zen practice of
shikantaza / edited by John Daido Loori ; with an introduction
by Taigen Dan Leighton.— 2nd ed.
      p. cm.
   Includes index.
   ISBN 0-86171-394-X (pbk. : alk. paper)
   1. Meditation—Sōtōshū. 2. Sōtōshū—Doctrines.
   I. Loori, John Daido. II. Leighton, Taigen Daniel.
   BQ9438.A78 2004
   294.3'4435--dc22

                                        2004002215

ISBN 978-0-86171-394-3   EBOOK ISBN 978-0-86171-949-5

Second Wisdom edition
24 23 22
6   5   4

Cover and interior design by Gopa&Ted2, Inc.
Set in Aldus 10.5/14. Cover photo by John Daido Loori

Wisdom Publications' books are printed on acid-free paper and meet the guidelines for permanence and durability of the Production Guidelines for Book Longevity set by the Council on Library Resources.

Printed in the United States of America.

Please visit fscus.org.

Contents

EDITOR'S PREFACE

Come said the muse,
Sing me a song no poet has yet chanted,
Sing me the universal.

In this broad earth of ours,
Amid the measureless grossness and the slag,
Enclosed and safe within its central heart,
Nestles the seed of perfection.

By every life a share or more or less,
None born but it is born, conceal'd or unconceal'd the seed is.

Walt Whitman

IN THE COLD, DAMP SHELTERS of our primitive ancestors, lit only by the flickering of a campfire, at day's end there was a time for recollection and stillness that would help to fuel the next day's events. Since the beginning of human history, the still point has served as the birthplace of all our activity. Virtually every creature on this great earth practices the backward step of quieting down and entering this still point. Birds, beasts, bugs, and fish all seem to find time in their daily existence to relax and recreate—to bring forth the flower from what Whitman called "the seed of perfection."

For us humans, relaxation is much more elusive, and even though its benefits are widely known, they are rarely appreciated. In the field of science, studies have shown that when the body is relaxed and free of tension, and the mind is not grasping at thoughts, remarkable physiological and psychological transformations take place. During deep relaxation, a person's respiration, heart rate, blood pressure, and rate of metabolism all slow down to a stable resting place. Since 1924, researchers have been able to measure the electrical activity in the brain and have discovered that alpha waves are created when the brain activity is stabilized, as when a person is in a meditative state. Beta waves, on the other hand, are present when a person is engaged in physical or mental activity. Though all this is now common knowledge, particularly interesting and relevant to us are the residual effects of these waves. While monitoring meditators, scientists found that alpha waves produced in meditation often continue on when activity is engaged. The energy to perform the activity is there, but not the tension.

Meditation in a variety of forms has been present worldwide since ancient times. A central spiritual practice for many of the great mystics, meditation has been used for both physical and spiritual restoration and as a potent preparation for strenuous undertakings. The warrior takes a moment to center himself as he gets ready for battle, as does the athlete for competition, or the musician for a performance. Meditation, in one form or another, has been intrinsic to most of the great religions of the world. Some traditions may have developed it more than others, but its presence is widespread and undeniable.

In the Buddhist tradition, meditation has been a core element of practice since the time of Shakyamuni Buddha, two thousand five hundred years ago. Different schools of Buddhism may emphasize other forms of practice, but meditation remains instrumental in all of them for attaining enlightenment. In the Zen school, meditation is the *sine qua non* of Zen practice and realization. The Five Houses of the Zen School during the T'ang Dynasty's Golden Age of Zen all recognized zazen (meditation) as the heart of their practice. In fact, by definition, Zen Buddhism is "meditation Buddhism"—the word *zen* is a derivative of the Chinese word *ch'an,* which in turn is derived from the Sanskrit term *dhyana,* or meditation.

Shikantaza, or "just sitting," is meditation without a goal. It is boundless—a process that is continually unfolding. Even students engaged in koan introspection, upon completion of their koan study, return to shikantaza during zazen. If you have ever wondered what kind of practice old Zen masters are doing, sitting so long and serenely year after year, the answer is: they are just sitting. The spiritual maturation resulting from this kind of practice is as subtle as it is profound. It shapes our spiritual character the way a river shapes the rocks it encounters on its journey to the sea. The resulting form has as much to do with the rock as with the action of the water, and the changes that take place are gradual and almost invisible. There is no definite way to chart this kind of activity. And so it is with sitting and the teachings that deal with it. We are left only with pointers, reminders that keep us moving in the right direction.

Given the importance placed on seated meditation in the Zen tradition, there is a surprisingly scant amount of written work addressing its practice. The volume of ancient and modern Zen literature is staggering, yet works that address meditation are few and far between. Is this because zazen is so simple and direct that all that can be said about it has already been said? Or is it that there is a profundity within the realm of zazen that is essentially ineffable? I am inclined to believe the latter. As Yasutani Roshi points out in his piece in this volume: "Shikantaza should be taught personally and individually by the right teacher." Zen practitioners, as they progress beyond the beginning stages of zazen, encounter a unique landscape that reflects their own personality and individual life experiences. There is no map for this terrain, so an experienced guide is required. Shikantaza, the zazen of "just sitting," is a continuous process of discovery that is aided by face-to-face encounters with an experienced teacher. Yet even teachers are limited in what they can do. Ultimately, the practitioners themselves must write their own rule book. They must go deep within themselves to find the foundations of zazen.

The Art of Just Sitting is an attempt to bring together some of the writings on shikantaza scattered over one thousand five hundred years of Zen history, from the time of its founder Bodhidharma in the fifth century down to the present time. A number of the pieces in this volume have been made previously available in English in a variety of publications, and, along with original material drawn from current teachings, they form a compilation of the best and most relevant of these widespread sources.

This book is inspiration for a sacred journey that, by its very nature, is wide open and limitless. But words can only take you so far. The journey is up to you. Like any practice that is worth doing, shikantaza demands commitment and personal discipline. Eventually, you may require the assistance of an experienced teacher. You will know when that time comes. Trust yourself and the process of zazen to guide you to the right teacher. If your sitting is strong and grounded, a teacher will appear and you will recognize him or her.

Like Whitman's muse, the ancient Zen masters beckon us to explore our own being, to discover the undiscovered, and in so doing, sing the song of the universal. We live at a time of great challenge and uncertainty, *amid the measureless grossness and the slag*. Yet, within each one of us lives a seed of perfection, the buddha nature. Every single one of us has it, *by every life a share or more or less*. And although some may realize the buddha nature and some may not, it is nevertheless present, waiting, as Whitman's poem suggests. It is my hope that the wisdom contained in these pages will awaken the spiritual journey for you, the reader, as it has for so many practitioners who have preceded us. *Enclosed and safe within its central heart* is your heart, your journey, your song. Please take it up, and realize the still point as it bursts into flower as this life itself.

John Daido Loori
Tremper Mountain, New York

Acknowledgments

My GRATITUDE goes to the many people whose generous work made this book possible. Thank you to Konrad Ryushin Marchaj and Vanessa Zuisei Goddard for their help in collecting the pieces included in the book, as well as editing and proofreading the whole manuscript. To Josh Bartok at Wisdom Publications for recognizing the importance and great need for this volume, and for persistently working towards its completion. To Taigen Dan Leighton for his excellent introduction on the practice of shikantaza within the context of Master Hongzhi's and Master Dogen's teachings. To those who provided assistance in the form of copyediting, graphic design, indexing and the like, thank you for your efforts.

Finally, deep bows to Master Dogen for his teachings on shikantaza, to my teacher Hakuyu Taizan Maezumi for making me aware of this profound practice, and to all the teachers who have tirelessly dedicated their lives to the transmission of the genuine dharma.

Introduction: Hongzhi, Dogen, and the Background of Shikantaza

Taigen Dan Leighton

ONE WAY TO CATEGORIZE the meditation practice of shikantaza, or "just sitting," is as an objectless meditation. This is a definition in terms of what it is *not*. One just sits, not concentrating on any particular object of awareness, unlike most traditional meditation practices, Buddhist and non-Buddhist, that involve intent focus on a particular object. Such objects traditionally have included colored disks, candle flames, various aspects of breath, incantations, ambient sound, physical sensations or postures, spiritual figures, mandalas (including geometric arrangements of such figures or of symbols representing them), teaching stories, or key phrases from such stories. Some of these concentration practices are in the background of the shikantaza practice tradition, or have been included with shikantaza in its actual lived experience by practitioners.

But objectless meditation focuses on clear, nonjudgmental, panoramic attention to all of the myriad arising phenomena in the present experience. Such objectless meditation is a potential universally available to conscious beings, and has been expressed at various times in history. This just sitting is not a meditation technique or practice, or anything at all. "Just sitting" is a verb rather than a noun, the dynamic activity of being fully present.

The specific practice experience of shikantaza was first articulated in the Soto Zen lineage (Caodong in Chinese) by the Chinese master Hongzhi Zhengjue (1091–1157; Wanshi Shogaku in Japanese), and further elaborated by the Japanese Soto founder Eihei Dogen (1200–1253). But prior to their expressions of this experience, there are hints of this practice in some of the earlier teachers of the tradition. The founding teachers of this lineage run from Shitou Xiqian (700–790; Sekito Kisen in Japanese), two generations after the Chinese Sixth Ancestor, through three generations to Dongshan Liangjie (807–869; Tozan Ryokai in Japanese), the usually recognized founder of the Caodong, or Soto, lineage in China. I will briefly mention a couple of these early practice intimations in their Soto lineage context before discussing the expressions of Hongzhi and Dogen.

Shitou/Sekito is most noted for his teaching poem "Sandokai," meaning "Harmony of Difference and Sameness," still frequently chanted in Soto Zen. "Sandokai" presents the fundamental dialectic between the polarity of the universal ultimate and the phenomenal particulars. This dialectic, derived by Shitou from Chinese Huayan thought based on the "Flower Ornament" *Avatamsaka Sutra*, combined with some use of Daoist imagery, became the philosophical background of Soto, as expressed by Dongshan in the Five Ranks teachings, and later elucidated by various Soto thinkers. But Shitou wrote another teaching poem, "Soanka"—"Song of the Grass Hut"—which presents more of a practice model for how to develop the space that fosters just sitting. Therein Shitou says, "Just sitting with head covered, all things are at rest. Thus this mountain monk does not understand at all."[1] So just sitting does not involve reaching some understanding. It is the subtle activity of allowing all things to be completely at rest just as they are, not poking one's head into the workings of the world.

Shitou also says in "Soanka": "Turn around the light to shine within, then just return…. Let go of hundreds of years and relax completely. Open your hands and walk, innocent." According to Shitou, the fundamental orientation of turning within, also later described by Hongzhi and Dogen, is simply in order to return to the world and to our original quality. Letting go of conditioning while steeped in completely relaxed awareness, one is able to act effectively, innocent of grasping and attachments. The context of this just sitting suggested by Shitou is the possibility of aware and responsive presence that is simple, open-hearted, and straightforward.

When discussing zazen, Dogen regularly quotes a saying by Shitou's successor, Yaoshan Weiyan (745–828; Yakusan Igen in Japanese): A monk asked Yaoshan what he thought of while sitting so still and stead-fastly. Yaoshan replied that he thought of not-thinking, or that he thought of that which does not think. When the monk asked how Yaoshan did that, he responded, "Beyond-thinking," (or, "Non-thinking"). This is a state of awareness that can include both cognition and the absence of thought, and is not caught up in either. Dogen calls this "the essential art of zazen."[2]

These early accounts would indicate that there was already a context of Caodong/Soto practitioners "just sitting" well before Hongzhi and Dogen. The Soto lineage almost died out in China a century before Hongzhi, but was revived by Touzi Yiqing (1032–1083; Tosu Gisei in Japanese), who brought a background in Huayan studies to enliven Soto philosophy. Touzi's successor, Furong Daokai (1043–1118; Fuyo Dokai in Japanese) was a model of integrity who solidified and developed the forms for the Soto monastic community. It remained for Hongzhi, two generations after Furong Daokai, to fully express Soto praxis. Hongzhi, easily the most prominent Soto teacher in the twelfth century, was a literary giant, a highly prolific, elegant, and evocative writer who com-prehensively articulated this meditation practice for the first time.

Hongzhi does not use the actual term, "just sitting," which Dogen quotes instead from his own Soto lineage teacher Tiantong Rujing (1163–1228; Tendo Nyojo in Japanese). But Tiantong Monastery, where Dogen studied with Rujing in 1227, was the same temple where Hongzhi had been abbot for almost thirty years up to his death in 1157. Dogen refers to Hongzhi as an "Ancient Buddha," and frequently quotes him, especially from his poetic writings on meditative experience. Clearly the meditative awareness that Hongzhi writes about was closely related to Dogen's meditation, although Dogen developed its dynamic orientation in his own writings about just sitting.

Hongzhi's meditation teaching is usually referred to as "silent, or serene, illumination," although Hongzhi actually uses this term only a few times in his voluminous writings. In his long poem, "Silent Illumi-nation," Hongzhi emphasizes the necessity for balance between serenity and illumination, which echoes the traditional Buddhist meditation prac-tice of shamatha-vipashyana, or stopping and insight. This was called *zhiguan* in the Chinese Tiantai meditation system expounded by the

great Chinese Buddhist synthesizer Zhiyi (538–597). Hongzhi emphasizes the necessity for active insight as well as calm in "Silent Illumination" when he says, "If illumination neglects serenity then aggressiveness
appears…. If serenity neglects illumination, murkiness leads to wasted
dharma."[3] Hongzhi's meditation values the balancing of both stopping, or
settling the mind, and its active illuminating functioning.

In his prose writings, Hongzhi frequently uses nature metaphors to
express the natural simplicity of the lived experience of silent illumination or just sitting. (I am generally using these terms interchangeably,
except when discussing differences in their usages by Hongzhi or
Dogen.) An example of Hongzhi's nature writing is:

> A person of the Way fundamentally does not dwell anywhere.
> The white clouds are fascinated with the green mountain's foun-
> dation. The bright moon cherishes being carried along with the
> flowing water. The clouds part and the mountains appear. The
> moon sets and the water is cool. Each bit of autumn contains vast
> interpenetration without bounds.[4]

Hongzhi here highlights the ease of this awareness and its function.
Like the flow of water and clouds, the mind can move smoothly to flow
in harmony with its environment. "Accord and respond without labor-
ing and accomplish without hindrance. Everywhere turn around freely,
not following conditions, not falling into classifications."[5]

In many places, Hongzhi provides specific instructions about how
to manage one's sense perceptions so as to allow the vital presence of
just sitting. "Respond unencumbered to each speck of dust without
becoming its partner. The subtlety of seeing and hearing transcends
mere colors and sounds."[6] Again he suggests, "Casually mount the
sounds and straddle the colors while you transcend listening and sur-
pass watching."[7] This does not indicate a presence that is oblivious to
the surrounding sense world. But while the practitioner remains
aware, sense phenomena do not become objects of attachment, or
objectified at all.

Another aspect of Hongzhi's practice is that it is objectless not only
in terms of letting go of concentration objects, but also in the sense of

avoiding any specific, limited goals or objectives. As Hongzhi says at the end of "Silent Illumination," "Transmit it to all directions without desiring to gain credit."[8] This serene illumination, or just sitting, is not a technique, or a means to some resulting higher state of consciousness, or any particular state of being. Just sitting, one simply meets the immediate present. Desiring some flashy experience, or anything more or other than "this" is mere worldly vanity and craving. Again invoking empty nature, Hongzhi says, "Fully appreciate the emptiness of all dharmas. Then all minds are free and all dusts evaporate in the original brilliance shining everywhere.... Clear and desireless, the wind in the pines and the moon in the water are content in their elements."[9]

This non-seeking quality of Hongzhi's meditation eventually helped make it controversial. The leading contemporary teacher in the much more prominent Linji lineage (Japanese Rinzai) was Dahui Zonggao (1089–1163; Daie Soko in Japanese). A popular historical stereotype is that Dahui and Hongzhi were rivals, debating over Hongzhi's "silent illumination" meditation as opposed to Dahui's "koan introspection" meditation teaching. Historians have now established that Hongzhi and Dahui were actually good friends, or at least had high mutual esteem, and sent students to each other. There was no such debate, at least until future generations of their successors, although Dahui did severely critique "silent illumination" practice as being quietistic and damaging to Zen. However, Dahui clearly was not criticizing Hongzhi himself, but rather, some of his followers, and possibly Hongzhi's dharma brother, Changlu Qingliao (1089–1151; Choryo Seiryo in Japanese), from whom Dogen's lineage descends.[10]

Dahui's criticism of silent illumination was partly valid, based on the legitimate danger of practitioners misunderstanding this approach as quietistic or passive. Dahui's critique was echoed centuries later by Japanese Rinzai critics of just sitting, such as Hakuin in the seventeenth century. Just sitting can indeed sometimes degenerate into dull attachment to inner bliss states, with no responsiveness to the suffering of the surrounding world. Hongzhi clarifies that this is not the intention of his practice, for example when he says, "In wonder return to the journey, avail yourself of the path and walk ahead.... With the hundred grass tips in the busy marketplace graciously share yourself."[11]

The meditation advocated by both Hongzhi and Dogen is firmly rooted in the bodhisattva path and its liberative purpose of assisting and awakening beings. Mere idle indulgence in peacefulness and bliss is not the point.

The other aspect of Dahui's criticism related to his own advocacy of meditation focusing on koans as meditation objects, explicitly aimed at generating flashy opening experiences. Such experiences may occur in just sitting practice as well, but generally have been less valued in the Soto tradition. The purpose of Buddhist practice is universal awakening, not dramatic experiences of opening any more than passive states of serenity. But contrary to another erroneous stereotype, use of koans has been widespread in Soto teaching as well as Rinzai.

Hongzhi himself created two collections of koans with his comments, one of which was the basis for the important anthology, the *Book of Serenity*. Dogen also created koan collections, and (ironically, considering his reputation as champion of just sitting meditation) far more of his voluminous writing, including the essays of his masterwork *Shobogenzo (True Dharma Eye Treasury)*, is devoted to commentary on koans than to discussion of meditation. Dogen was actually instrumental in introducing the koan literature to Japan, and his writings demonstrate a truly amazing mastery of the depth and breadth of the range of that literature in China. Steven Heine's modern work, *Dogen and the Koan Tradition*, clearly demonstrates how Dogen actually developed koan practice in new expansive modes that differed from Dahui's concentrated approach.[12] Although Hongzhi and Dogen, and most of the traditional Soto tradition, did not develop a formal koan meditation curriculum as did Dahui, Hakuin, and much of the Rinzai tradition, the koan stories have remained a prominent context for Soto teaching. Conversely, just sitting has often been part of Rinzai practice, such that some Soto monks in the nineteenth and early twentieth centuries went to Rinzai masters for training in just sitting.

Although a great deal of Dogen's writing focuses on commentary on koans and sutras, and on monastic practice expressions, the practice of just sitting is clearly in the background throughout his teaching career. Dogen builds on the descriptions of Hongzhi to emphasize the dynamic function of just sitting.

In one of his first essays, "Bendowa," or "Talk on Wholehearted Practice of the Way," written in 1231, a few years after his return from training in China, Dogen describes this meditation as the samadhi of self-fulfillment (or enjoyment), and elaborates the inner meaning of this practice. Simply just sitting is expressed as concentration on the self in its most delightful wholeness, in total inclusive interconnection with all of phenomena. Dogen makes remarkably radical claims for this simple experience. "When one displays the buddha mudra with one's whole body and mind, sitting upright in this samadhi for even a short time, everything in the entire dharma world becomes buddha mudra, and all space in the universe completely becomes enlightenment."[13] Proclaiming that when one just sits all of space itself becomes enlightenment is an inconceivable statement, deeply challenging our usual sense of the nature of reality, whether we take Dogen's words literally or metaphorically. Dogen places this activity of just sitting far beyond our usual sense of personal self or agency. He goes on to say that "even if only one person sits for a short time, because this zazen is one with all existence and completely permeates all times, it performs everlasting buddha guidance" throughout space and time.[14] At least in Dogen's faith in the spiritual or "theological" implications of the activity of just sitting, this is clearly a dynamically liberating practice, not mere blissful serenity.

Through his writings, Dogen gives ample indication as to how to engage this just sitting. In another noted early writing, "Genjokoan," or "Actualizing the Fundamental Point," from 1233, Dogen gives a clear description of the existential stance of just sitting: "To carry yourself forward and experience myriad things is delusion. That myriad things come forth and experience themselves is awakening."[15] That we are conditioned to project our own conceptions onto the world as a dead object-screen is the cause of suffering. When all of phenomena (including what we usually think of as "ours") join in mutual self-experience and expression, the awakened awareness that Hongzhi described through nature metaphors is present, doing Buddha's work, as Dogen says.

Some modern Dogen scholars have emphasized the shift in his later teaching to the importance of strict monastic practice, and supposedly away from the universal applicability of shikantaza practice. In 1243

Dogen moved his community far from the capital of Kyoto to the snowy north coast mountains, where he established his monastery, Eiheiji. His teaching thereafter, until his death in 1253, was mostly in the form of often brief talks to his monks, presented in *Eihei Koroku*, "Dogen's Extensive Record." These are certainly focused on training a core of dedicated monks to preserve his practice tradition, a mission he fulfilled with extraordinary success. But through his work, both early and late, instructions and encouragements to just sit appear regularly.

In 1251 Dogen was still proclaiming,

> The family style of all buddhas and ancestors is to engage the way in zazen. My late teacher Tiantong [Rujing] said, "Cross-legged sitting is the dharma of ancient buddhas.... In just sitting it is finally accomplished."... We should engage the way in zazen as if extinguishing flames from our heads. Buddhas and ancestors, generation after generation, face to face transmit the primacy of zazen.[16] (Discourse 319)

In 1249 he exhorted his monks, "We should know that zazen is the decorous activity of practice after realization. Realization is simply just sitting zazen.... Brothers on this mountain, you should straightforwardly, single-mindedly focus on zazen." For Dogen, all of enlightenment is fully expressed in the ongoing practice of just sitting. That same year, he gave a straightforward instruction for just sitting:

> Great assembly, do you want to hear the reality of just sitting, which is the Zen practice that is dropping off body and mind?
>
> After a pause [Dogen] said: Mind cannot objectify it; thinking cannot describe it. Just step back and carry on, and avoid offending anyone you face. At the ancient dock, the wind and moon are cold and clear. At night the boat floats peacefully in the land of lapis lazuli. (Discourse 337)

The concluding two sentences of this talk are quoted from a poem by Hongzhi, further revealing the continuity of their practice teachings.

Dogen also frequently describes this just sitting as "dropping away body and mind," *shinjin datsuraku* in Japanese, a phrase traditionally associated with Dogen's awakening experience in China.[17]

For Dogen this "dropping off body and mind" is the true nature both of just sitting and of complete enlightenment, and is the ultimate letting go of self, directly meeting the cold, clear wind and moon. After turning within while just sitting, it is carried on in all activity and throughout ongoing engagement with the world. Although just sitting now has been maintained for 750 years since Dogen, the teachings of Hongzhi and Dogen remain as primary guideposts to its practice.

Notes:

1. Shitou does not use the words for shikantaza, but the reference to the iconic image of Bodhidharma just sitting, or "wall-gazing" in his cold cave with a quilt over his head is unquestionable. For "Soanka," see Taigen Dan Leighton, with Yi Wu, trans., *Cultivating the Empty Field: The Silent Illumination of Zen Master Hongzhi*, revised, expanded edition (Boston: Tuttle Publishing, 2000), pp. 72–73.

2. In Dogen's *Fuganzazengi*; see Kazuaki Tanahashi, ed., *Enlightenment Unfolds: The Essential Teachings of Zen Master Dogen* (Boston: Shambhala Publications, 1999), p. 55; or the groundbreaking translation by Norman Waddell and Masao Abe later in this book.

3. Leighton, *Cultivating the Empty Field*, pp. 67–68 (reprinted in this book). For more on Hongzhi and his meditation teaching, see also Morton Schlutter, "Silent Illumination, Kung-an Introspection, and the Competition for Lay Patronage in Sung Dynasty Chan," in Peter Gregory and Daniel Getz, eds., *Buddhism in the Sung* (Honolulu: University of Hawai'i Press, 1999), pp. 109–47.

4. Leighton, *Cultivating the Empty Field*, pp. 41–42.

5. Ibid., p. 31.

6. Ibid., p. 30.

7. Ibid., p. 55.

8. Ibid., p. 68.

9. Ibid., p. 43.

10. Schlutter, "Silent Illumination, Kung-an Introspection," in Gregory and Getz, eds., *Buddhism in the Sung*, pp. 109–110.

11. Leighton, *Cultivating the Empty Field*, p. 55.

12. Steven Heine, *Dogen and the Koan Tradition: A Tale of Two* Shobogenzo *Texts* (Albany: State University of New York Press, 1994).

13. Shohaku Okumura and Taigen Dan Leighton, trans., *The Wholehearted Way: A Translation of Eihei Dogen's Bendowa with Commentary by Kosho Uchiyama Roshi* (Boston: Tuttle Publishing, 1997), p. 22.

14. Ibid., p. 23.

15. Kazuaki Tanahashi, ed., *Moon in a Dewdrop: Writings of Zen Master Dogen* (New York: North Point Press, division of Farrar, Straus and Giroux), 1985, p. 69.

16. *Eihei Koroku*, Dharma Discourse 319, from Taigen Dan Leighton and Shohaku Okumura, trans., *Dogen's Extensive Record: A Translation of Eihei Koroku* (Boston: Wisdom Publications, forthcoming). All later quotes from *Eihei Koroku* in this introduction are from this translation, identified in the text after the quote by Dharma Discourse number.

17. See Leighton, *Cultivating the Empty Field*, pp. 20–23 (reprinted in this book).

EDITOR'S NOTE

THE SELECTIONS included in this volume use both the Pinyin and Wade-Giles romanization styles of Chinese names. For the sake of fidelity to the original sources, we have kept the spelling used in each piece, adding the Pinyin version in parenthesis when applicable. Certain writers also include the Japanese version of the master's name.

Also, we have retained each piece's capitalization and spelling of words like "Buddhas" and "Buddha-nature," as well as the use of the pronoun "he" to refer to monks or Buddhist practitioners.

The appendix includes six pieces we have called "Foundational Texts." Though they are directly related to Zen meditation, they do not explicitly refer to it as shikantaza or "just sitting." These terms were first referred to by Hongzhi Zhengjue, who called the practice of just sitting "silent illumination."

GUIDEPOST OF SILENT ILLUMINATION

Hongzhi Zhengjue

Translated by Taigen Dan Leighton with Yi Wu

Silent and serene, forgetting words, bright clarity appears before you.

*When you reflect it you become vast, where you embody
it you are spiritually uplifted.*

Spiritually solitary and shining, inner illumination restores wonder,

*Dew in the moonlight, a river of stars, snow-covered pines,
clouds enveloping the peak.*

In darkness it is most bright, while hidden it is all the more manifest.

*The crane dreams in the wintry mists. The autumn waters flow
far in the distance.*

Endless kalpas *are totally empty, all things completely the same.*

*When wonder exists in serenity, all achievement is forgotten
in illumination.*

What is this wonder? Alertly seeing through confusion

Is the way of silent illumination and the origin of subtle radiance.

Vision penetrating into subtle radiance is weaving gold on a jade loom.

*Upright and inclined yield to each other; light and dark are
interdependent.*

*Not depending on sense faculty and object, at the right time
they interact.*

Drink the medicine of good views. Beat the poison-smeared drum.

When they interact, killing and giving life are up to you.

Through the gate the self emerges and the branches bear fruit.

Only silence is the supreme speech, only illumination the universal response.

Responding without falling into achievement, speaking without involving listeners,

The ten thousand forms majestically glisten and expound the dharma.

All objects certify it, every one in dialogue.

Dialoguing and certifying, they respond appropriately to each other;

But if illumination neglects serenity then aggressiveness appears.

Certifying and dialoguing, they respond to each other appropriately;

But if serenity neglects illumination, murkiness leads to wasted dharma.

When silent illumination is fulfilled, the lotus blossoms, the dreamer awakens,

A hundred streams flow into the ocean, a thousand ranges face the highest peak.

Like geese preferring milk, like bees gathering nectar,

When silent illumination reaches the ultimate, I offer my teaching.

The teaching of silent illumination penetrates from the highest down to the foundation.

The body being shunyata, *the arms in* mudra;

From beginning to end the changing appearances and ten thousand differences have one pattern.

Mr. Ho offered jade [to the Emperor; Minister] Xiangru pointed to its flaws.

Facing changes has its principles, the great function is without striving.

The ruler stays in the kingdom, the general goes beyond the frontiers.

Our school's affair hits the mark straight and true.

Transmit it to all directions without desiring to gain credit.

Cultivating the Empty Field

Hongzhi Zhengjue

Translated by Taigen Dan Leighton
with Yi Wu

The Practice of True Reality

The practice of true reality is simply to sit serenely in silent introspection. When you have fathomed this you cannot be turned around by external causes and conditions. This empty, wide-open mind is subtly and correctly illuminating. Spacious and content, without confusion from inner thoughts of grasping, effectively overcome habitual behavior and realize the self that is not possessed by emotions. You must be broad-minded, whole without relying on others. Such upright independent spirit can begin not to pursue degrading situations. Here you can rest and become clean, pure, and lucid. Bright and penetrating, you can immediately return, accord, and respond to deal with events. Everything is unhindered, clouds gracefully floating up to the peaks, the moonlight glitteringly flowing down mountain streams. The entire place is brightly illumined and spiritually transformed, totally unobstructed and clearly manifesting responsive interaction like box and lid or arrow-points [meeting]. Continuing, cultivate and nourish yourself to embody maturity and achieve stability. If you accord everywhere with thorough clarity and cut off sharp corners without dependence on doctrines, like the white bull or wildcat [helping to arouse wonder], you can be called a complete person. So we hear that this is how one on the way of non-mind acts, but before realizing non-mind we still have great hardship.

Performing the Buddha Work

[The empty field] cannot be cultivated or proven. From the beginning it is altogether complete, undefiled and clear down to the bottom. Where everything is correct and totally sufficient, attain the pure eye that illuminates thoroughly, fulfilling liberation. Enlightenment involves enacting this; stability develops from practicing it. Birth and death originally have no root or stem; appearing and disappearing originally have no defining signs or traces. The primal light, empty and effective, illumines the headtop. The primal wisdom, silent but also glorious, responds to conditions. When you reach the truth without middle or edge, cutting off before and after, then you realize one wholeness. Everywhere sense faculties and objects both just happen. The one who sticks out his broad long tongue transmits the inexhaustible lamp, radiates the great light, and performs the great buddha work, from the first not borrowing from others one atom from outside the dharma. Clearly this affair occurs within your own house.

With Total Trust Roam and Play in Samadhi

Empty and desireless, cold and thin, simple and genuine, this is how to strike down and fold up the remaining habits of many lives. When the stains from old habits are exhausted, the original light appears, blazing through your skull, not admitting any other matters. Vast and spacious, like sky and water merging during autumn, like snow and moon having the same color, this field is without boundary, beyond direction, magnificently one entity without edge or seam. Further, when you turn within and drop off everything completely, realization occurs. Right at the time of entirely dropping off, deliberation and discussion are one thousand or ten thousand miles away. Still no principle is discernible, so what could there be to point to or explain? People with the bottom of the bucket fallen out immediately find total trust. So we are told simply to realize mutual response and explore mutual response, then turn around and enter the world. Roam and play in samadhi. Every detail clearly appears before you. Sound and form, echo and shadow, happen instantly without leaving traces. The outside and myself do not dominate each other, only because no perceiving [of objects] comes between us. Only this nonperceiving encloses the empty space of the dharma realm's majestic ten thousand forms. People with the original face should enact and fully investigate [the field] without neglecting a single fragment.

THE BACKWARD STEP AND THE UPRIGHT CAULDRON

With the depths clear, utterly silent, thoroughly illuminate the source, empty and spirited, vast and bright. Even though you have lucidly scrutinized your image and no shadow or echo meets it, searching throughout you see that you still have distinguished between the merits of a hundred undertakings. Then you must take the backward step and directly reach the middle of the circle from where light issues forth. Outstanding and independent, still you must abandon pretexts for merit. Carefully discern that naming engenders beings and that these rise and fall with intricacy. When you can share your self, then you may manage affairs, and you have the pure seal that stamps the ten thousand forms. Traveling the world, meeting conditions, the self joyfully enters samadhi in all delusions and accepts its function, which is to empty out the self so as not to be full of itself. The empty valley receives the clouds. The cold stream cleanses the moon. Not departing and not remaining, far beyond all the changes, you can give teachings without attainment or expectation. Everything everywhere comes back to the olden ground. Not a hair has been shifted, bent, or raised up. Despite a hundred uglinesses or a thousand stupidities, the upright cauldron is naturally beneficent. Zhaozhou's answers "wash out your bowl" and "drink your tea" do not require making arrangements; from the beginning they have always been perfectly apparent. Thoroughly observing each thing with the whole eye is a patch-robed monk's spontaneous conduct.

THE CONDUCT OF THE MOON AND CLOUDS

The consistent conduct of people of the way is like the flowing clouds with no [grasping] mind, like the full moon reflecting universally, not confined anywhere, glistening within each of the ten thousand forms. Dignified and upright, emerge and make contact with the variety of phenomena, unstained and unconfused. Function the same toward all others since all have the same substance as you. Language cannot transmit [this conduct], speculation cannot reach it. Leaping beyond the infinite and cutting off the dependent, be obliging without looking for merit. This marvel cannot be measured with consciousness or emotion. On the journey accept your function, in your house please sustain it. Comprehending birth and death, leaving causes and conditions, genuinely realize that from the outset your spirit is not halted. So we have been told that the mind that embraces all the ten directions does not stop anywhere.

The Amazing Living Beings

Our house is a single field, clean, vast, and lustrous, clearly self-illuminated. When the spirit is vacant without conditions, when awareness is serene without cogitation, then buddhas and ancestors appear and disappear transforming the world. Amid living beings is the original place of nirvana. How amazing it is that all people have this but cannot polish it into bright clarity. In darkness unawakened, they make foolishness cover their wisdom and overflow. One remembrance of illumination can break through and leap out of the dust of kalpas. Radiant and clear white, [the single field] cannot be diverted or altered in the three times; the four elements cannot modify it. Solitary glory is deeply preserved, enduring throughout ancient and present times, as the merging of sameness and difference becomes the entire creation's mother. This realm manifests the energy of the many thousands of beings, all appearances merely this [field's] shadows. Truly enact this reality.

Zazengi: Rules for Zazen

Eihei Dogen

*Translated by Dan Welch
and Kazuaki Tanahashi*

PRACTICING ZEN IS ZAZEN. For zazen a quiet place is suitable. Lay out a thick mat. Do not let in drafts or smoke, rain or dew. Protect and maintain the place where you settle your body. There are examples from the past of sitting on a diamond seat and sitting on a flat stone covered with a thick layer of grass.

Day or night the place of sitting should not be dark; it should be kept warm in winter and cool in summer.

Set aside all involvements and let the myriad things rest. Zazen is not thinking of good, not thinking of bad. It is not conscious endeavor. It is not introspection.

Do not desire to become a buddha; let sitting or lying down drop away. Be moderate in eating and drinking. Be mindful of the passing of time, and engage yourself in zazen as though saving your head from fire. On Mount Huangmei the Fifth Ancestor practiced zazen to the exclusion of all other activities.

When sitting zazen, wear the kashaya and use a round cushion. The cushion should not be placed all the way under the legs, but only under the buttocks. In this way the crossed legs rest on the mat and the backbone is supported with the round cushion. This is the method used by all buddha ancestors for zazen.

Sit either in the half-lotus position or in the full-lotus position. For the full-lotus put the right foot on the left thigh and the left foot on the right thigh. The toes should lie along the thighs, not extending beyond. For the half-lotus position, simply put the left foot on the right thigh.

Loosen your robes and arrange them in an orderly way. Place the right hand on the left foot and the left hand on the right hand, lightly touching the ends of the thumbs together. With the hands in this position, place them next to the body so that the joined thumb-tips are at the navel.

Straighten your body and sit erect. Do not lean to the left or right; do not bend forward or backward. Your ears should be in line with your shoulders, and your nose in line with your navel.

Rest your tongue against the roof of your mouth, and breathe through your nose. Lips and teeth should be closed. Eyes should be open, neither too wide, nor too narrow. Having adjusted body and mind in this manner, take a breath and exhale fully.

Sit solidly in samadhi and think not-thinking. How do you think not-thinking? Nonthinking. This is the heart of zazen.

Zazen is not learning to do concentration. It is the dharma gate of great ease and joy. It is undefiled practice-enlightenment.

In the eleventh month, first year of Kangen [1243], this was taught to the assembly at Yoshimine Monastery, Yoshida County, Echizen Province.

FUKANZAZENGI: UNIVERSAL RECOMMENDATIONS FOR ZAZEN

Eihei Dogen

Translated by Norman Waddell and Abe Masao

THE WAY IS BASICALLY PERFECT and all-pervading. How could it be contingent upon practice and realization? The Dharma-vehicle is free and untrammeled. What need is there for man's concentrated effort? Indeed, the whole body is far beyond the world's dust. Who could believe in a means to brush it clean? It is never apart from one right where one is—what is the use of going off here and there to practice?

And yet, if there is the slightest discrepancy, the way is as distant as heaven from earth. If the least like or dislike arises, the Mind is lost in confusion. Suppose one gains pride of understanding and inflates one's own enlightenment, glimpsing the wisdom that runs through all things, attaining the Way and clarifying the Mind, raising an aspiration to escalade the very sky. One is making the initial, partial excursions about the frontiers but is still somewhat deficient in the vital Way of total emancipation.

Need I mention the Buddha, who was possessed of inborn knowledge? The influence of his six years of upright sitting is noticeable still. Or Bodhidharma's transmission of the mind-seal? The fame of his nine years of wall-sitting is celebrated to this day. Since this was the case with the saints of old, how can men of today dispense with negotiation of the Way?

You should therefore cease from practice based on intellectual understanding, pursuing words and following after speech, and learn the backward step that turns your light inwardly to illuminate your self. Body and mind of themselves will drop away, and your original face will be manifest. If you want to attain suchness, you should practice suchness without delay.

For sanzen a quiet room is suitable. Eat and drink moderately. Cast aside all involvements and cease all affairs. Do not think good or bad. Do not administer pros and cons. Cease all the movements of the conscious mind, gauging of all thoughts and views. Have no thoughts of becoming a buddha. Sanzen has nothing whatever to do with sitting or lying down.

At the site of your regular sitting, spread out thick matting and place a cushion above it. Sit either in the full-lotus or half-lotus position. In the full-lotus position you first place your right foot on your left thigh and your left foot on your right thigh. In the half-lotus you simply press your left foot against your right thigh. You should have your robes and belt loosely bound and arranged in order. Then place your right hand on your left leg and your left palm (facing upwards) on your right palm, thumb tips touching. Thus sit upright in correct bodily posture, neither inclining to the left nor to the right, neither leaning forward nor backward. Be sure your ears are on a plane with your shoulders and your nose in line with your navel. Place your tongue against the front roof of your mouth, with teeth and lips both shut. Your eyes should always remain open, and you should breathe gently through your nose.

Once you have adjusted your posture, take a deep breath, inhale and exhale, rock your body right and left and settle into a steady, immobile sitting position. Think of not thinking. How do you think of not thinking? Non-thinking in itself is the essential art of zazen.

The zazen I speak of is not learning meditation. It is simply the Dharma-gate of repose and bliss, the practice-realization of totally culminated enlightenment. It is the manifestation of ultimate reality. Traps and snares can never reach it. Once its heart is grasped, you are like the tiger when he enters the mountain. For you must know that just there (in zazen) the right Dharma is manifesting itself and that from the first, dullness and distraction are struck aside.

When you arise from sitting, move slowly and quietly, calmly and deliberately. Do not rise suddenly or abruptly. In surveying the past, we find that transcendence of both unenlightenment and enlightenment, and dying while either sitting or standing, have all depended entirely on the strength [of zazen].

In addition, the bringing out of enlightenment by the opportunity provided by a finger, a banner, a needle, or a mallet, and the effecting of realization with the aid of a *hossu*, a fist, a staff, or a shout, cannot be fully understood by man's discriminative thinking. Indeed, it cannot be fully known by the practicing or realizing of supernatural powers either. It must be deportment beyond man's hearing and seeing—is it not a principle that is prior to his knowledge and perceptions?

This being the case, intelligence or lack of it does not matter; between dull- and sharp-witted there is no distinction. If you concentrate your effort singlemindedly, that in itself is negotiating the Way. Practice-realization is naturally undefiled. Going forward [in practice] is a matter of everydayness.

In general, this world and other worlds as well, both in India and China, equally hold the Buddha-seal and over all prevails the character of this school, which is simply devotion to sitting, total engagement in immobile sitting. Although it is said that there are as many minds as there are men, still they [all] negotiate the Way solely in zazen. Why leave behind the seat that exists in your home and go aimlessly off to the dusty realms of other lands? If you make one misstep you go astray from [the Way] directly before you.

You have gained the pivotal opportunity of human form. Do not use your time in vain. You are maintaining the essential working of the Buddha Way. Who would take wasteful delight in the spark from the flint stone? Besides, form and substance are like the dew on the grass, destiny like the dart of lightning—emptied in an instant, vanished in a flash.

Please, honored followers of Zen, long accustomed to groping for the elephant, do not be suspicious of the true dragon. Devote your energies to a way that directly indicates the absolute. Revere the man of complete attainment who is beyond all human agency. Gain accord with the enlightenment of the buddhas; succeed to the legitimate lineage of the patriarchs' samadhi. Constantly perform in such a manner and you are assured of being a person such as they. Your treasure-store will open of itself, and you will use it at will.

Zazenshin: Lancet of Seated Meditation

Eihei Dogen

Translated by Carl Bielefeldt

Once, when the Great Master Hung-tao (Hongdao) of
Yüeh-shan (Yaoshan) was sitting [in meditation], a monk
asked him, "What are you thinking, [sitting there] so fixedly?"
The master answered, "I'm thinking of not thinking."
The monk asked, "How do you think of not thinking?"
The master answered, "Nonthinking."

VERIFYING THAT SUCH ARE THE WORDS of the Great Master, we should study and participate in the correct transmission of fixed sitting. This is the investigation of fixed sitting transmitted in the way of the Buddha. Although he is not alone in thinking fixedly, Yüeh-shan's words are singular: he is thinking of not thinking. [These words express] what is the very skin, flesh, bones, and marrow of thinking and the very skin, flesh, bones, and marrow of not thinking.

The monk asked, "How do you think of not thinking?" Indeed, though [the notion of] not thinking may be old, here it is [the question] how do you think of it? Could there be no thinking [in sitting] fixedly? In [sitting] fixedly, how could we fail to penetrate [this]? If we are not the sort of fool that despises what is near, we ought to have the strength—and the thinking—to question [sitting] fixedly.

The master answered, "Nonthinking."

Although the employment of nonthinking is crystal clear, when we think of not thinking, we always use nonthinking. There is someone in nonthinking, and this someone maintains us. Although it is we who are [sitting] fixedly, [our sitting] is not merely thinking: it presents itself as [sitting] fixedly. Although sitting fixedly is sitting fixedly, how could it think of [sitting] fixedly? Therefore, [sitting] fixedly is not the measure of the Buddha, not the measure of awakening, not the measure of comprehension.

The single transmission of this [sitting fixedly] by Yüeh-shan represents the thirty-sixth generation directly from the Buddha Shakyamuni: if we trace back from Yüeh-shan thirty-six generations, we come to the Buddha Shakyamuni. And in what was thus correctly transmitted [from the Buddha] there was already [Yüeh-shan's] thinking of not thinking.

Recently, however, some stupid illiterates say, "Once the breast is without concerns, the concentrated effort at seated meditation is a state of peace and calm." This view does not compare with that of the Hinayana scholastics; it is inferior even to the vehicles of men and gods. How could one [who holds such a view] be called a man who studies the teaching of the Buddha? At present, there are many such practitioners in the Great Sung. How sad that the path of the Patriarchs has become overgrown.

Then there is another type [which holds] that to pursue the way through seated meditation is a function essential for the beginner's mind and the late student, but it is not necessarily an observance of the Buddhas and Patriarchs. Walking is Zen, sitting is Zen; whether in speech or silence, motion or rest, the substance is at ease. [Therefore, they say,] do not adhere solely to the present concentrated effort [of seated meditation]. This view is common among those calling themselves a branch of the Lin-chi (Linji) lineage. It is because of a deficiency in the transmission of the orthodox lineage of the teaching of the Buddha that they say this. What is the "beginner's mind?" Where is there no beginner's mind? Where do we leave the beginner's mind?

Be it known that, for studying the way, the established [means of] investigation is pursuit of the way in seated meditation. The essential point that marks this [investigation] is the understanding that there is a practice of a Buddha that does not seek to make a Buddha. Since the practice of a Buddha is not to make a Buddha, it is the realization of the koan. The embodied Buddha does not make a Buddha; when the baskets and cages are broken, a seated Buddha does not interfere with making a Buddha. At just such a time—from one thousand, from ten thousand ages past, from the very beginning—we have the power to enter into Buddha and enter into Mara. Walking forward or back, its measure fills the ditches and moats.

> *When the Chan (Zen) master Ta-chi (Daji) of Chiang-hsi (Jiangxi) was studying with the Chan master Ta-hui (Dahui) of Nan-yüeh (Nanyue), after intimately receiving the mind seal, he always sat in meditation. Once Nan-yüeh went to Ta-chi and said, "Worthy one, what are you figuring to do, sitting there in meditation?"*

We should calmly give concentrated effort to the investigation of this question. Does it mean that there must be some figuring above and beyond seated meditation? Is there no path to be figured outside of seated meditation? Should there be no figuring at all? Or does it ask what kind of figuring occurs at the very time we are practicing seated meditation? We should make a concentrated effort to understand this in detail. Rather than love the carved dragon, we should go on to love the real dragon. We should learn that both the carved and the real dragons have the ability [to produce] clouds and rain. Do not value what is far away, and do not despise it; become completely familiar with it. Do not despise what is near at hand, and do not value it; become completely familiar with it. Do not take the eyes lightly, and do not give them weight. Do not give weight to the ears, and do not take them lightly. Make your eyes and ears clear and sharp.

> *Chiang-hsi said, "I'm figuring to make a Buddha."*

We should clarify and penetrate the meaning of these words. What does it mean to speak of making a Buddha? Does it mean to be made a Buddha by the Buddha? Does it mean to make a Buddha of the Buddha? Does it mean that one or two faces of the Buddha emerge? Is it that figuring to make a Buddha is sloughing off [body and mind], and [that what is meant here is] figuring to make a Buddha as the act of sloughing off? Or does figuring to make a Buddha mean that, while there are ten thousand ways to make a Buddha, they become entangled in this figuring?

It should be recognized that Ta-chi's words mean that seated meditation is always figuring to make a Buddha, is always the figuring of making a Buddha. This figuring must be prior to making a Buddha; it must be subsequent to making a Buddha; and it must be at the very moment of making a Buddha. Now what I ask is this: How many [ways of] making a Buddha does this one figuring entangle? These entanglements themselves intertwine with entanglements. At this point, entanglements, as individual instances of the entirety of making a Buddha, are all direct statements of that entirety and are all instances of figuring. We should not seek to avoid this one figuring: when we avoid the one figuring, we destroy our body and lose our life. When we destroy our body and lose our life, this is the entanglement of the one figuring.

At this point, Nan-yüeh took up a tile and began to rub it on a stone. At length, Ta-chi asked, "Master, what are you doing?"

Who could fail to see that he was polishing a tile? Who could see that he was polishing a tile? Still, polishing a tile has been questioned in this way: "What are you doing?" This "What are you doing?" is itself always polishing a tile. This land and the other world may differ, but the essential message of polishing a tile never ceases. Not only should we avoid deciding that what we see is what we see, we should be firmly convinced that there is an essential message to be studied in all the ten thousand activities. We should know that, just as we may see the Buddha without knowing or understanding Him, so we may see rivers and yet not know rivers, may see mountains and yet not know mountains. The precipitate assumption that the phenomena before one's eyes offer no further passage is not Buddhist study.

Nan-yüeh said, "I'm polishing this to make a mirror."

We should be clear about the meaning of these words. There is definitely a principle in polishing [a tile] to make a mirror: there is the koan of realization; this is no mere empty contrivance. A tile may be a tile and a mirror a mirror, but when we exert ourselves in investigating the principle of polishing, we shall find there are many examples of it. The old mirror and the bright mirror—these are mirrors made through polishing a tile. If we do not realize that these mirrors come from polishing a tile, then the Buddhas and Patriarchs have nothing to say; they do not open their mouths, and we do not perceive them exhaling.

Ta-chi said, "How can you produce a mirror by polishing a tile?"

Indeed, though [the one who is] polishing the tile be a man of iron, who borrows no power from another, polishing a tile is not producing a mirror. And even if it is producing a mirror, it must be quick about it.

Nan-yüeh replied, "How can you make a Buddha by sitting in meditation?"

This is clearly understood: there is a principle that seated meditation does not await making a Buddha; there is nothing obscure about the essential message that making a Buddha is not connected with seated meditation.

Ta-chi asked, "Then, what is right?"

These words resemble a simple question about this [practical matter of what to do], but they are also asking about that [final] rightness. You should realize [that the relationship between what and right here is like], for example, the occasion when one friend meets another: the fact that he is my friend means that I am his friend. [Similarly, here the meanings of] "what" and "right" emerge simultaneously.

Nan-yüeh replied, "When a man is driving a cart, if the cart doesn't go, should he beat the cart or beat the ox?"

Now, when we say the cart doesn't go, what do we mean by the cart's going or not going? For example, is the cart going [analogous to] water flowing, or is it [analogous to] water not flowing? [There is a sense in which] we can say that flowing is water's not going, and that water's going is not its flowing. Therefore, when we investigate the words "the cart doesn't go," we should approach them both in terms of not going and in terms of not not going; for it is a question of time. The words, "if [the cart] doesn't go," do not mean simply that it does not go.

Should he beat the cart or beat the ox? Does this mean there is a beating of the cart as well as a beating of the ox? Are beating the cart and beating the ox the same or not? In the world, there is no method of beating the cart; but, though ordinary men have no such method, we know that on the path of the Buddha there is a method of beating the cart, and this is the very eye of [Buddhist] study. Even though we study that there is a method of beating the cart, we should give concentrated effort to understanding in detail that this is not the same as beating the ox. And even though the method of beating the ox is common in the world, we should go on to study the beating of the ox on the path of the Buddha. Is this ox-beating the water buffalo, or ox-beating the iron bull or the clay ox? Is this beating with a whip, with the entire world, the entire mind? Is this to beat by using the marrow? Should we beat with the fist? The fist should beat the fist, and the ox beat the ox.

Ta-chi did not reply.

We should not miss [the import of] this. In it, there is throwing out a tile to take in a jade; there is turning the head and reversing the face. By no means should we do violence to his silence.

Nan-yüeh went on, "Are you studying seated meditation or are you studying seated Buddha?"

Investigating these words, we should distinguish the essential activity of the Patriarchal ancestors. Without knowing what the full reality of studying seated meditation is, we do know here that it is studying seated Buddha. Who but a scion of true descent could say that studying seated meditation is studying seated Buddha? We should know indeed that the seated meditation of the beginner's mind is the first seated meditation, and the first seated meditation is the first seated Buddha. In speaking of this seated meditation, [Nan-yüeh] said,

"If you're studying seated meditation, meditation is not sitting still."

The point of what he says here is that seated meditation is seated meditation and is not sitting still. From the time the fact that it is not sitting still has been singly transmitted to us, our unlimited sitting still is our own self. Why should we inquire about close or distant familial lines? How could we discuss delusion and awakening? Who would seek wisdom and eradication? Then Nan-yüeh said,

"If you're studying seated Buddha, Buddha is no fixed mark."

Such is the way to say what is to be said. The reason the seated Buddha is one or two Buddhas is that He adorns Himself with no fixed mark. When [Nan-yüeh] says here that Buddha is no fixed mark, he is describing the mark of the Buddha. Since he is a Buddha of no fixed mark, the seated Buddha is difficult to avoid. Therefore, since it is adorned with this [mark of] Buddha is no fixed mark, if you're studying seated meditation, you are a seated Buddha. In a nonabiding dharma, [as Nan-yüeh goes on to say,] who would grasp or reject [something] as not the Buddha? Who would grasp or reject it as the Buddha? It is because [seated meditation] has sloughed off all grasping and rejecting that it is a seated Buddha. Nan-yüeh continues,

"If you're studying seated Buddha, this is killing Buddha."

This means that, when we investigate further [the notion of] seated Buddha, [we find] it has the virtue of killing Buddha. At the very moment that we are a seated buddha we are killing Buddha. Indeed, when we pursue it, [we find] that the [thirty-two] marks and [eighty] signs and the radiance of killing Buddha are always a seated Buddha. Although the word "kill" here is identical with that used by ordinary people, [its meaning] is not the same. Moreover, we must investigate in what form it is that a seated Buddha is killing Buddha. Taking up the fact that it is itself a virtue of the Buddha to kill Buddha, we should study whether we are killers or not.

> *"If you grasp the mark of sitting, you're not reaching its principle."*

To grasp the mark of sitting here means to reject the mark of sitting and to touch the mark of sitting. The principle behind this is that, in being a seated Buddha, we cannot fail to grasp the mark of sitting. Since we cannot fail to grasp it, though our grasping the mark of sitting is crystal clear, we are not reaching its principle. This kind of concentrated effort is called "sloughing off body and mind."

Those who have never sat do not talk like this: [such talk] belongs to the time of sitting and the man who sits, to the seated Buddha and the study of the seated Buddha. The sitting that occurs when the ordinary man sits is not [the sitting of] the seated Buddha. Although a man's sitting naturally resembles a seated Buddha, or a Buddha's sitting, the case is like that of a man's making a Buddha, or the man who makes a Buddha: though there are men who make Buddhas, not all men make Buddhas, and Buddhas are not all men. Since all the Buddhas are not simply all men, man is by no means a Buddha, and a Buddha is by no means a man. The same is true of a seated Buddha.

Here, then, in Nan-yüeh and Chiang-hsi we have a superior master and a strong disciple: Chiang-hsi is the one who verifies making a Buddha as a seated Buddha; Nan-yüeh is the one who points out the seated Buddha for making a Buddha. There was this kind of concentrated effort in the congregation of Nan-yüeh and words like the above in the congregation of Yüeh-shan.

Know this, that it is the seated Buddha that Buddha after Buddha and Patriarch after Patriarch have taken as their essential activity. Those who are Buddhas and Patriarchs have employed this essential activity, while those who are not have never even dreamt of it. To say that the dharma of the Buddha has been transmitted from the Western Heavens to the Eastern Earth implies the transmission of the seated Buddha, for it is the essential function [of that dharma]. And where the dharma of the Buddha is not transmitted, neither is seated meditation. What has been inherited by successor after successor [in this transmission] is just this message of seated meditation; one who does not participate in the unique transmission of this message is not a Buddha or a Patriarch. When one is not clear about this one dharma, he is not clear about the ten thousand dharmas or about ten thousand practices. And without being clear about each of these dharmas, he cannot be said to have a clear eye. He has not attained the way; how could he represent the present or past [in the lineage] of the Buddhas and Patriarchs? By this, then, we should be firmly convinced that the Buddhas and Patriarchs always transmit seated meditation.

To be illuminated by the radiance of the Buddhas and the Patriarchs means to concentrate one's efforts in the investigation of this seated meditation. Some fools, misunderstanding the radiance of the Buddha, think it must be like the radiance of the sun or moon or the light from a pearl or a fire. But the light of the sun and moon is nothing but a mark of action within [the realm of] transmigration in the six destinies; it is not to be compared with the radiance of the Buddha. The radiance of the Buddha means receiving and hearing a single phrase, maintaining and protecting a single dharma, participating in the single transmission of seated meditation. So long as one is not illuminated by the radiance [of the Buddha], he is not maintaining, nor has he accepted, [the Buddha's dharma].

This being the case, [throughout history] there have been few who understood seated meditation as seated meditation. And at the present, in the [Ch'an] mountains of the great Sung, many of those who are heads of the principal monasteries do not understand, and do not study, seated meditation. There may be some who have clearly understood it but not many. Of course, the monasteries have fixed periods for seated meditation; the monks, from the abbot down, take seated meditation as their basic task; and, in leading their students, [the teachers] encourage its practice. Nevertheless, there are few abbots who understand it.

For this reason, although from ancient times to the present there have been one or two old worthies who have written [texts known as] "Inscriptions on Seated Meditation," "Principles of Seated Meditation," or "Lancets of Seated Meditation," among them there is nothing worth taking from any of the "Inscriptions on Seated Meditation," and the "Principles of Seated Meditation" are ignorant of its observances. They were written by men who do not understand, and do not participate in, its unique transmission. Such are the "Lancet of Seated Meditation" in the *Ching-te ch'uan teng lu* and the "Inscription on Seated Meditation" in the *Chia-t'ai p'u teng lu*. What a pity that, though [the authors of such texts] spend their lives passing among the [Ch'an] groves of the ten directions, they do not have the concentrated effort of a single sitting—that sitting is not their own, and concentrated effort never encounters them. This is not because seated meditation rejects their bodies and minds but because they do not aspire to the true concentrated effort and are precipitately given over to their delusion. What they have collected [in their texts] is nothing but models for reverting to the source and returning to the origin, vain programs for suspending considerations and congealing in tranquillity. [Such views of meditation] do not approach the stages of observation, exercise, infusion, and cultivation, or the understandings of [those on the path of] the ten stages and the equivalence of enlightenment; how, then, could they be the single transmission of the seated meditation of the Buddhas and Patriarchs? The Sung chroniclers were mistaken to record [these texts], and later students should cast them aside and not read them.

Among the "Lancets of Seated Meditation," the only one that is [an expression of] the Buddhas and Patriarchs is that by the Reverend Cheng-chüeh (Zhengjue), the Chan Master Hung-chih (Hongzhi) of the Ching-te (Jingde) Monastery at T'ien t'ung (Tiantong), renowned Mount T'ai-po (Daibo), in the district of Ching-yüan (Jingyuan) in the Great Sung. This one is a [true] "Lancet of Seated Meditation." This one says it right. It alone radiates throughout the surface and interior of the realm of the dharma. It is the statement of a Buddha and Patriarch among the Buddhas and Patriarchs of past and present. Prior Buddhas and later Buddhas have been lanced by this "Lancet"; present Patriarchs and past Patriarchs appear from this "Lancet." Here is that "Lancet of Seated Meditation":

LANCET OF SEATED MEDITATION
by Cheng-chüeh
by imperial designation the Chan Master Hung-chih

> *Essential function of all the Buddhas,*
> *Functioning essence of all the Patriarchs—*
> *It knows without touching things,*
> *It illumines without facing objects.*
> *Knowing without touching things,*
> *Its knowledge is inherently subtle;*
> *Illumining without facing objects,*
> *Its illumination is inherently mysterious.*
> *Its knowledge inherently subtle,*
> *It is ever without discriminatory thought;*
> *Its illumination inherently mysterious,*
> *It is ever without a hair's breadth of sign.*
> *Ever without discriminatory thought,*
> *Its knowledge is rare without peer;*
> *Ever without a hair's breadth of sign,*
> *Its illumination comprehends without grasping.*
> *The water is clear right through to the bottom,*
> *A fish goes lazily along.*
> *The sky is vast without horizon,*
> *A bird flies far away.*

The lancet in this lancet of seated meditation means the manifestation of the great function, the comportment beyond sight and sound; it is the juncture before your parents were born. It means you had better not slander the Buddhas and Patriarchs; you do not avoid destroying your body and losing your life; it is a head of three feet and a neck of two inches.

Essential function of all the Buddhas,

The Buddhas always take the Buddhas as their essential function: this is the essential function that is realized here; this is seated meditation.

Functioning essence of all the Patriarchs—

My master had no such saying—this principle is [what is meant here by] the Patriarchs. [It is in this that] the dharma and the robe are transmitted. The faces [that are reversed] when we turn the head and reverse the face are the essential function of all the Buddhas; the heads [that turn] when we reverse the face and turn the head are the functioning essence of all the Patriarchs.

It knows without touching things,

Knowing, here, of course, does not mean perception; for perception is of little measure. It does not mean understanding; for understanding is artificially constructed. Therefore, this knowing is not touching things, and not touching things is knowing. [Such knowing] should not be measured as universal knowledge; it should not be categorized as self-knowledge. This not touching things means, when they come in the light, I hit them in the light; when they come in the dark, I hit them in the dark. It means sitting and breaking the skin born of mother.

It illumines without facing objects.

This illumining does not mean the illumining of luminosity or of spiritual illumination: it means simply without facing objects. [In this meaning,] the illumining does not change into the object, for the object itself is illumining. Without facing means it is never hidden throughout the world; it does not emerge when you break the world. It is subtle; it is mysterious; it is interacting while not interacting.

Its knowledge inherently subtle,
It is ever without discriminatory thought;

Thought is itself knowing, without dependence on another's power. Its knowing is its form, and its form is the mountains and rivers. These mountains and rivers are subtle, and this subtlety is mysterious. When we put it to use, it is brisk and lively. When we make a dragon, it does not matter whether we are inside or out of the Yü (Yu) Gate. To put this single knowing to the slightest use is to take up the mountains and rivers of the entire world and know them with all one's power. Without our intimate knowing of the mountains and rivers, we do not have a single knowing or a half understanding. We should not lament the late arrival of discriminatory thinking: the Buddhas of previous discrimination have already been realized. "Ever without" here means "previously"; "previously" means "[already] realized." Therefore, "ever without discriminatory thought" means you do not meet a single person.

> *Its illumination inherently mysterious,*
> *It is ever without a hair's breadth of a sign.*

A hair's breadth here means the entire world; yet it is inherently mysterious, inherently illumining. Therefore, it is as if it is never brought out. The eyes are not to be doubted, nor the ears to be trusted. You should clarify the essential meaning apart from the sense; do not look to words to grasp the rule—this is [what is meant by] illumining. Therefore, it is without peer; therefore, it is without grasping. This has been preserved as being rare and maintained as comprehending, but I have doubts about it.

> *The water is clear right through to the bottom,*
> *A fish goes lazily along.*

The water is clear: the water that has to do with the sky does not get right through to the bottom of [what is meant here by] clear water; still less is that which forms clear, deep pools in the vessel world the water [intended by the expression] the water is clear. That which has no shore as its boundary—this is what is meant by clear water penetrated right through to the bottom. If a fish goes through this water, it is not that it does not go; yet, however many tens of thousands the degree of its progress, its going is immeasurable, inexhaustible. There is no shoreline by which it is gauged; there is no sky to which it ascends, nor bottom to which it sinks. And therefore there is no one who can take its measure. If we try to discuss its measure, [all we can say is that] it is only clear water penetrated right through to the bottom. The virtue of seated meditation is like the fish going: who can calculate its degree in thousands or tens of thousands? The degree of the going that penetrates right through to the bottom is [like that on] the path of the bird along which the body as a whole does not go.

The sky is vast without horizon,
A bird flies far away.

[The expression] "the sky is vast" here has nothing to do with the heavens: the sky that has to do with the heavens is not the vast sky. Still less is that [space] which extends everywhere here and there the vast sky. Neither hidden nor manifest, without surface or interior—this is what is meant by the vast sky. When the bird flies this sky, it is the single dharma of flying the sky. This conduct of flying the sky is not to be measured: flying the sky is the entire world, for it is the entire world flying the sky. Although we do not know how far this flying goes, to express what is beyond our calculation, we call it far, far away. This is [equivalent to saying] you should go off without a string beneath your feet. When the sky flies off, the bird flies off; when the bird flies off, the sky flies off. To express the investigation of this flying off, we say, "It is just here." This is the lancet of [sitting] fixedly: through how many tens of thousands of degrees does it express this "it is just here."

Such then, is the Chan Master Hung-chih's "Lancet of Seated Meditation." Among the old worthies throughout all the generations, there has never been another "Lancet of Seated Meditation" like this one. If the stinking skin bags throughout all quarters were to attempt to express a "Lancet of Seated Meditation" like this one, they could not do so though they exhaust the efforts of a lifetime or two. This is the only "Lancet" in any quarter; there is no other to be found. When he ascended the hall to lecture, my former master often said, "Hung-chih is an old Buddha." He never said this about any other person. When one has the eye to know a man, he will know as well the voice of the Buddhas and Patriarchs. In truth, we know that there are Buddhas and Patriarchs in [the tradition of] Tung-shan.

Now some eighty years and more since the days of the Chan Master Hung-chih, reading his "Lancet of Seated Meditation," I compose my own. The date is the eighteenth day of the third month in [the cyclical year] Mizunoetora, the third year of Ninji [1242]; if we calculate back from this year to the eighth day of the tenth month in the twenty-seventh year of [the Southern Sung era of] Shao-hsing (Shaoxing) [1157, when Hung-chih died], there are just eighty-five years. The "Lancet of Seated Meditation" I now compose is as follows:

Lancet of Seated Meditation

Essential function of all the Buddhas,
Functioning essence of all the Patriarchs—
It is present without thinking,
It is completed without interacting.
Present without thinking,
Its presence is inherently intimate;
Completed without interacting,
Its completion is inherently verified.
Its presence inherently intimate,
It is ever without any stain or defilement;
Its completion inherently verified,
It is ever without the upright or inclined.
Intimacy ever without stain or defilement,
Its intimacy sloughs off without discarding;
Verification ever without upright or inclined,
Its verification makes effort without figuring.
The water is clear right through the earth,
A fish goes along like a fish.
The sky is vast straight into the heavens,
A bird flies just like a bird.

It is not that the "Lancet of Seated Meditation" by the Chan Master Hung-chih has not yet said it right, but it can also be said like this. Above all, the descendants of the Buddhas and Patriarchs should study seated meditation as the one great concern. This is the orthodox seal of the single transmission.

Zazen Yojinki: Notes on What to Be Aware of in Zazen

Keizan Jokin

Translated by Yasuda Joshu and Anzan Hoshin

1

SITTING IS THE WAY to clarify the ground of experiences and to rest at ease in your Actual Nature. This is called "the display of the Original Face" and "revealing the landscape of the basic ground."

Drop through this bodymind and you will be far beyond such forms as sitting or lying down. Beyond considerations of good or bad, transcend any divisions between usual people and sages, pass beyond the boundary between sentient beings and Buddha.

Putting aside all concerns, shed all attachments. Do nothing at all. Don't fabricate any things with the six senses.

Who is this? Its name is unknown; it cannot be called "body," it cannot be called "mind." Trying to think of it, the thought vanishes. Trying to speak of it, words die.

It is like a fool, an idiot. It is as high as a mountain, deep as the ocean. Without peak or depths, its brilliance is unthinkable, it shows itself silently. Between sky and earth, only this whole body is seen.

This one is without compare—he has completely died. Eyes clear, she stands nowhere. Where is there any dust? What can obstruct such a one?

Clear water has no back or front, space has no inside or outside. Completely clear, its own luminosity shines before form and emptiness were fabricated. Objects of mind and mind itself have no place to exist.

This has always already been so, but it is still without a name. The great teacher, the Third Ancestor Sengcan temporarily called it "mind," and the Venerable Nagarjuna once called it "body." Enlightened essence and form, giving rise to the bodies of all the Buddha, it has no "more" or "less" about it.

This is symbolized by the full moon, but it is this mind that is enlightenment itself. The luminosity of this mind shines throughout the past and brightens as the present. Nagarjuna used this subtle symbol for the samadhi of all the Buddhas, but this mind is signless, nondual, and differences between forms are only apparent.

Just mind, just body. Difference and sameness miss the point. Body arises in mind, and when the body arises, they appear to be distinguished. When one wave arises, a thousand waves follow; the moment a single mental fabrication arises, numberless things appear. So the four elements and five aggregates mesh, four limbs and five senses appear, and on and on to the thirty-six body parts and the twelvefold chain of interdependent emergence. Once fabrication arises, it develops continuity, but it still existsonly through the piling up of myriad dharmas.

The mind is like the ocean waters, the body like the waves. There are no waves without water and no water without waves; water and waves are not separate, motion and stillness are not different. So it is said, "A person comes and goes, lives and dies, as the imperishable body of the four elements and five aggregates."

Zazen is going right into the Ocean of Awareness, manifesting the body of all Buddhas. The natural luminosity of mind suddenly reveals itself and the original light is everywhere. There is no increase or decrease in the ocean and the waves never turn back.

2

Thus Buddhas have arisen in this world for the one Great Matter of teaching people the wisdom and insight of Awakening and to give them true entry. For this, there is the peaceful, pure practice of sitting. This is the complete practice of self-enjoyment of all the Buddhas. This is the sovereign of all samadhis. Entering this samadhi, the ground of mind is clarified at once. You should know that this is the true gate to the Way of the Buddhas.

If you want to clarify the mind-ground, give up your jumble of limited knowledge and interpretation, cut off thoughts of usualness and holiness, abandon all delusive feelings. When the true mind of reality manifests, the clouds of delusion dissipate and the moon of the mind shines bright.

3

The Buddha said, *"Listening and thinking about it are like being shut out by a door. Zazen is like coming home and sitting at ease."* This is true! Listening and thinking about it, views have not ceased and the mind is obstructed; this is why it's like being shut out by a door. True sitting puts all things to rest and yet penetrates everywhere. This sitting is like coming home and sitting at ease.

Being afflicted by the five obstructions arises from basic ignorance, and ignorance arises from not understanding your own nature. Zazen is understanding your own nature. Even if you were to eliminate the five obstructions, if you haven't eliminated basic ignorance you have not yet realized yourself as the Buddhas and Awakened Ancestors. If you want to release basic ignorance, the essential key is to sit and practice the Way.

An old master said, *"When confusion ceases, clarity arises; when clarity arises, wisdom appears; and when wisdom appears, Reality displays itself."*

If you want to cease your confusion, you must cease involvement in thoughts of good or bad. Stop getting caught up in unnecessary affairs. A mind "unoccupied" together with a body "free of activity" is the essential point to remember.

When delusive attachments end, the mind of delusion dies out. When delusion dies out, the Reality that was always the case manifests and you are always clearly aware of it. It is not a matter of extinction nor of activity.

4

Avoid getting caught up in arts and crafts, prescribing medicines and fortune-telling. Stay way from songs and dancing, arguing and babbling, fame and gain. Composing poetry can be an aid in clarifying the mind but don't get caught up in it. The same is true for writing and calligraphy. This is the superior precedent for practitioners of the Way and is the best way to harmonize the mind.

Don't wear luxurious clothing or dirty rags. Luxurious clothing gives rise to greed and then the fear that someone will steal something. This is a hindrance to practitioners of the Way. Even if someone offers them to you, to refuse is the excellent tradition from ancient times. If you happen to have luxurious clothing, don't be concerned with it; if it's stolen, don't bother to chase after it or regret its loss. Old, dirty clothes should be washed and mended; clean them thoroughly before putting them on. If you don't take care of them you could get cold and sick and hinder your practice. Although we shouldn't be too anxious about bodily comforts, inadequate clothing, food, and sleep are known as the "three insufficiencies" and will cause our practice to suffer.

Don't eat anything alive, hard, or spoiled. Such impure foods will make your belly churn and cause heat and discomfort of bodymind, making your sitting difficult. Don't indulge in rich foods. Not only is this bad for bodymind, it's just greed. You should eat to promote life so don't fuss about taste. Also, if you sit after eating too much you will feel ill. Whether the meal is large or small, wait a little while before sitting. Monks should be moderate in eating and hold their portions to two-thirds of what they can eat. All healthy foods, sesame, wild yams, and so on, can be eaten. Essentially, you should harmonize bodymind.

5

When you are sitting in zazen, do not prop yourself up against a wall, meditation brace, or screen. Also, do not sit in windy places or high, exposed places, as this can cause illness.

Sometimes, when you are sitting, you may feel hot or cold, discomfort or ease, stiff or loose, heavy or light, or sometimes startled. These sensations arise through disharmonies of mind and breath-energy. Harmonize your breath in this way: open your mouth slightly, allow long breaths to be long, and short breaths to be short, and it will harmonize naturally. Follow it for awhile until a sense of awareness arises and your breath will be natural. After this, continue to breathe through the nose.

The mind may feel as if it were sinking or floating, it may seem dull or sharp. Sometimes you can see outside the room, the insides of the body, the forms of Buddhas or Bodhisattvas. Sometimes you may believe that you have wisdom and now thoroughly understand all the sutras and commentaries. These extraordinary conditions are diseases that arise through disharmony of mind and breath. When this happens, sit placing the mind in the lap. When the mind sinks into dullness, raise attention above your hairline or before your eyes. When the mind scatters into distraction, place attention at the tip of the nose or at the tanden [hara]. After this, rest attention in the left palm. Sit for a long time and do not struggle to calm the mind and it will naturally be free of distraction.

Although the ancient Teachings are a long-standing means to clarify the mind, do not read, write about, or listen to them obsessively because such excess only scatters the mind.

Generally, anything that wears out bodymind causes illness. Don't sit where there are fires, floods, or bandits, by the ocean, near bars, brothels, where widows or virgins live, or near where courtesans sing and play music. Don't live near kings, ministers, powerful or rich families, people with many desires, those who crave name and fame, or those who like to argue meaninglessly. Although large Buddhist ceremonials and the construction of large temples might be good things, one who is committed to practice should not get involved.

Don't be fond of preaching the Dharma, as this leads to distraction and scattering. Don't be delighted by huge assemblies or run after disciples. Don't try to study and practice many different things.

Do not sit where it is too bright or too dark, too cold or too hot. Do not sit where pleasure-seekers or whores live. Go and stay in a monastery where there is a true teacher. Go deep into the mountains and valleys. Practice kinhin by clear waters and verdant mountains. Clear the mind by a stream or under a tree. Observe impermanance without fail and you will keep the mind that enters the Way.

The mat should be well padded so that you can sit comfortably. The practice place should always be kept clean. Burn incense and offer flowers to the Dharma Protectors, the Buddhas and Bodhisattvas, and your practice will be protected. Put a statue of a Buddha, Bodhisattva, or arhat on the altar and demons of distraction will not overwhelm you.

Remain always in Great Compassion, and dedicate the limitless power of zazen to all living beings.

Do not become arrogant, conceited, or proud of your understanding of the Teachings; that is the way of those outside of the Way and of usual people. Maintain the vow to end afflictions, the vow to realize Awakening and just sit. Do nothing at all. This is the way to study Zen.

Wash your eyes and feet, keep bodymind at ease and deportment in harmony. Shed worldly sentiments and do not become attached to sublime feelings about the Way. Though you should not begrudge the Teachings, do not speak of it unless you are asked. If someone asks, keep silent three times; if still they ask from their heart, then give the teachings. If you wish to speak ten times, keep quiet nine; it's as if moss grew over your mouth or like a fan in winter. A wind-bell hanging in the air, indifferent to the direction of the wind—this is how people of the Way are.

Do not use the Dharma for your own profit. Do not use the Way to try to make yourself important. This is the most important point to remember.

6

Zazen is not based upon teaching, practice, or realization; instead these three aspects are all contained within it. Measuring realization is based upon some notion of enlightenment—this is not the essence of zazen. Practice is based upon strenuous application—this is not the essence of zazen. Teaching is based upon freeing from evil and cultivating good—this is not the essence of zazen.

Teaching is found in Zen but it is not the usual teaching. Rather, it is a direct pointing, just expressing the Way, speaking with the whole body. Such words are without sentences or clauses. Where views end and concept is exhausted, the one word pervades the ten directions without setting up so much as a single hair. This is the true Teaching of the Buddhas and Awakened Ancestors.

Although we speak of "practice," it is not a practice that you can do. That is to say, the body does nothing, the mouth does not recite, the mind doesn't think things over, the six senses are left to their own clarity and unaffected. So this is not the sixteen-stage practice of the hearers (the path of insight or *darsanamarga* into the four noble truths at four different levels). Nor is it the practice of understanding the twelve nidanas of interdependent emergence of those whose practice is founded upon isolation. Nor is it the six perfections within numberless activities of the Bodhisattvas. It is without struggle at all, so it is called Awakening or enlightenment. Just rest in the Self-Enjoyment Samadhi of all the Buddhas, wandering playfully in the four practices of peace and bliss of those open to Openness. This is the profound and inconceivable practice of Buddhas and Awakened Ancestors.

Although we speak of realization, this realization does not hold to itself as being "realization." This is practice of the supreme samadhi, which is the knowing of unborn, unobstructed, and spontaneously arising Awareness. It is the door of luminosity that opens out onto the realization of the Those Who Come Thus, born through the practice of the great ease. This goes beyond the patterns of holy and profane, goes beyond confusion and wisdom. This is the realization of unsurpassed enlightenment as our own nature.

Zazen is also not based upon discipline, practice, or wisdom. These three are all contained within it.

Discipline is usually understood as ceasing wrong action and eliminating evil. In zazen the whole thing is known to be non-dual. Cast off the numberless concerns and rest free from entangling yourself in the "Buddhist Way" or the "worldly way." Leave behind feelings about the path as well as your usual sentiments. When you leave behind all opposites, what can obstruct you? This is the formless discipline of the ground of mind.

Practice usually means unbroken concentration. Zazen is dropping the bodymind, leaving behind confusion and understanding. Unshakable, without activity, it is not deluded, but still—like an idiot, a fool. Like a mountain, like the ocean. Without any trace of motion or stillness. This practice is no-practice because it has no object to practice and so is called great practice.

Wisdom is usually understood to be clear discernment. In zazen, all knowledge vanishes of itself. Mind and discrimination are forgotten forever. The wisdom-eye of this body has no discrimination but is clear seeing of the essence of Awakening. From the beginning it is free of confusion, cuts off concept, and open and clear luminosity pervades everywhere. This wisdom is no-wisdom; because it is traceless wisdom, it is called great wisdom.

The teaching that the Buddhas have presented all throughout their lifetimes are just this discipline, practice, and wisdom. In zazen there is no discipline that is not maintained, no practice that is uncultivated, no wisdom that is unrealized. Conquering the demons of confusion, attaining the Way, turning the wheel of the Dharma and returning to tracelessness all arise from the power of this. Siddhis [supernatural powers] and inconceivable activities, emanating luminosity and proclaiming the Teachings— all of these are present in this zazen. Penetrating Zen *is* zazen.

7

To practice sitting, find a quiet place and lay down a thick mat. Don't let wind, smoke, rain, or dew come in. Keep a clear space with enough room for your knees. Although in ancient times there were those who sat on diamond seats or on large stones for their cushions. The place where you sit should not be too bright in the daytime or too dark at night; it should be warm in winter and cool in summer. That's the key.

Drop mind, intellect, and consciousness; leave memory, thinking, and observing alone. Don't try to fabricate Buddha. Don't be concerned with how well or how poorly you think you are doing; just understand that time is as precious as if you were putting out a fire in your hair.

The Buddha sat straight, Bodhidharma faced the wall; both were wholehearted and committed. Shishuang was like a gnarled, dead tree. Rujing warned against sleepy sitting and said, *"Just-sitting is all you need. You don't need to make burning incense offerings, meditate upon the names of Buddhas, repent, study the scriptures or do recitation rituals."*

When you sit, wear the kesa (except in the first and last parts of the night when the daily schedule is not in effect). Don't be careless. The cushion should be about twelve inches thick and thirty-six in circumference. Don't put it under the thighs but only from mid-thigh to the base of the spine. This is how the Buddhas and Ancestors have sat. You can sit in the full or half lotus postures. To sit in the full lotus, put the right foot on the left thigh and the left foot on the right thigh. Loosen your robes, but keep them in order. Put your right hand on your left heel and your left hand on top of your right, thumbs together and close to the body at the level of the navel. Sit straight without leaning to left or right, front or back. Ears and shoulders, nose and navel should be aligned. Place the tongue on the palate and breathe through the nose. The mouth should be closed. The eyes should be open but not too wide nor too slight. Harmonizing the body in this way, breathe deeply with the mouth once or twice. Sitting steadily, sway the torso seven or eight times in decreasing movements. Sit straight and alert.

Now think of what is without thought. How can you think of it? Be Before Thinking. This is the essence of zazen. Shatter obstacles and become intimate with Awakening Awareness.

When you want to get up from stillness, put your hands on your knees, sway seven or eight times in increasing movements. Breathe out through the mouth, put your hands to the floor and get up lightly from the seat. Slowly walk, circling to right or left.

If dullness or sleepiness overcome your sitting, move to the body and open the eyes wider, or place attention above the hairline or between your eyebrows. If you are still not fresh, rub the eyes or the body. If that still doesn't wake you, stand up and walk, always clockwise. Once you've gone about a hundred steps you probably won't be sleepy any longer. The way to walk is to take a half step with each breath. Walk without walking, silent and unmoving.

If you still don't feel fresh after doing kinhin, wash your eyes and forehead with cold water. Or chant the Three Pure Precepts of the Bodhisattvas. Do something; don't just fall asleep. You should be aware of the Great Matter of birth and death and the swiftness of impermanence. What are you doing sleeping when your eye of the Way is still clouded? If dullness and sinking arise repeatedly you should chant, "Habituality is deeply rooted and so I am wrapped in dullness. When will dullness disperse? May the compassion of the Buddhas and Ancestors lift this darkness and misery."

If the mind wanders, place attention at the tip of the nose and tanden and count the inhalations and exhalations. If that doesn't stop the scattering, bring up a phrase and keep it in awareness—for example: "What is it that comes thus?" or "When no thought arises, where is affliction?— Mount Meru!" or "What is the meaning of Bodhidharma's coming from the West?—The cypress in the garden." Sayings like this that you can't draw any flavor out of are suitable.

If scattering continues, sit and look to that point where the breath ends and the eyes close forever and where the child is not yet conceived, where not a single concept can be produced. When a sense of the two-fold emptiness of self and things appears, scattering will surely rest.

8

Arising from stillness, carry out activities without hesitation. This moment is the koan. When practice and realization are without complexity then the koan is this present moment. That which is before any trace arises, the scenery on the other side of time's destruction, the activity of all Buddhas and Awakened Ancestors, is just this one thing.

You should just rest and cease. Be cooled, pass numberless years as this moment. Be cold ashes, a withered tree, an incense burner in an abandoned temple, a piece of unstained silk.

This is my earnest wish.

Shikantaza

Hakuun Yasutani

SHIKANTAZA should be personally and individually taught to you by a qualified teacher. While practicing shikantaza by yourself based only on what you've read is less harmful than unsupervised koan study, proper instructions are very rare.

The *Fukanzazengi* by Dogen Zenji is good instruction, but is very difficult to understand. It is especially hard to comprehend how to work with the mind, and how the practice relates to enlightenment. I will briefly explain how to practice shikantaza.

Generally speaking, zazen can be described in three phases: first, adjusting the body, second, the breathing, and third, the mind. The first and second are the same in both koan Zen and shikantaza. However, the third, adjusting the mind, is done very differently in the two practices.

To do shikantaza, one must have a firm faith in the fact that all beings are fundamentally buddhas. Dogen Zenji says in the ninth chapter of *Gakudo Yojin-shu (Precautions on Learning the Way):*

> You should practice along with the Way. Those who believe in the Buddha Way must believe in the fact that their own self is in the midst of the Way from the beginning, so that there is no confusion, no delusion, no distorted viewpoint, no increase or decrease, and no errors. To have such faith and to understand such a way and practice in accordance with it, is the very fundamental aspect of the learning of the Way. You try to cut off the root of

consciousness by sitting. Eight, even nine out of ten will be able to see the Way—have kensho—suddenly.

This is the key to practicing shikantaza. But this does not at all mean that one must believe that one's small-minded, self-centered life is Buddha's life—on the contrary! Casting all sorts of self-centeredness away and making yourself as a clean sheet of paper; sit, just firmly sit. Sit unconditionally, knowing that sitting itself is the actualization of buddhahood—this is the foundation of shikantaza. If one's faith in that fact is shaky, one's shikantaza is also shaky.

In doing shikantaza you must maintain mental alertness, which is of particular importance to beginners—and even those who have been practicing ten years could still be called beginners! Often due to weak concentration, one becomes self-conscious or falls into a sort of trance or ecstatic state of mind. Such practice might be useful to relax yourself, but it will never lead to enlightenment and is not the practice of the Buddha Way.

When you thoroughly practice shikantaza you will *sweat*—even in the winter. Such intensely heightened alertness of mind cannot be maintained for long periods of time. You might think that you can maintain it for longer, but this state will naturally loosen. So sit half an hour to an hour, then stand up and do a period of *kinhin,* walking meditation.

During kinhin, relax the mind a little. Refresh yourself. Then sit down and continue shikantaza.

To do shikantaza does not mean to become without thoughts, yet, doing shikantaza, do not let your mind wander. Do not even contemplate enlightenment or becoming Buddha. As soon as such thoughts arise, you have stopped doing shikantaza. Dogen says very clearly: "Do not attempt to become Buddha."

Sit with such intensely heightened concentration, patience, and alertness that if someone were to touch you while you are sitting, there would be an electrical spark! Sitting thus, you return naturally to the original Buddha, the very nature of your being.

Then, almost anything can plunge you into the sudden realization that all beings are originally buddhas and all existence is perfect from the beginning. Experiencing this is called enlightenment. Personally experiencing this is as vivid as an explosion; regardless of how well you know the theory of explosions, only an actual explosion will do anything. In the same manner, no matter how much you know about enlightenment, until you actually experience it, you will not be intimately aware of yourself as Buddha.

In short, shikantaza is the actual practice of buddhahood itself from the very beginning—and, in diligently practicing shikantaza, when the time comes, one will realize that very fact.

However, to practice in this manner can require a long time to attain enlightenment, and such practice should never be discontinued until one fully realizes enlightenment. Even after attaining great enlightenment and even if one becomes a roshi (Zen master), one must continue to do shikantaza forever, simply because shikantaza is the actualization of enlightenment itself.

The *Tenzo Kyokun* and Shikantaza

Kosho Uchiyama

ONE DAY WU-CHAO (Wuzhao) was working as the *tenzo* (head cook) at a monastery in the Wu-t'ai (Wutai) Mountains. When the Bodhisattva Manjushri suddenly appeared above the pot where he was cooking, Wu-chao beat him. Later he said, "Even if Shakyamuni were to appear above the pot, I would beat him, too!"

I find this story both intriguing and accessible. Here we have Wu-chao working as a tenzo in the Wu-t'ai Mountains, when suddenly one day while cooking rice, who should appear above the pot but Manjushri, the bodhisattva of wisdom, the very figure enshrined in the *sodo* (monks' hall)! Upon seeing this, Wu-chao struck Manjushri and exclaimed, "Even if Shakyamuni were to appear above the pot, I would beat him, too!"

I was ordained as a monk on the very day that war was declared in the Pacific, December 8, 1941. Throughout the entire war, I lived in harsh poverty. Afterward, things began to settle down, and other disciples of my teacher, Kodo Sawaki Roshi, were able to come together again, gradually restoring the semblance of a community. In 1948 and 1949 I was going through the most difficult years of my life. Despite the fact that I had been a monk for seven or eight years, I still had not figured out just what was the aim of zazen practice. It was also a time when food was scarce in Japan and many people were actually starving, a condition that most people today in the industrialized countries cannot even imagine. I thought it was great during those days to get to be a tenzo, because I could snitch a little extra food on the side. Yet, it seemed like every time my turn as tenzo came around, I would get distracted thinking about getting a little extra to eat. Inevitably, I would mess up something in my work. Actually, it was not only then that something would go wrong. Whenever I would ponder over what troubled me most during those days, such as what the aim of zazen ought to be, sure enough there would be a disaster in the kitchen! During the war, I had no spare time to read through the *Eihei Shingi* nor, as an old Zen expression instructs, to carry on my practice while reflecting on myself in the light of the ancient teachings. Just after the war, about the only thing I did have plenty of was time, and when I got around to reading the passage about Wu-chao, it greatly affected my attitude toward being a tenzo. When I thought carefully about Wu-chao beating Manjushri when he appeared above the pot and going right on with the cooking, I felt miserable about my inability to do the same thing, even though all that appeared above my pot was some "hungry ghost." I worked hard after that to chase away the ghosts whenever they showed up.

Dogen Zenji writes that "the directly transmitted buddhadharma of the ancient buddhas and patriarchs is just zazen." Zazen has the highest value in our practice of Buddhism. However, in the *Tenzo Kyokun* there are three passages which read: "The Three Treasures [Buddha, Dharma, and Sangha] are the highest and most worthy of respect of all things.... Given the opportunity to prepare meals for the Three Treasures,...our attitude should truly be one of joy and gratefulness"; and, a bit further in the chapter, "My sincerest desire is that you exhaust all the strength and effort of all your lives—past, present, and future—and of every moment of every day into your practice through the work of the tenzo."

You might conclude from studying these passages that to take up the problem of the meaning of zazen while working in the role of tenzo, or vice versa, to ponder the significance of the tenzo's work while sitting in zazen, would be the perfect way to carry on your practice. Such is not the case. When you sit in zazen, *just* sit, and when you work as a tenzo, *just* do that. It is the spirit of *just* sitting or *just* working that is common to both zazen and to the work of a tenzo. This idea of concentrating wholly on one thing is the cornerstone of the teachings of Dogen

Zenji. In Japanese, this is called *shikan,* and the ramifications this teaching of shikan may have in our lives are important.

Here I'd like to examine the connection between shikantaza (just doing zazen) and the work of the tenzo. Despite the fact that a great deal has been written about shikantaza, there is no other writing that brings the work of the tenzo and shikantaza together, and herein lies our problem. What I shall try to do is explain how I understand Dogen Zenji's teaching of shikantaza, and then take a look at the connection this has to the *Tenzo Kyokun.*

We already know that shikantaza means to just do zazen, but what does that mean, "to just do zazen"? Dogen Zenji describes the type of zazen we do as the "King of Samadhis." We can trace the word "zazen" back to the Sanskrit words *dhyana* and *samadhi.* Samadhi is sometimes called *toji,* to hold or see all things equally (and is sometimes written with different Chinese characters), or in Sanskrit, *samapatti.* Another definition of samadhi is that mind and environment are innately one. And finally, samadhi has been defined in this way: "The buddhadharma should be grasped so that mind and object become one."

The problem centers around this word "mind," in Japanese, *shin.* How we understand the use of this word is naturally going to affect our understanding of zazen.

When we think of mind in its ordinary use, we usually think of the psychological mind or conscious awareness. In Sanskrit, mind used in this sense is referred to as *citta,* in which case the expression *shin ikkyosho* would mean to gather our confused mind together and concentrate on one thing. By definition, zazen would become some sort of exercise in mental or psychic concentration, or a method for training the mind to attain a state whereby all of one's ideas or thoughts about some object would disappear, leaving the person completely unperturbed. This is the superficial implication of *munen muso,* no notion, no thought. Zazen of the Theravada teachings and of the non-Buddhist teachings are of this type of psychic concentration. Any method of psychic concentration works from the assumption that our mind is always in disorder and aims to still it by doing zazen. Dogen Zenji, however, never taught that zazen was merely a method of working to improve yourself, nor a simplistic straightening out of your own life with no concern for those around you. Dogen once said: "Even if you have the mind of a wily fox, do not practice the Theravada way of trying only to improve yourself!"

I would not want to suggest that when the word "mind" is used in Buddhist literature it never means psychological mind or conscious awareness, but by and large it is not used in such a narrow sense. We see that this is particularly true when Dogen Zenji used mind in a passage in the chapter entitled "Sokushin Zebutsu" ("Mind Is Buddha") of the *Shobogenzo*: "The meaning and scope of mind that has been directly transmitted from buddha to buddha is that mind extends throughout all phenomena, and all phenomena are inseparable from mind."

Mind as the directly transmitted buddhadharma is used in the sense of mind extending throughout all things, and of all things being included within mind. When we speak of a zazen based on the innate oneness of mind and environment, it should not be understood that zazen is a method of psychic concentration or of trying to still one's mind.

What, then, is the meaning of mind extending throughout all things, and all things being included within mind? First of all, I would like to express it in my own words and to examine how I see it applying to myself. Looking at the volumes and volumes of Buddhist teachings that had their origins in India with Shakyamuni, and which became more and more refined down through the ages, the words and expressions that arose have never been used loosely; they have almost always carried deep meaning and broad implications. For example, when this word "mind" was first used, I am sure that it was used in the same psychological sense we ordinarily think of today. However, when we come to the expression about mind extending through all phenomena and all phenomena being inseparable from mind, the implications of the word go far beyond psychology. The meaning here is total, nondualistic. It surpasses mental or psychological implications.

To talk of our being alive implies at the same time that there is also a world of phenomena in which we live. We usually assume that the world existed long before we were born and that our birth is our entrance onto the stage of an already existing world. At the same time, we often assume that our death means our departure from this world, and that after our death this world continues to exist. Within this way of thinking a fabrication is taking shape that is not the actualization of reality itself. The actuality of the world that I live in and experience is not merely a conglomeration of ideas or abstractions.

When we look at a cup that is set down between two of us, we have the feeling that we are looking at the same cup, though actually that is not so. You look at the cup with your vision, and from a certain angle. Moreover, you see it in the rays of light and shadows that come from your side of the room. This applies equally to me as well. In a very rough sense, we proceed to separate the reality of the situation by entertaining the idea that we both see the same cup. This is what I mean by the fabrication of ideas.

In the same way, we assume that a world exists that you and I experience in common with all other human beings, that this world existed prior to our births, and that it will continue to exist even after our deaths. But again, this is nothing more than an idea. Not only that, we wind up thinking that we live and die within this world of fabrication. This is an utterly inverted way of looking at one's life. My true Self lives in reality, and the world I experience is one I alone can experience, and not anyone else can experience it along with me. To express this as precisely as possible, as I am born, I simultaneously give birth to the world I experience; I live out my life along with that world, and at my death the world I experience also dies.

From the standpoint of reality, my own life experience (which in Buddhist terminology equals mind) and reality (which means the dharma or phenomena I encounter in life) can never be abstractly separated from each other. They must be identical. However, to take what I have just said and conclude that everything must therefore be "in my mind" (thinking, emotional, or psychological mind) would be to fall into another philosophical trap. On the other hand, to conclude that mind is totally dependent on the environment would be to relegate the matter of mind to a sort of naive realism. The teachings of Buddhism are neither a simplistic idealism nor some sort of environmentalism.

Shin, or mind, in terms of buddhadharma should be understood as follows: the mind that has been directly transmitted from buddha to buddha is the mind that extends throughout all phenomena, and all phenomena are inseparable from that mind. My personal life experience is at the same time the world of reality. Conversely, the world of reality constitutes my mind. Hence, the use of the word "mind" in this case goes far beyond having only a mental or psychological meaning. In our age, perhaps "pure life" would be a clearer expression than mind. In the daily course of things I encounter a world of phenomena, and it is through those encounters and my experience of them that I live out my life.

With the definition of mind that I have explained above, it is necessary to take another look at the expression, "The dharma should be grasped so that mind and object become one." This expression means that we must learn to see all phenomena (everything in life) from the foundation of a pure-life experience. All too often we while away our lives, creating general assumptions and ideologies out of the thoughts that arise in our minds, and, after having fabricated those ideas, we finally dissipate our life energy by living in the world we have abstracted from them. "The dharma should be grasped so that mind and object become one" means that we must see all of the worlds that our lives encompass from the foundation of our own personal life experience; our life experience is our mind. This means that all things in life function as parts of our bodies. This is also the meaning of toji, holding all things equally.

Dogen Zenji, then, did not intend that we get rid of all the delusions, fantasies, or thoughts that come into our heads during zazen. Yet, if we go about pursuing these thoughts, we are sitting in the zazen posture thinking, and not actually doing zazen. Trying to get rid of our thoughts is just another form of fantasy. Zazen, understood as mind being innately one with all phenomena, is a means of seeing all things from the foundation of pure life, wherein we give up both pursuing thought and trying to chase it away. Then we see everything that arises as the scenery of our lives. We let arise whatever arises and allow to fall away whatever falls away.

What I have just explained is the rationale behind the passage in the *Fukanzazengi*, written by Dogen Zenji, that says:

> Drop all relationships, set aside all activities. Do not think about what is good or evil, and do not try to judge right from wrong. Do not try to control perceptions or conscious awareness, nor attempt

to figure out your feelings, ideas, or viewpoints. Let go of the idea
of trying to become a buddha as well.

Human beings happen to be living creatures endowed with a head
inside of which thoughts and feelings appear and disappear. The occur-
rence of this phenomenon, even while doing zazen, is perfectly normal.
In the same way that various secretions and hormones flow through
the organs of the body, thoughts can be likened to secretions of the
mind. It is just that if we are not careful—or sometimes even if we
are!—we put these secretions into action, invest all our energy working
them out, and end up crippled, unable to act or move. The most important thing to bear in mind when practicing zazen is to completely let go
of everything, since secretion is nothing more than a normal function.
When we do that, everything that arises can be viewed as the scenery
of our lives. This has been described as "the most fundamental appearance of things." Chan (in Chinese), Zen (in Japanese), or dhyana (in
Sanskrit) also carry this meaning, while later on, historically, it was
referred to as *joryo*. "The deep sky never obstructs the floating white
clouds" is yet another expression of this scenery. Finally, an expression
sometimes used to describe the zazen of the Soto tradition, *mokusho-
zen,* which means to be silently illuminating, points to this scenery as
well. The basis for silent illumination is to entrust everything to the
posture of zazen, letting go of all that comes up without trying to work
out solutions for what we ought to do about this or that. This is what is
called shikantaza. When we do zazen with this attitude, it is no longer
sitting for the purpose of fulfilling some artificial fantasy such as gaining enlightenment or improving our minds.

In the *Shobogenzo* "Zuimonki," Dogen Zenji writes: "Sitting is the
practice of the Reality of life. Sitting is nonactivity. This is the true
form of the Self. Outside of this, there is nowhere to search for the
buddhadharma."

During zazen, if we are not very careful, we are apt to doze off or
daydream about something in our day-to-day lives. Since both these
conditions cloud over the natural purity of our life force, the essential
point is to wake up from either one and return to firmly maintaining the

zazen posture. This is the activity of shikantaza. This practice is in itself enlightenment; it is the wholehearted practice of this enlightenment that we should carry on.

So far, I have tried to outline my understanding of shikantaza. The spirit of the *Tenzo Kyokun* coincides with what I have been talking about up to now, that is, living out the reality of pure life. The attitude of the tenzo that Dogen Zenji writes about is one of living in the reality of pure life day by day. As I mentioned earlier, if we are not careful we are apt to smother the vitality of our lives through the fabrication of our ideas. The teachings in the *Tenzo Kyokun* operate from the foundation of the reality of life to thoroughly cut through the ideas and homespun philosophies we so often set up and attempt to carry out, and seek, rather, to truly allow that reality to function in our lives.

In the very beginning of the text, Dogen Zenji talks about the importance of the tenzo, cutting through the notion that this work is the same as that performed by "an ordinary cook or kitchen helper," to state that "the monks holding each office are all disciples of the Buddha and all carry out the activities of a buddha." In other words, the text shows us that the tenzo practices the reality of life just as validly as those practicing zazen. In Zen, this is called practicing single-mindedly with all one's energies. This attitude is completely different from the cut-and-dried assumptions people too often hold when looking at the world. Living by ordinary social or worldly values is a typical example of what I mean by living in a realm of fabricated thoughts and ideas, and relative values. That is why our practice consists of cutting through the ordinary social and market values of things and human beings, and of practicing with a life attitude based upon the practice of the reality of the life of one's total Self.

THE WHOLEHEARTED WAY

Eihei Dogen

ALL BUDDHA-TATHAGATAS TOGETHER have been simply transmitting wondrous dharma and actualizing *anuttara samyak sambodhi* for which there is an unsurpassable, unfabricated, wondrous method. This wondrous dharma, which has been transmitted only from buddha to buddha without deviation, has as its criterion *jijuyu zanmai*.

For disporting oneself freely in this samadhi, practicing zazen in an upright posture is the true gate. Although this dharma is abundantly inherent in each person, it is not manifested without practice, it is not attained without realization. When you let go, the dharma fills your hands; it is not within the boundary of one or many. When you try to speak, it fills your mouth; it is not limited to vertical or horizontal. Buddhas continuously dwell in and maintain this dharma, yet no trace of conceptualization remains. Living beings constantly function in and use this dharma, yet it does not appear in their perception.

The wholehearted practice of the Way that I am talking about allows all things to exist in enlightenment and enables us to live out oneness in the path of emancipation. When we break through the barrier and drop off all limitations, we are no longer concerned with conceptual distinctions....

For all ancestors and buddhas who have been dwelling in and maintaining buddha-dharma, practicing upright sitting in jijuyu zanmai is the true path for opening up enlightenment. Both in India and in China, those who have attained enlightenment have followed this way. This is

because each teacher and each disciple has been intimately and correctly transmitting this subtle method and receiving and maintaining
its true spirit.

According to the unmistakenly handed-down tradition, the straightforward buddha-dharma that has been simply transmitted is supreme
among the supreme. From the time you begin practicing with a teacher,
the practices of incense burning, bowing, nembutsu, repentance, and reading sutras are not at all essential; just sit, dropping off body and mind.

When one displays the buddha mudra with one's whole body and
mind, sitting upright in this samadhi even for a short time, everything
in the entire dharma world becomes buddha mudra, and all space in
the universe completely becomes enlightenment. Therefore, it enables
buddha-tathagatas to increase the dharma joy of their own original
grounds and renew the adornment of the way of awakening. Simultaneously, all living beings of the dharma world in the ten directions and
six realms become clear and pure in body and mind, realize great emancipation, and their own original face appears. At that time, all things
together awaken to supreme enlightenment and utilize the buddha-
body, immediately go beyond the culmination of awakening, and sit
upright under the kingly bodhi tree. At the same time, they turn the
incomparable, great dharma wheel and begin expressing ultimate and
unfabricated profound prajna.

There is a path through which the anuttara samyak sambodhi of all
things returns [to the person in zazen], and whereby [that person and
the enlightenment of all things] intimately and imperceptibly assist each
other. Therefore this zazen person without fail drops off body and
mind, cuts away previous tainted views and thoughts, awakens genuine buddha-dharma, universally helps the buddha work in each place,
as numerous as atoms, where buddha-tathagatas teach and practice, and
widely influences practitioners who are going beyond buddha, thereby
vigorously exalting the dharma that goes beyond buddha. At that time,
because earth, grasses and trees, fences and walls, tiles and pebbles, all
things in the dharma realm in ten directions, carry out buddha work,
therefore everyone receives the benefit of wind and water movement
caused by this functioning, and all are imperceptibly helped by the wondrous and incomprehensible influence of buddha to actualize the

enlightenment at hand. Since those who receive and use this water and fire extend the buddha influence of original enlightenment, all who live and talk with these people also share and universally unfold the boundless buddha virtue and they circulate the inexhaustible, ceaseless, incomprehensible, and immeasurable buddha-dharma within and without the whole dharma world. However, these various [mutual influences] do not mix into the perceptions of this person sitting, because they take place within stillness without any fabrication, and they are enlightenment itself. If practice and enlightenment were separate, as people commonly believe, it would be possible for them to perceive each other. But that which is associated with perceptions cannot be the standard of enlightenment because deluded human sentiment cannot reach the standard of enlightenment.

Moreover, although both mind and object appear and disappear within stillness, because this takes place in the realm of self-receiving and self-employing (jijuyu) without moving a speck of dust or destroying a single form, extensive buddha work and profound, subtle buddha influence are carried out. The grass, trees, and earth affected by this functioning radiate great brilliance together and endlessly expound the deep, wondrous dharma. Grasses and trees, fences and walls demonstrate and exalt it for the sake of living beings, both ordinary and sage; and in turn, living beings, both ordinary and sage, express and unfold it for the sake of grasses and trees, fences and walls. The realm of self-awakening and awakening others is fundamentally endowed with the quality of enlightenment with nothing lacking, and allows the standard of enlightenment to be actualized ceaselessly.

Therefore, even if only one person sits for a short time, because this zazen is one with all existence and completely permeates all time, it performs everlasting buddha guidance within the inexhaustible dharma world in the past, present, and future. [Zazen] is equally the same practice and the same enlightenment for both the person sitting and for all dharmas. The melodious sound continues to resonate as it echoes, not only during sitting practice, but before and after striking *shunyata*, which continues endlessly before and after a hammer hits it. Not only that, but all things are endowed with original practice within the original face, which is impossible to measure.

You should know that even if all the buddhas in the ten directions, as numerous as the sands of the Ganges River, together engage the full power of the buddha wisdom, they could never reach the limit, or measure or comprehend the virtue, of one person's zazen.

No Dualism

Shunryu Suzuki

WE SAY OUR PRACTICE should be without gaining ideas, without any expectations, even of enlightenment. This does not mean, however, just to sit without any purpose. This practice free from gaining ideas is based on the *Prajnaparamita Sutra*. However, if you are not careful, the sutra itself will give you a gaining idea [an idea of gaining something]. It says, "Form is emptiness and emptiness is form." But if you attach to that statement, you are liable to be involved in dualistic ideas: here is you, form, and here is emptiness, which you are trying to realize through your form. So "form is emptiness, and emptiness is form" is still dualistic. But fortunately, our teaching goes on to say, "Form is form and emptiness is emptiness." Here there is no dualism.

When you find it difficult to stop your mind while you are sitting and when you are still trying to stop your mind, this is the stage of "form is emptiness and emptiness is form." But while you are practicing in this dualistic way, more and more you will have oneness with your goal. And when your practice becomes effortless, you can stop your mind. This is the stage of "form is form and emptiness is emptiness."

To stop your mind does not mean to stop the activities of mind. It means your mind pervades your whole body. Your mind follows your breathing. With your full mind you form the mudra in your hands. With your whole mind you sit with painful legs without being disturbed by them. This is to sit without any idea of gain. At first you feel some restriction in your posture, but when you are not disturbed by the restriction, you have found the meaning of "emptiness is emptiness and form is form." So to find your own way under some restriction is the way of practice.

Practice does not mean that whatever you do, even lying down, is zazen. When the restrictions you have do not limit you, this is what we mean by practice. When you say, "Whatever I do is Buddha nature, so it doesn't matter what I do, and there is no need to practice zazen," that is already a dualistic understanding of our everyday life. If it really does not matter, there is no need for you even to say so. As long as you are concerned about what you do, that is dualistic. If you are not concerned about what you do, you will not say so. When you sit, you will sit. When you eat, you will eat. That is all. If you say, "It doesn't matter," it means that you are making some excuse to do something in your own way with your small mind. It means you are attached to some particular thing or way. That is not what we mean when we say, "Just to sit is enough," or "Whatever you do is zazen." Of course whatever we do is zazen, but if so, there is no need to say it.

When you sit, you should just sit without being disturbed by your painful legs or sleepiness. That is zazen. But at first it is very difficult to accept things as they are. You will be annoyed by the feeling you have in your practice. When you can do everything, whether it is good or bad, without disturbance or without being annoyed by the feeling, that is actually what we mean by "form is form and emptiness is emptiness."

When you suffer from an illness like cancer, and you realize you cannot live more than two or three years, then seeking something upon which to rely, you may start practice. One person may rely on the help of God. Someone else may start the practice of zazen. His practice will be concentrated on obtaining emptiness of mind. That means he is try-ing to be free from the suffering of duality. This is the practice of "form is emptiness and emptiness is form." Because of the truth of emptiness, he wants to have the actual realization of it in his life. If he practices in this way, believing and making an effort, it will help him, of course, but it is not perfect practice.

Knowing that your life is short, to enjoy it day after day, moment after moment, is the life of "form is form, and emptiness is emptiness." When Buddha comes, you will welcome him, when the devil comes, you will welcome him. The famous Chinese Zen Master Baso (Mazu), said,

"Sun-faced Buddha and moon-faced Buddha." When he was ill, some-one asked him, "How are you?" And he answered, "Sun-faced Buddha and moon-faced Buddha." That is the life of "form is form and empti-ness is emptiness." There is no problem. One year of life is good. One hundred years of life are good. If you continue your practice, you will attain this stage.

At first you will have various problems, and it is necessary for you to make some effort to continue your practice. For the beginner, practice without effort is not true practice. For the beginner, the practice needs great effort. Especially for young people, it is necessary to try very hard to achieve something. You must stretch out your arms and legs as wide as they will go. Form is form. You must be true to your own way until at last you actually come to the point where you see it is necessary to forget all about yourself. Until you come to this point, it is completely mistaken to think that whatever you do is Zen or that it does not mat-ter whether you practice or not. But if you make your best effort just to continue your practice with your whole mind and body, without gain-ing ideas, then whatever you do will be true practice. Just to continue should be your purpose. When you do something, just to do it should be your purpose. Form is form and you are you, and true emptiness will be realized in your practice.

Commentary on *Fukanzazengi*

Hakuyu Taizan Maezumi

THE TITLE OF THIS ESSAY by Dogen Zenji, *Fukanzazengi,* could be translated in a number of ways. Some translators have used *The Universal Pro-
motion of the Principles of Zazen.* Here it is translated as *The Principles
of Seated Meditation.* The thing to understand about this title is that, first
of all, Dogen Zenji isn't just giving a lecture on *how* to do zazen; he is, in
fact, really urging everybody to do it. Furthermore, he uses the word
fukan in the title to convey the universality of these principles, applying
them without exception to all beings. Of course, when we talk about how
to sit, we may say "just sit." But merely putting your body in a sitting
position isn't quite enough. *Zazen* literally means, "sitting Zen." And that
raises the question of "what is Zen?" Our practice should be real zazen,
and we must clarify what this is for ourselves. And yet, zazen can be done
by anybody and everybody. In order to do zazen, we don't need to have
anything more than this body. That much is quite sufficient.

When Dogen Zenji returned from China, he wasn't quite satisfied
with the kind of Zen practice then prevalent in Japan. He felt that it was
somehow less precise, less vital than it should be. For example, Eisai
Zenji himself combined the principles of Zen and the teachings of the
Tendai and Shingon Schools. So it wasn't really Zen alone that was being
taught and practiced.

But Dogen Zenji, after his great realization under Master Tendo, was
strongly convinced that just zazen alone should be practiced. In writing
this piece, Dogen Zenji wanted not only to promote the practice of zazen
as such, but to encourage people to do the kind of genuine zazen which
he had himself experienced and come to understand deeply.

It is characteristic of Dogen Zenji's writing style that he says the most important thing immediately, in the first couple of lines or in the first paragraph. Yasutani Roshi once told me that Harada Roshi used to stress the significance of the opening words of the *Fukanzazengi. "Tazunuru ni sore…,"* which I would translate roughly as "After searching exhaustively…" And yet in many English translations, this introductory phrase is not translated at all, being regarded as an untranslatable formal opening. But that may not be quite correct in this instance, for it greatly affects the meaning of the first paragraph.

Let us examine *Fukanzazengi* thoroughly.

Fundamentally speaking, the basis of the way is perfectly pervasive…

The sense of this opening passage, along with the introduction I just mentioned, is something like this: "After a thorough search for the truth, Dogen Zenji came to the realization that the very essence of the Way is basically perfect and all-pervading." The character *moto,* translated here as "the essence," is translated as a noun: the "essence of the Way." Or we could read it as "the fundamental Way." It is fundamental because it is universal; it is all-pervading; it is complete. It is *shunyata,* emptiness, buddha-nature.

It is our life!

We may speak of the Way as perfectly pervasive, but perhaps "free" might be clearer. But the Japanese word that means "perfectly pervasive" can also mean "unhindered functioning" and this functioning is active and positive. Before we go further, let me explain the two aspects of our practice and our life: the intrinsic, or absolute; and the experiential or relative. The intrinsic refers to an ultimate reality; the way things really are, whether or not we are aware of it. The experiential or relative level refers to what we directly and consciously experience as "real."

So looking at this passage from the experiential perspective, if we don't practice zazen and the Way correctly, then we miss the point. And so we create a gap between ourselves and externals—and we cannot recognize the Way.

But when we examine it from the intrinsic perspective, just being as we are is perfect. Perhaps the word "perfect" is not quite adequate; let me add the word "complete." Nothing is lacking; nothing is in excess. No two things are identical. Each of us is distinctly different; perfect and complete.

All of us enter into Zen to find our true self, the real implication of life and death. But here it says, "Fundamentally speaking, the basis of the way is perfectly pervasive...." What is the Way? In technical terms, it's *anuttara-samyaksambodhi,* unsurpassable supreme enlightenment. In Chinese this is translated as the "Supreme Way," the "very best Way," the "unsurpassable Way," or as "Perfect Wisdom," which is what enlightenment actually is. Enlightenment is synonymous with the Way. The Supreme Way, complete realization, is perfect in itself, by itself.

And again, we may ask, "What is wisdom? What is anuttara-samyaksambodhi?" It is our life itself. We not only have that wisdom; we are constantly using it. When it's cold, we put on more clothing. When it's hot, we take some clothes off. When hungry, we eat. When sad, we cry. Being happy, we laugh. That's perfect wisdom.

And this perfect wisdom doesn't only pertain to humans, but to anything and everything. Birds chirp, dogs run, mountains are high, valleys low. It's all perfect wisdom! The seasons change, the stars shine in the heavens; it's perfect wisdom. Regardless of whether we realize it or not, we are always in the midst of the Way. Or, more strictly speaking, we are nothing but the Way itself.

Of course, there are always reasons and causes for our being the way we are. The law of causation applies to everybody; no one escapes from it. In a sense, that law is everything. So the key is actually how clearly we realize the Way, which is, after all, nothing but ourselves. And realizing that the Way is all-pervading, perfect and complete, what have we to worry about?

In the Soto School, the emphasis is more on this original realization or fundamental enlightenment, which is nothing but our life itself. Then what we should do is take care of it and not stain or defile it. Whatever we do then becomes the act of the Buddha.

That's what the first line refers to when it says: "Fundamentally speaking, the basis of the Way is perfectly pervasive; how could it be contingent on practice and verification?"

The vehicle of the ancestors is naturally unrestricted;
why should we expend sustained effort?

The vehicle which is this very essence of life is totally free, without
bondage or restriction. That vehicle is nothing but our life, and thus our
life is also originally free, unrestricted. Of course, as long as we are alive
we have to live under certain conditions, which, in a sense, is a limitation. But within limitation there is always freedom. Regardless of where
you go or what you do, in one way or another your life is restricted.
Don't look to circumstances or the environment for your freedom. You
won't find it. You can always find freedom within limitation.

Surely the Whole Being is far beyond defilement;
who could believe in a method to polish it?

We have all sorts of defilements, but altogether it's far beyond defilements. This alone is a nice koan!
The Whole Being. What is the Whole Being? Again, it's nothing but
the body of each of us. Each one of us must go beyond all sorts of defilement. It's unnecessary to wipe off the dust of defilement as such. Isn't
it wonderful?
There is a famous passage from the *Platform Sutra,* quoting poems
by the Sixth Ancestor Huineng, and the monk Shenxiu.
Shenxiu's verse was:

Our body is the Bodhi tree,
Our mind a mirror bright.
Take care to wipe them hour by hour,
And let no dust alight.

And the Sixth Ancestor responded:

There is in fact no Bodhi tree,
Nor stand of mirror bright.
Since all is emptiness itself,
Where can dust alight?

Do you see? It's not a matter of dusting off, or of shining or polishing. Our original self, our original nature, buddha-nature—*that is the Way*. The Way, the whole being, is complete, perfect, free, all-pervading.

> *Never is it apart from this very place; what is the use of*
> *a pilgrimage to practice it?*

This is very important: The Way is always here; always right here and right now. Always, wherever you go, wherever you are, it's right here and right now, complete, free, all-pervading. Isn't it wonderful? That is our life. Just be so, be so. Don't defile it or stain this moment, right here and right now.

> *And yet if a hair's breadth of distinction exists, the gap*
> *is like that between heaven and earth....*

That means our individual existence or being is absolute and as obvious as the nose on your face. Each of us is perfect and free. This is a very strong affirmation of our life.

The point of our practice is not to become something other than what we already are, such as a buddha or enlightened person, but to realize or become aware of the fact that we *are* intrinsically, originally the Way itself, free and complete. If we practice to become something else, we simply put another head on top of our own, making ourselves ghosts. One head is enough!

So then, how do we realize that our life is complete and free? Or, if we realize it, how *clearly* do we realize that point? Clarifying this matter is why we practice.

Dogen Zenji says, "To study the enlightened Way is to study the self. And to study the self is to forget the self." To forget the self is not to create any distance between oneself and the Way. Then what creates our experience of separateness?

What creates the separation is always our limited, self-centered consciousness. There is nothing at all wrong with consciousness per se. Consciousness is a plain, pure function of the body-mind, and not a matter of right or wrong, problematical or not problematical. But our trouble is that we give too much value, too much authority, to our conscious functioning. We think that we can figure out everything by our intelligence, by our thinking, by our ideas and thoughts and concepts. That's how we get into trouble.

So, in practicing zazen, set aside those ideas and preconceived notions. Just stop that entire process of analysis and idea formation.

> *Once the slightest like or dislike arises, all is confused*
> *and the mind is lost.*

When you start having ideas of liking or disliking, right or wrong, good or bad, enlightened or deluded, then you lose the mind. Again, this mind is synonymous with the Way.

> *Though you are proud of your understanding and replete with*
> *insight, getting hold of the wisdom that knows at a glance, though*
> *you attain the Way and clarify the mind, giving rise to the spirit*
> *that assaults the heavens, you may loiter in the precincts of the*
> *entrance and still lack something of the vital path of liberation.*

Even attaining very clear enlightenment, still such attainment is just a beginning. There is a saying in Zen, "The head is through, but the body is still sticking out." Attaining enlightenment, clear vision, wisdom, seeing that the whole world is nothing but myself, such understanding is nothing but the beginning. And as long as you are stuck at that level, then you have fallen into the ocean of poison and can never liberate yourself.

Consider the story of Hakuin Zenji, who at the age of twenty-four years, attained very clear enlightenment upon hearing the temple gong at dawn. He was caught by a terrific sensation of delight and the thought that nobody in the last hundred years had had such a clear enlightenment as he. Much later, reflecting upon his youth, he wrote of this experience that "conceit and arrogance came up just like the ocean tide." Later on, he met Shoju Roshi, who deflated him thoroughly and helped him attain a still clearer realization.

We must be careful about how we proceed in our practice. Dogen

Zenji warns against attaining a little bit of realization and getting prematurely satisfied and conceited. To the extent that we do so, we tie ourselves up instead of becoming liberated.

> *Even in the case of the one of Jetavana, innately wise though he was, we can see the traces of his six years sitting erect.*

The Buddha, who was born in the grove of Jetavana, was born a prince. Even prior to becoming a monk, he was the finest youth in his country, excelling in all kinds of learning, literature, and sports. Yet even having such extraordinary talents and such a fine character, he still had to struggle for six years. Actually, it was more than that, because for six years prior to beginning his meditation under the bodhi tree, his zazen, he practiced the most severe asceticism. Finally he realized that asceticism was not the best way to practice, and started to sit by himself. So even having such tremendous capacity and such extraordinary character, still he had to struggle, to go through that much difficulty. So we too should practice hard.

In a way it seems contradictory, for Dogen Zenji has written that it's not really a matter of practice or enlightenment. If this is true, then why do we have to practice? But again that goes back to the two aspects of our practice: Speaking from the intrinsic perspective, of course, we say that fundamentally we are all buddhas and there is no need for anything such as practice or enlightenment since that is our true nature anyway. But the problem is that we may only believe that theoretically; we don't know it firsthand. To become directly aware of it and know it fully is why we practice.

> *...and in the case of the one of Shaolin, though he succeeded to the mind-seal, we still hear of the fame of his nine years facing the wall. When even the ancient sages were like this, how could men today dispense with pursuing [the Way]?*

What is the mind-seal? Again it is a synonym for the Way and also for the mind-to-mind transmission of the Dharma. In a sense, there is nothing to be transmitted. Realization is itself the transmission; a teacher just approves the realization. That is to say, you transmit yourself to yourself—by realizing that this very body, this very mind, this very place where we stand is nothing but the Buddha. What more could there be?

Generation after generation, the ancestral teachers did this. And their self-transmitted mind-seal approved, it is then handed down to the next generation who transmit it to themselves. Self-styled understanding is insufficient. For this reason, we emphasize the importance of the transmission by a teacher who really knows what it is and how it should be taken care of.

> *Therefore, stop the intellectual practice of investigating words and chasing after talk; study the backward step of turning the light and shining it back. Body and mind will drop away of themselves, and your original face will appear. If you want such a state, urgently work at such a state.*

Don't waste your time intellectualizing instead of really practicing, lest your intellectual activities become a kind of obstacle.

Dogen Zenji refers to the "the backward step." This is the key. In our everyday lives, our impulse is to go forward. However, instead of going forward, what if we were to step back and carefully consider practice in that very moment? How do we defile ourselves? We create gaps. These gaps, created by our self-centered, habitual consciousness, divide us from so-called externals or others. It is this kind of consciousness that discriminates.

Of course, the recognition of differences is a very important matter, too. Especially in koan study, you deal with the relationship between oneness and differences in a very special way—but only after having realized oneness. Without this ground of realization, we create all kinds of value judgments that divide ourselves from ourselves or set ourselves apart from externals. Value judgments are, in a way, necessary, and yet because of them we create problems. So the thing to do is step backward and not rush forward. Then examine and reflect upon yourself carefully.

"Body and mind will drop away of themselves." You don't need to concern yourself about body and mind dropping away. When you practice as Dogen Zenji describes, it will happen. So first you sit, then get into samadhi; then, in samadhi, that limited, self-centered consciousness disappears. You recognize that you and the universe are one. It just happens automatically.

"Body and mind will drop away of themselves, and your original face will appear."

"Original face" means enlightenment.

"If you want such a state, urgently work at such a state."

"Such a state" also refers to enlightenment. If you want to attain enlightenment, you should practice enlightenment without delay. And the practice of enlightenment is zazen.

> *For studying Zen, one should have quiet quarters. Be moderate in food and drink. Cast aside all involvements and discontinue all affairs. Do not think of good or evil; do not deal with right or wrong. Halt the revolutions of mind, intellect, and consciousness; stop the calculations of thoughts, ideas, and perceptions. Do not intend to make a buddha, much less be attached to sitting still.*
>
> *In the place where you regularly sit, spread a thick mat and use a cushion on top of it. Sit in either the full cross-legged or half cross-legged position. For the full position, first place your right foot on your left thigh; then place your left foot on your right thigh. For the half position, simply rest your left foot on your right thigh.*
>
> *Loosen your robe and belt, and arrange them properly. Next, place your right hand on your left foot, and your left hand on your right palm. Press the tips of your thumbs together. Then straighten your body and sit erect. Do not lean to the left or right, forward or backward.*
>
> *Your ears should be in line with your shoulders, and your nose in line with your navel. Press your tongue against the front of your palate and close your lips and teeth. The eyes should always remain open. Breathe gently through the nose.*

"Studying Zen" is one translation of the Japanese word *sanzen*.

Sanzen usually refers to the private face-to-face interview with a teacher, which is also called *nishitsu*. Nishitsu literally means "entering the room," and refers to entering the teacher's room for private dharma combat and dharma dialogue. But Dogen Zenji also says that zazen itself is sanzen. It's that important! Zazen itself is as important as private teachings from a master. In the word *sanzen, san* means "penetration"— you should really penetrate yourself. Really become yourself which is equal to everything. That's sanzen, and that's zazen.

One should have quiet quarters.

When we really get used to sitting, sound doesn't bother us much, but if our zazen is still getting established, noise may bother us. It's interesting; a constant noise, such as the ticking of a clock, is less disturbing, but music or the human voice are among the worst distractions, since they carry meaning and are constantly changing, and so tend to deflect our attention from zazen. Nevertheless, although a quiet room is preferable, just do your best wherever you are.

Be moderate in food and drink.

Moderation is important. And it's better to avoid sitting right after eating. Take a good rest, give your stomach a good chance to digest the meal, for at least an hour or so, then start sitting.

Cast aside all involvements and discontinue all affairs.

How, you might ask, can we live our lives with all the responsibilities we have to take care of, if we "cast aside all involvements"? At least when sitting, put aside all considerations of work, household duties, and family responsibilities.

Sitting and just thinking about all sorts of things, one after another, is not zazen; in fact, it's daydreaming! So when sitting, cast aside all these involvements and affairs; just try to sit well.

Occasionally I say "just sit," but you may find that a little hard to do. So you can do it gradually: First try to make yourself empty. If you are working on koans or on breathing, totally put yourself into your koan or into your breathing. Let it occupy you completely.

If you are practicing shikantaza, it's especially hard to do this. In all probability, you are not "just sitting," but "just thinking," "just imagining," or just something else. So in order to get past all that and truly just sit, you must try to cut off clinging to the senses.

When you hear a sound, instead of remaining outside of it, and thereby fighting it, just become that sound yourself. Really being that sound yourself, that sound won't disturb you anymore. The "me" that perceives the sound becomes one with the sound, leaving only the sound itself. This is emptying yourself.

With a koan it's the same process. Really put yourself into the koan, then you'll forget about yourself. That's what we call *ninku*, "person emptied" or "subject emptied." But still there remains the dharma, the object. So next, empty that too! Again, by really being *thus,* you become unaware of even being *thus.* This is a state of samadhi: both person and dharma are empty; subject and object are both empty. This is called the great death. In describing the great death, Dogen Zenji says, "body and mind drop away." When body and mind spontaneously drop away, you transcend the bondage of limited consciousness.

However, this is not necessarily an easy thing to do. So your sitting should be very solid and yet free of any physical strain.

Do not think of good or evil; do not deal with right or wrong. Halt the revolutions of mind, intellect, and consciousness; stop the calculations of thoughts, ideas, and perceptions.

When sitting, put thoughts aside. But this doesn't imply that we deny the value of consciousness; Dogen Zenji isn't urging us merely to become like logs or stones. Without any thoughts or views, we can still function clearly, like a bright mirror. The mirror is there, and simply reflects whatever is before it. When the object vanishes, so does the reflection; not a trace remains behind, but the mirror is still there. That's the state of mind to maintain during the practice of zazen. It's hard, but encourage yourself to sit like this.

I often compare the mind to a pond. When the water is clear and undisturbed, the reflection of the moon is perfectly clear. But if the water is stirred up by winds, the surface of the pond is disturbed, and then waves arise and distort the reflections. The wind of thoughts, opinions, and ideas causes waves in the mind. If a pond only had a few ripples, at least we could still recognize the moon and tell where it is. But when it's really choppy, we cannot locate the moon, even though the pond, of course, is still reflecting. Although we ourselves are nothing but buddha-nature, nothing but *mu*, nothing but mind, we cannot recognize this because of the choppy condition of our minds. But nonetheless, the pond is still always reflecting—and so are we.

Only when we are calm will we see the reflection of the moon clearly on the surface of the water. Then we'll recognize it for what it is. That recognition is always instantaneous; sudden, not gradual. But once this recognition comes, if we don't continue to sit, it may fade away—unless it's *extremely* clear to begin with. And when you have that kind of clarity, then you simply cannot stop practicing.

Practicing in this fashion you realize the true nature, or as Dogen Zenji says, "Your original face will manifest." This process occurs automatically.

Do not intend to make a buddha....

If you have any expectations, right there you have created a split. Right there is where duality comes into being. So when you do zazen, you don't need to expect anything, just do so, just be so "...much less be attached to sitting still." We can appreciate this in two ways. On the one hand, zazen is not simply sitting still; on the other, you must really be constantly practicing from morning to night. Whatever you do must be zazen. That kind of solid, powerful practice has nothing to do with physical posture; rather it is the practice of zazen in each activity throughout the day.

Dogen Zenji goes on to tell us:

Breathe gently through the nose.

This last sentence is interesting. Some teachers place great emphasis on breathing technique, but see how little Dogen Zenji says about breathing: "Breathe gently through the nose." Those who find themselves having difficulty in zazen, straining to breathe deeply or slowly, should just breathe, as Dogen Zenji says, "gently through the nose." By carefully balancing the body without overemphasizing breathing technique, you can sit quite well.

Regarding the disposition of the eyes, just gaze downward at a point about four feet in front of you. Let your gaze move toward the tip of your nose, and then let it rest upon the floor at a distance of three or four feet.

This is a good eye position, and when you maintain it, the eyelids usually will shut halfway. Thus without any special effort, you can have proper eye position. But if you are facing a wall and it is very close, or if your eyelids are naturally droopy, you can even close your eyes—but watch out for the tendency to become drowsy or to drift into thinking or daydreaming. Of course, it's better to keep the eyes half-opened, but even so, once you've established your practice fairly regularly, you'll not find closed eyes much of a problem. Make whatever adjustments of this sort you find most helpful in your sitting.

Dogen Zenji also speaks about the position of the mouth and tongue. Place the tip of your tongue against the roof of your mouth, leaving less room for air in the mouth. Close your lips, so that your teeth are touching lightly. By doing this, you can decrease your rate of salivation without any special effort—because when you become conscious of your saliva, you tend to produce more of it! But by leaving your mouth like this, you can forget about your salivation and strengthen your sitting.

Now, let me discuss posture briefly. The body should be perpendicular and not lean or incline in any direction. Sit up straight, carefully balanced. If you sit with poor posture, your body will ache. But over time, good posture will allow your body to adjust and you will sit more comfortably.

Even though Dogen Zenji doesn't mention the arm position, it is still important. Let your hands rest naturally either on your legs or feet, forming a circle with your arms. Be careful not to position your hands too high up on your abdomen. Your shoulder muscles should not be used to support your arms and hands; they should just rest naturally. Let the thumb-tips be about level with the navel, and, if you are sitting in half- or full-lotus, rest the hands on the soles or heels; otherwise just let your hands rest on your thighs.

Notice the lower back, the lower abdomen, the joints of the legs, the soles of the feet, and the hands—all these are in the same general area, and this area forms the very center of your sitting. Each of us has slight differences in bone and muscle structure, but we can adjust our posture accordingly. So please sit strongly—but sit without any tension. By being tense, you can strain yourself to the point of exhaustion. To sit strongly requires that your body be free of tension. When you really sit strongly, it's almost as though you are generating electricity; if anybody were to accidentally touch you, sparks would leap out!

When you do shikantaza, sit as if your very life depended on it, as if you were in a duel to the death. What kind of intense concentration would you have? You would need to be physically relaxed, and yet in a state of greatly heightened alertness. When we sit, two major types of hindrances may occur: a scattered, busy mind, and a dull, drowsy mind. And the way to eliminate both these hindrances while we sit is to concentrate in zazen as though engaged in the fight for our very lives.

When you really concentrate, it involves the entire body-mind. The power you generate with strong concentration can keep you warm, even in the coldest winter weather. So when you sit, please be attentive.

Once you have regulated your posture, take a breath and exhale fully. Swing to the left and right. Sitting fixedly, think of not-thinking. How do you think of not-thinking? Nonthinking. This is the essential art of zazen.

"Think of not-thinking. How do you think of not-thinking? Nonthinking." Dogen Zenji is quoting the famous words of Master Yakusan Igen (Yaoshan Weiyan). A phrase like this could be certainly elaborated quite a bit—for our purposes, we can plainly take it to mean that we should stop grasping at thoughts and just sit. That unconditioned state is a state of nonthinking. So what is the unconditioned state? Don't develop or cling to *any* thoughts.

It is very important not to hold on to your ideas, opinions, emotions—all the forms of thinking. That very unconditioned, unadorned state of mind, that's the state of nonthinking. Sit in that state. Don't even think of becoming Buddha. Trying to become Buddha or trying to become enlightened becomes a hindrance.

This kind of preconception is a hindrance because we don't know what enlightenment *is* until we experience it firsthand. Thus, whatever we think of as enlightenment merely becomes an idea, and enlightenment is not an idea. As soon as we form an idea, right there a gap opens. By sitting we empty ourselves of ourselves and of our objects. Thus the subject-object relationship is eliminated altogether and you are one. Zazen itself manifests ultimate reality. That's shikantaza.

Please understand that it is not denying the functioning of our mind when we say think nonthinking. Consciousness is vividly functioning, alive with ideas or thoughts. But that functioning is conditioned, and if we don't let go of the conditioned functioning of consciousness—the thoughts and ideas that arise—then we falsely find ourselves in those thoughts and ideas, and to the extent we do that, we restrict ourselves.

When we don't see this fact clearly, we imagine problems have origins outside ourselves. But this is not so: If there is any difficulty or problem, it's a problem of our own making.

And this is always the case! It may not seem so but it is. In a narrower sense it is so, and in a broader sense it is so too. Sometimes it is hard to grasp. For example, if the house next door catches fire, so the building in which we live is also burned up. We can blame others, and yet if we look at it from a larger perspective, they too are a part of ourselves. Ultimately, there is no one at all to blame.

When we really see into the nature of the self, then "my" becomes identical with "your" and "their" and even "its." That is the state of nonthinking. So again, we make ourselves as plain as possible, then just be as we are—and then our being becomes an absolute thing.

The zazen I speak of is not learning meditation. It is simply the dharma-gate of repose and bliss, the practice-realization of totally culminated enlightenment. It is the manifestation of ultimate reality.

The term used here is *practice-realization:* Practice *is* realization itself; we are practicing realization, or realizing our practice. That's our zazen.

This is to have deep faith in the fact that you are nothing but the Three Treasures. And having that faith, then sit, work, study. So whatever you do is nothing but the Buddha's action, expounding and manifesting the Dharma yourselves. And that is nothing but perfect unity and harmony altogether. Where's the problem? Even difficulties are nothing but the Dharma itself. What is there to complain about? What to be frustrated by? What to be annoyed about? "The practice-realization of totally culminated enlightenment" is the manifestation of absolute reality. In a way it's zazen; and in a way it's yourself. Your zazen is a total thing, and being so you also become ultimate and absolute.

> *Traps and snares can never reach it. Once its heart is grasped, you are like the dragon when he gains the water, like the tiger when he enters the mountain. For you must know that just there [in zazen] the right Dharma is manifesting itself and that from the first, dullness and distraction are struck aside.*

"Traps and snares can never reach it." Our own ideas, our own thoughts, these are the traps and snares and that very plain, mirrorlike state is the state that traps and snares can never reach. We snare ourselves with our fixed ideas.

Regardless of how fine a teacher you have or where you got your fine ideas, if you cling to any of them, then you're trapped! The monks who followed the Buddha knew this: At the beginning of the *Lotus Sutra*, as Buddha prepares to expound it on Mount Gridhrakuta, it says that five hundred monks just stood up and left.

> *When you arise from sitting, move slowly and quietly, calmly and deliberately. Do not rise suddenly or abruptly. In surveying the past, we find that transcendence of both unenlightenment and enlightenment, and dying while either sitting or standing have all depended entirely on the strength [of zazen].*

Now actually, this kind of thing happens—you would be amazed how much we can train ourselves. The Third Ancestor, Kanchi Sosan Daishi (Jianzhi Sengcan), died standing. Many monks died sitting. Some even died amid fire in a sitting position. We have a saying, "Emancipating the mind, even fire becomes cool." It's one of the lines of poetry one monk composed just before he was burned up.

Morita Goryu Roshi, who was the head of Eiheiji five or six generations ago, had to have a tumor removed from his neck and asked not to have any anesthetic. The doctor was amazed, but Morita Roshi didn't move once during surgery or cry out in pain. That's how much you can train yourself. Now that's what Dogen Zenji mentions here. "Dying while either sitting or standing have all depended entirely on the strength of zazen." He is talking about *joriki*.

> *In addition, the bringing about of enlightenment by the opportunity provided by a finger, a banner, a needle or a mallet, and the effecting of realization with the aid of a hossu, a fist, a staff, or a shout, cannot be fully understood by man's discriminative thinking. Indeed, it cannot be fully known by the practicing or realizing of supernatural powers either. It must be deportment beyond man's hearing and seeing—is it not a principle that is prior to his knowledge and perceptions?*

This is the place we get stuck. We try to understand enlightenment by our discriminative mind; yet, our discriminative, our discursive thought, is the very thing that binds us. The question really is how to go beyond, how to transcend that dichotomy. But we all have to start with that discriminative mind.

All of us want to liberate ourselves, to become free and peaceful. But that is not quite enough. That's just the *shravaka* spirit, the spirit of simply wanting one's own salvation. Of course, the shravaka spirit could also be interpreted differently, but that's one interpretation. But the bodhisattva is something else again. That is simply to care more about others than about oneself. Since we are altogether one to begin with, regardless of how fully we realize it, it works out beautifully. To think of others first, we do something for them; then, in one way or another, sooner or later it benefits ourselves. Dogen Zenji said that only the foolish think that concern for others is at one's own expense. It is not so; benefiting others and oneself is altogether one thing.

I really want you to have strong, inclusive aspiration and vows to accomplish the Buddha Way together with all beings. Then with such deep aspiration we encourage our practice. We just keep on going, and deep enlightened experiences will take place in one way or another. Here Dogen Zenji enumerates examples of such cases.

"The bringing about of enlightenment by the opportunity provided by a finger." The finger referred to is, of course, that of Gutei (Juzhi)—that famous koan "Gutei's Finger," which appears in the *Gateless Gate* and also in the *Book of Equanimity*. Whatever Gutei was asked, he just held up his finger. And when he was dying, he told his disciples, "I got this one-finger Zen from Master Tenryu (Tianlong), and I've used it all my life and have never exhausted it." Then, holding his finger up, he died.

Each of these objects Dogen Zenji mentions relates to famous cases of enlightenment: Ananda and the banner in front of the temple; Shishuang's "take a step from the top of a hundred-foot-high pole"; Kanadaiba's needle; Manjushri and the mallet; Baizhang and the fly whisk; Mazu's shout; Deshan's staff. All these are instances of ancestors and bodhisattvas whose enlightenment experiences involved certain objects. In each of these instances there is no room for dichotomy or dualism, no room for thinking. For example, if you burn your finger or you get hurt, there's no room for thinking. You just shriek, "AAAR-RGGGHH!" That's all. That totality, that absoluteness, that's what you should experience by yourself. How? Again the same principle of forgetting yourself, of really becoming a total being.

"Indeed, it cannot be fully known by the practicing or realizing of supernatural powers either." Some people are attracted by supernatural powers. I've heard that even these days a number of people have certain occult powers. By increasing your samadhi power you can train yourself in that path if you wish to. But the point is that even acquiring such supernatural powers won't give us the wisdom by which we liberate ourselves and others from the tie of birth and death. The gatha we chant every evening says, "Life and death are of grave importance." To really take care of them or take care of our lives altogether, that is the aim of our practice.

This being the case, intelligence or lack of it does not matter; between the dull and the sharp-witted there is no distinction.

Regardless of being intelligent or dull, female or male, we have the same opportunity, the same chance to realize ourselves, and it all depends on each of us. It's not a matter of any distinction whatsoever.

If you concentrate your effort single-mindedly, that in itself is negotiating the Way. Practice-realization is naturally undefiled.

What makes defilement are self-centered, ego-centered ideas. When the time comes, we get up; when the time comes, we eat. Everything goes smoothly; that is the functioning of our wisdom. Ideally, whatever comes along, day after day, we just put ourselves into it.

Then "practice-realization is naturally undefiled." "Going forward in practice is a matter of ordinariness." This is one of the most important statements in the *Fukanzazengi*: "Going forward is a matter of ordinariness." Going forward regardless of how much we achieve or accomplish, still it's ordinary. Still it's everyday. The word *ordinary* is etymologically related to *orderliness*, and orderliness is extremely important. Orderliness of mind, orderliness of body, orderliness of daily life, orderliness of surroundings, orderliness of groups, orderliness of society, country, even of the moon—everything. No matter how far we go, we are just whatever we are. So we don't need to lose our heads, or put an extra head on top of ours. We just need to be ordinary. If we can live every day like that, there is no problem. Then practice-realization is naturally undefiled.

In our world and the other quarters, from the Western Heaven to the Eastern Earth, all equally maintain the Buddha seal, while each enjoys its own style of teaching. They devote themselves only to sitting; they are obstructed by fixedness. Though they speak of ten thousand distinctions and a thousand differences, they only study Zen and pursue the Way. Why abandon the seat in your own home to wander in vain through the dusty regions of another land? If you make one false step, you miss what is right before you.

Here again we see Dogen Zenji's strong emphasis on zazen. "In our world" is the world where Shakyamuni resides, the Western Heaven is the world of Amida Buddha, and the Eastern Earth is the Medicine Buddha's realm. Each direction of the compass is governed by a different Tathagata. Thousands of buddhas are living, taking care of us and of everything. How do we relate to them?

What is the Buddha seal? It is understanding our lives as awareness and wisdom. Everything depends on our devoting ourselves to zazen.

If all of us were to sit like that, attaining enlightenment would be as simple as eating three meals a day. But since we don't sit like that, it won't happen that easily. So at least when we sit, we try to really sit well, like immovable mountains.

Though they speak of ten thousand distinctions and a thousand differences, they only study Zen and pursue the Way.

Although each of us is different, we should all practice, penetrating into zazen and accomplishing the Way.

Why abandon the seat in your own home to wander in vain through the dusty regions of another land?

When we read this line, we think that Dogen Zenji is talking about going abroad to practice. But there is another implication. Sometimes the objects of our senses are called the "six dusts." When we are conditioned by what we see, hear, smell, taste, think, and feel, it's like dust. So instead of being in the conditioned state, adjust.

The seat Dogen Zenji mentions is the diamond seat, where the Buddha sits. That's our zazen. The very zafu on which we sit is the diamond seat, the seat of the Buddha; so we don't need to go anyplace. The seat of the Tathagata is always right here now.

If you make one false step, you miss what is right before you.

There is a story in the Lotus Sutra of the beggar who is the long-lost son of a millionaire. Wandering around all his life thinking himself a beggar, he finally ends up at his father's house. His father recognizes him immediately, but only when the son becomes comfortable in his father's house does his father reveal himself and leave him his possessions. In the same way, we mistakenly believe ourselves to be impoverished, and our practice is to return home and know who we really are.

Since you have already attained the functioning essence of a human body, do not pass your days in vain; when one takes care of the essential function of the way of the Buddha, who can carelessly enjoy the spark from a flint? Verily form and substance are like the dew on the grass, and the fortunes of life like the lightning flash: in an instant they are emptied, in a moment they are lost.

How precious and how rare it is to be born as a human! To be human is truly precious. As humans, we are able to be Tathagatas.

The concluding passage of the *Diamond Sutra* says, "All composite things are like a dream, a fantasy, a bubble and a shadow; like a dewdrop and a flash of lightning—they are thus to be regarded." In a way, life is long, between seventy and a hundred years, but when we compare it to infinite time, it's short. The time we can put into our practice is also very limited. So the time we have right now is really precious time. Let us reflect upon ourselves, how we can have a stronger, better practice together. And not only make ourselves happy and content, but share such understanding, freedom and peace with other people.

Eminent students [of the Dharma], long accustomed to groping for the elephant, pray do not doubt the true dragon. Apply yourselves to the way that points directly at reality; honor the man who is through with learning and free from action. Accord with the bodhi of all the Buddhas; succeed to the samadhi of all the Patriarchs. If you act this way for a long time, you will be this

*way. Your treasure store will open of itself, and you will use it as
you will.*

In this last paragraph Dogen Zenji sums up again what zazen is and
what it does for us. The line "long accustomed to groping..." refers to
the parable of the blind men and the elephant, in which a group of blind
men try to find out what an elephant is like, using only their sense of
touch. One, feeling the trunk, says that elephants are shaped like
snakes; another, feeling the legs, says that elephants are like trees; each
blind man clings to his own limited perception, and so jumps to a false
conclusion.

In the same way we have our own self-styled ideas, understandings,
and concepts, and we stick to them and regard them as measurements
and to that extent we can't accept anything else. A larger container
can contain more, but our practice is to be bottomless. We do this by
forgetting the self. To study the Buddha Way, to transmit the samadhi
of the ancestors, we've got to be bottomless. Otherwise the Dharma
won't fit.

"Do not doubt the true dragon." The true dragon represents freedom.
We are bound by whatever we cling to, even enlightenment. We can be
bound by enlightenment, freedom, even peace, in which case there is
actually no enlightenment, freedom, or peace. Similarly, if, like the blind
men, we get attached to our limited perceptions of the elephant, of reality, we miss the true dragon, which is life as it really is.

This "true dragon," by the way, is a reference to still another story.
There was a man by the name of Shoko, who loved dragons. And all
over his room, there were pictures, sculptures, and paintings of dragons.
A true dragon up in heaven was very impressed and appreciated Shoko's
love of dragons. He wanted to visit Shoko and show him a true dragon.
So one night this dragon came down to visit Shoko and stuck his face in
through one window and his tail through the other window. Shoko was
so shocked, he fainted.

*Long accustomed to imitations, do not be suspicious of what is
true. Apply yourselves to the Way that points directly at reality.*

That is zazen. This is what we are doing.

Honor the man who is through with learning and free from action.

Honor the man who has, in Japanese, *zetsu gaku mui.* This is an idiomatic expression, and the translation here doesn't capture all of the aspects of it. *Zetsu gaku* means "stopped learning" or "no-learning." There are the "ten no-learnings": adding two to the Eightfold Path, a ninth one, "right wisdom," and the last one, "right liberation," we get ten "no-learnings." That's zetsu gaku—being liberated. And *mui* means "non-doing, doing nothing." Not doing nothing physically, though: doing anything, everything, whatever's necessary, yet not doing it. In other words, be totally absorbed by whatever you are doing.

Dogen Zenji says that when you meet the person who expounds the Dharma, don't think of the caste that person came from, don't think of the appearance, don't think of conduct or behavior—but paying reverence to the prajna wisdom, every day, day after day, make three bows to him three times daily. Don't raise any frustrations, complications, or agitations within yourself. Making yourself empty and unconditioned as much as possible; listen carefully. Then whatever he says comes in without any friction. "Revere the man of complete attainment who is beyond all human agency." The man of complete attainment is always in the midst of all human agency, and goes with it without disturbance or friction. Otherwise, what is the use?

Gain accord with the enlightenment of the Buddhas.

Perhaps better than "gain accord" we should say " become one." In becoming one with the enlightenment of the Buddhas, we become the Buddha ourselves. "Succeed to the legitimate lineage of the Ancestors' samadhi." Really sit and become zazen yourself. But it's not you doing zazen, but zazen doing zazen. That's what samadhi is. And when you get into that samadhi, right there the lineage of the Ancestors is manifested, is succeeded.

Constantly perform in such a manner and you are assured of being a person such as they.

When we read it as "constantly perform in such a manner," it becomes a kind of conditional, "if you do such-and-such, then such-and-such." That's the way it's usually translated. But instead of reading "if you do such-and-such," we can read it "since it is this suchness." "Since it is already this, just do it in that way, or just be that." And when we really do that, the treasure-house opens by itself and then we can use that treasure freely. It's not a matter of something happening in the future, but it's always right now, right here.

Let's share that treasure together.

How to Sit

P.T.N.H. Jiyu-Kennett

When sitting, one should take care that one's spine follows the natural curvature of a healthy spine, as seen in any good medical book, as much as possible. It is very important for a person learning to sit to get this right. What happens with the feet is not important; what happens to one's spine is of the utmost importance. If the spine is not correct for the individual concerned, stiffness, pain, and perhaps even hallucinations may result. The weight of the body is carried easily by the lower back muscles if this position is correct; one does tend, however, to develop something of a bulge in the front, popularly called a "Zazen pot." This cannot be helped and should not be worried about. It sometimes happens that a person may have had a back injury of some sort during his or her earlier years and this may make sitting with a spine exactly right extraordinarily difficult. You should know that what we are attempting to do is to find the place where a person can sit best so as to have the very best results possible.

One never sits completely back upon the cushion or chair. When sitting on the floor, only the tip of the base of the spine should actually be on the cushion itself so that there is a slight slope from the buttocks, just seated on the edge of the cushion, to the floor where the knees rest comfortably. This posture prevents anything from pressing upon the thighs which may restrict the blood flow. If one sits fully upon the cushion, without allowing this free space for the thighs, it will be impossible to move from the cushion without considerable pain at a later time. The head should feel naturally comfortable and weightless upon the shoulders, with the ears in line with the latter and the nose in line with the navel. No two people are exactly the same physically so it is very important to experiment carefully for yourself so that you can be certain that you have found the right place for your head and the right place for your feet. If your ears are not exactly in line with your shoulders as a result of a back injury of some sort, do not feel that you cannot meditate. Find that place in which you are most comfortable, that is, the place where you are most weightless, and commence your meditation in that position. One sways one's body from left to right, after the correct sitting position has been achieved, starting with large sways and ending with smaller and smaller ones; one can do circular swaying instead of this if one wishes. These types of movement enable a person to find the best position of rest for him or her as an individual; the place at which all his or her weight seems to drop straight down the spine and into the cushion or onto the chair.

The hands must not be pushed together but held in the lap with the thumbs lightly touching the ends of each other. A left-handed person places the right hand over the left, and a right-handed person the left hand over the right, for the following reason: one side of the body is always slightly more active than the other, usually the side that one uses most; therefore, during seated meditation, one puts the hand of the less active side over the hand of the more active one since it is believed that this helps to equate the unevenness of the body's activity.

No one should ever close their eyes completely. They should be lowered so that they rest upon a spot on the floor that the meditator can see comfortably. No two people are ever comfortable at exactly the same distance of focus; therefore, although it is customary to say that it is best to allow the eyes to rest upon the floor at a distance of about one meter, it should be understood that this is not a hard and fast rule. Neither a short-sighted nor a long-sighted person could achieve this. One does not sit in meditation to do that which is unnatural for oneself; therefore, if it is normal for a person to wear spectacles, he should continue to do so while meditating; he should not remove them. The natural inheritance and right of all of us is to know our True Selves, that is, to be peaceful and at one with the Eternal; in order to achieve this we must not do something that is unnatural for us, as individuals, simply because meditation instructions that have been written for the perfect body say that we should....

It is important to do much the same thing with the eyes that one does with one's mind. One must neither try to see anything specific, such as the patterns on the wall or floor, nor try to make such things blurry and indistinct. One should simply keep the eyes downcast and in focus. One keeps one's eyes open so as to be able to stay awake and alert. A person is not trying to see and, at the same time, he is not trying not to see.

It is important to breathe through the nose and not through the mouth. This is achieved quite simply by keeping the mouth shut and nothing more. It is not a hard, tight shutting that may cause the teeth to grind; it is just a simple, comfortable closing of the mouth.

When breathing, a person must not do anything that is unnatural. There are many and varied forms of so-called meditation, all of which give varying degrees of spiritual comfort. There is no form that gives greater spiritual comfort, and deeper understanding and awareness, than serene reflection meditation as far as I am concerned; however, these benefits can only be achieved if one breathes naturally. It is important to synchronize one's breathing with the natural state of one's own body. If the breathing is rough, that is, strained or made unusual by the individual concerned, there can be no harmonization whatsoever of body and mind. Some of us breathe more quickly than others, others more slowly. Each person must breathe in his or her own normal, natural rhythm so that no unusual stresses or strains are caused. Again, the accent is on not being unnatural.

One must not deliberately try to think nor deliberately try not to think. Thoughts come and go in our heads and we can either play with them or just sit there and allow them to pass. Too many of us allow ourselves to be hijacked by our thoughts, while some try to deliberately push them away; both of these activities are completely incorrect. The Japanese distinguish between deliberate thought and natural thought. There is absolutely nothing wrong with natural thought. Because our ears are not plugged up during meditation, it is normal for us to hear cars passing on the roads and birds singing; because our eyes are not closed, it is only reasonable that we will notice patterns on the carpet, floor, or wall: these things will only disturb us if we permit ourselves to discuss them in our own minds. If one merely notices that a car is going by there will be no problem. However, if one notices that a car is going by and becomes annoyed or pleased about it, then meditation has already ceased. All that is required in meditation is that one sit with a positive attitude of mind, knowing that, if one does so, one will indeed find the True Buddha within oneself.

I have often used the example of sitting under a bridge to illustrate the above. One sits beneath a bridge across which traffic is traveling in both directions. One does not climb upon the bridge to hitch a ride in one of the cars, nor does one chase after them; one also makes no attempt to push the cars off the bridge. One cannot ignore that the cars are there; one does not have to be bothered by them. If a person does get caught by his or her thoughts (which, in the beginning, is quite likely), it is important not to worry about it. One merely accepts the fact that one was caught and continues to sit, without worrying about the fact that one was caught or feeling guilty about it. No matter what one does, one cannot change the fact that one was caught and, if one worries about it, one just does not become peaceful enough to return to meditation. One should avoid guilt at all costs concerning this; there is nothing so destructive as guilt in this regard.

When the meditation is over, one sways the body from side to side or in a circular motion, exactly as one did at the beginning, except that one commences with small sways and ends with large ones.

It is important not to wear anything that is either tight or constricting. It is equally important to dress adequately so that one is neither too hot nor too cold. The great Master Dogen, when speaking of excesses, that is, too much warmth, too much clothing, too much food, not enough warmth, not enough clothing, not enough food, makes the following comment: "Six parts of a full stomach support the man, the other two support his doctor." One must make sure that one is adequately fed and clothed, with just the right amount of rest, and thereafter not indulge oneself. Great Master Dogen gives a very important warning concerning what he calls the three lacks, that is, lack of sleep, lack of food, and lack of warmth. Unless these three are exactly right, neither too much nor too little of any, the harmonization of body and mind is impossible.

Question: What happens if a person is halfway through a meditation period and cannot continue to hold the same sitting position?
It is advisable to move and not worry about doing so. Seated meditation is not an endurance test. If a person feels that he or she cannot maintain the meditation position, there is nothing whatsoever wrong with changing it. Should it become necessary to move, it is very important to remember that the spine should again be correctly aligned. It is also important to discipline oneself to a certain extent. I have always maintained that a person who feels that he can sit for ten minutes should push himself to sit for twelve minutes and that, when he is able to sit for twelve minutes, he should push himself to sit for fourteen minutes. He should continue in this way until he can maintain the same position during the full forty-five-minute sitting period without discomfort. By such means the body is disciplined gently and naturally while recognizing that it has rights. If it is not done in this way, sitting may become something that is dreaded; I know of nothing worse than this.

Question: What about fidgeting?
If a person wishes to progress in meditation, it is very important for him or her to learn to sit still. Fidgeting, if the body is not uncomfortable, is a sign of a person's dislike of discipline and is a measure of the ego that is, as yet, unconverted. The debate of the opposites in our minds is not always as clear-cut as we think, and the urge to fidget is sometimes a reaction to our unwillingness to do something about ourselves. If a person finds himself suffering from the urge to fidget, he should take two or three deep breaths and again realign his body since he will probably have become tense and stiff in the shoulders.

If we were all short, fat, thin, or tall, had exactly the same eyesight or were in exactly the same state of health, it would be extraordinarily easy to teach meditation. However, each one of us is totally different, and this means that it is impossible to write a chapter on the mode of physical sitting necessary for meditation that will be exactly the same for everyone. It is important for a person to have himself or herself checked carefully by a competent teacher to find what is exactly the right position for him or her as an individual. Too many people try to keep to the letter of the physical *Rules for Meditation* without realizing that the purpose of them is to help them learn to meditate, not to cause them physical pain and unnatural discomfort.

To Live Is Just to Live

Dainin Katagiri

BASED ON SHAKYAMUNI BUDDHA'S EXPERIENCE and the experience of the buddhas in the past, the main point of Dogen Zenji's teaching is that zazen is to just become present in the process of zazen itself; this is shikantaza. It is not something you acquire after you have done zazen. It is not a concept of the process; it is to focus on the process itself. It is very difficult to understand this because even though we are always in the process, we don't focus on it. There are even many schools in Buddhism that still handle Buddhism as a concept. But real Buddhism is to focus completely on the process itself. The process is you.

Zazen is completely different from other meditations. It is not a matter of philosophical or metaphysical discussion. All we have to do is do what we are doing, right now, right here. Whatever kind of experience we have through zazen is secondary. Whatever happens, all we have to do is to be constantly present right in the middle of the process of zazen. This is the beginning and also the end. You can do it; it is open to all people, whoever they are. This is shikantaza.

We are already exactly peaceful and harmonious. But still, when we do zazen, we want to try to be peaceful. Trying to be peaceful is no longer to be peaceful. Just sit down. We do not have to try or not try or say that we do not care. If I say something is this way, immediately you rush and try to grasp it. And then if I say it is not this way, you immediately try to grasp that. Then I say it is not that either, and then you are confused. Finally, you say you are neutral, but that is not good either. What we have to do is realize we are buddha; this is a big koan for us.

This practice is called shikantaza and is our koan for our whole life. There are hundreds of koans, but those koans are just leaves and branches, that is all; the root is shikantaza. We have to understand this. This is perfect peace, perfect harmony.

We are always thinking about something, always trying to acquire something. Some people criticize Soto Zen, because it teaches not to expect enlightenment, to just sit down. They say if one cannot expect enlightenment, then what are we doing? Even Soto priests do not always understand what shikantaza is. Then if they are criticized, their faith starts to wobble. This is very common. This is to be a human being, and includes not only my friends, and others, but it includes me. If someone criticizes us, then our faith starts to wobble. If we look around, there are many things for people to be interested in. Very naturally, we think some other way would be better. So we pick it up and use it. But if we are wobbling, our feet are already not completely grounded. It is just like walking during a big earthquake. Even though we believe we are walking stably, we are not. If we are going to walk, we have to walk stably, no matter what happens. This is completely beyond being a matter of discussion. To walk in stability means to just walk. "Just walk" is to be present in the process itself. The process of walking is exactly that our body and mind are nothing but the process. There is no gap between us and the process. This is shikantaza; this is to be peace. We are peaceful, we are harmonious from the very beginning. That is why we should not expect to acquire peace. Take off all conceptual clothes, and then what is left? Finally, there is nothing to think about. All we have to do is just plunge in.

For twenty-five hundred years the Buddha has been teaching us that we are buddha, that we lack nothing of the highest enlightenment. Still we do not completely understand, and even though we understand, it has not settled down in our hearts. That is why we have to practice constantly. We have to practice because we have a mind.

Mind is tranquility; it means peace and harmony. What is wrong with mind? Nothing is wrong with mind. What *is* wrong is that for many years we have given our mind the chance, the environment, the circumstances for it to be a monkey mind. Monkey mind means the mind is always going out, in many directions, picking up many things that are fun and exciting. If we always leave the mind to take its own course, finally before we are conscious of it we are going in a different direction than we expected and we become completely confused. That is why we have to take care of mind. We have to take care of chances, circumstance, time, and occasions.

For zazen, we arrange the circumstances in the zendo so that it is not too bright or too dark, not too cold or too hot, not dry or wet. We also arrange the external physical conditions, such as our posture and the amount of food we eat. If we eat too much we fall asleep pretty easily, so we have to fill just sixty or seventy percent of our stomach. Also, we keep our eyes open, because if we close our eyes we might fall asleep, or we are more likely to enjoy ourselves with lots of imaginings and daydreams. Next we arrange our internal physical condition, that is, our heart, our intestines, our stomach, and our blood. But these things are beyond our control, so how can we take care of them? The only way is to take care of the breath. If we take care of the breath, very naturally, internal physical conditions will work pretty well. This is important. If we arrange the circumstances around our body, our mind, and all internal and external conditions, then, very naturally, the mind is also engaged in our activities. Then we are not bothered by the workings of our mind; the mind does not touch the core of our existence; it is just with us, that is all. When all circumstances are completely peaceful, just our center blooms. This is our zazen; this is shikantaza.

Shikan is translated as wholeheartedness, which seems to be sort of a psychological state or pattern. But shikan is not a psychological pattern. Shikan is exactly becoming one with the process itself. Literally, *za* of *taza* is zazen, and *ta* means to hit; so, from moment to moment, we have to hit the bull's-eye of zazen itself. This is not a technique. In the sword practice of *kendo*, one has to hit right in the middle of the opponent's head to get a point. This is not a technique; it is the practice that has been accumulated day after day. Our practice must be very deep, unfathomable, and then we can hit the bull's-eye. Shikan is exactly taza—full devotion to zazen itself, that is, to the process itself and not to a concept. This is the practice of zazen mentioned by buddhas and ancestors.

Dogen Zenji says in "The King of Samadhis Samadhi": "Even though some may have known experientially that sitting is the Buddhadharma, no one knows sitting as sitting." Even in Dogen Zenji's time, no one knew this except his master, Ju-ching (Rujing). Sitting as sitting is just the process of zazen itself; this is exactly life and death. If we look at our life, it is very clear. How often in our lives have we had feelings of happiness, unhappiness, pros and cons, success and failure? Countless numbers of times. But we are still alive. Regardless of whether or not we awaken to how important the essence of human life is, basically we are peaceful and harmonious. In other words, our life is just a continuation of living, that is all, "being living" constantly. That is why everyone can survive, no matter what happens. Is it our effort that makes it possible for us to survive for twenty years or forty years? No. Is it our judgment? No. Strictly speaking, it is just a continuation of becoming one with the process of living, that is all. This is the essence of living. The truth of living is just to live. This is a very simple practice.

To Study the Self

Shohaku Okumura

*To study the Buddha Way is to study the self.
To study the self is to forget the self. To forget the self
is to be verified by all things. To be verified by all things
is to let the body and mind of the self, and the body
and mind of others, drop off. There is a trace of realization
that cannot be grasped. We endlessly keep expressing
the ungraspable trace of realization.*

—Dogen Zenji from "Genjokoan"

To study the Buddha Way is to study the self. This is the most essential point of Dogen's as well as Buddha's teaching. In the *Dhammapada,* one of the earliest scriptures in Buddhism, Shakyamuni Buddha said, "The self is the only foundation of the self."

But what does this really mean? When we say that we study the Buddha Way, we think "I," this person, studies some objective thing called the "Buddha Way." "I" is the subject and the "Buddha Way" is the object. This person called "I" wants to understand it and make it "my possession." This is our common understanding of "I" "study" "something."

The original Japanese word Dogen uses for "study" is *narau*. Narau comes from *nareru,* which means "to get accustomed to," "to become familiar with," "to get used to," or "to become intimate with." This is not simply intellectual study.

In the Chinese character for narau, the upper part of the *kanji* means "bird's wings." The lower part of the kanji refers to "self." This study is like a baby bird studying or learning how to fly with its parents. By nature, a baby bird has the ability to fly, but a baby bird does not know how to fly. So the baby watches its parents and learns how to fly. It tries again and again, and finally it can fly like its parents. This is the origi-nal meaning of "to study" here. This is not simply intellectual study. Of course, intellection is included in the case of a human being, in the capac-ity of studying or learning, but merely accumulating knowledge does not allow us to fly (to live out ourselves in its true meaning). As flying is the essential thing for a bird (except a bird like a penguin or an ostrich), to be a bird, to study the self is the essential thing for us human beings to be human. A human being is a living being that needs to study the self to become the self.

This is the meaning of "to study" here. When we study the self, we cannot see ourselves as objects. We have to live out ourselves. We have to practice with this body and mind to study the self. Intellectual inves-tigation is only a small part of it, though it is not less important.

Even when we say, "I study the Buddha Way," still there is a subject "I" and an object—the Buddha Way. When we speak in that way, "I," "study," and "the Buddha Way" are separate. In the case of the Buddha Way, this is a mistaken way of thinking. This creates a basic problem for us human beings to see actual reality as it is. When we practice the Buddha Way or study the self, there is no separation between "I" and "the self" or "the Buddha Way," nor between the action of "study" and "practice." When we study the self, "I" is the "self," and there is noth-ing called "I" beside the action of "studying." Subject, action, and object are completely the same thing. But as soon as we start to think or speak using words and concepts, we have to say, "I study the self" or "I study the Buddha Way." The important point here is just study or practice. Within the action both "the self" and "the Buddha Way" are mani-fested. Keep studying, practicing, manifesting. Dogen Zenji said, "When buddhas are truly buddhas, they don't need to perceive that they are buddhas. However, they are enlightened buddhas, and they continue actualizing buddha." Sawaki Roshi elucidated Dogen Zenji's expression, *jijuyu zanmai*, when he said, "In zazen, the self does the self by the self."

In our daily lives, we say, "I drink water." That works within the sphere of our daily lives. That is the way to communicate with people using language. We can transmit what we want to communicate with others in speaking this way. When I say, "I want to drink a cup of water," someone may bring a cup of water. And we have no problem with this on the ground of conventional living in human society.

But when we talk of Buddha Dharma, it does not work. This is the point where our language or our way of thinking using words and concepts starts to be a problem. We need to go beyond words, concepts, language, and logic to be free from the problem of separation. But this does not mean we have to stop thinking and see things in some mysterious way beyond our usual way of thinking.

What I am saying is that the reality of our life is a very obvious, ordinary thing, but once we start to talk about it, we lose the vivid, immediate reality.

In our practice we just sit with this body and mind on a cushion in the zendo. Or we do various things outside the zendo, but when we practice the Buddha Way there is no separation between the "self" that is studying the self and the "self" that is studied by the self. Self is studying the self. And the action of studying is also the self. There is no such thing called the self outside of our action. There is no runner beside the action of running. Runner and running are exactly the same thing. If there is a runner outside of "running" then the runner is not running. That is, the runner cannot be called a runner because the runner is not running. This is the one point of discussion made by Nagarjuna to show emptiness and negate the existence of a fixed ego that is permanent and the owner of our body and mind.

We run. This is a very ordinary thing, just like we sit, we eat, we drink, or we breathe. But when we say, "There is no 'I' besides running" or "running without a runner," we feel that we are discussing something mysterious. But that is not a correct way to understand the discussion by people like Nagarjuna or Dogen. They are trying to express the very ordinary thing in the truly realistic way without fabrication. They use language in a way that words negate the words themselves and show the reality beyond our thoughts.

When we practice the Buddha Way, there is no self, no Buddha Way, no others. Self and all others are working together. The working done by self and all others are called our actions. When we drive a car, we think "we" are "driving" "a car." We are operators (subject) and the car is operated upon (object). But, actually, we are also operated by the car.

Depending upon the style or the quality of the car, we have to drive in a different way. Depending upon whether we drive a cheap old truck carrying junk or a luxurious, brand-new car carrying a VIP, our feelings and attitude are totally different. In a sense the car is driving us.

We are owned by the car. I and the car work together and the action of driving is manifested. This is not only about a special practice done by a group of people called Buddhists. This is the actual way all beings are working within the circle of independent origination.

The Buddha Way includes both self and objects. The Buddha Way includes both people sitting and sitting done by the people. It is one thing actually. This is very difficult to explain but it is really an obvious, plain reality of our lives. This is not some special state or condition accomplished by only certain, so-called enlightened people. Even when we don't know it, the self, others, and action are working together as one reality. We don't need to train ourselves to make those three into one thing. If those are really three separate things, they cannot become one. They are always one reality.

"To study the self is to forget the self." When we study ourselves as the Buddha Way, we find that there is no such self that is separate from "others." The self is connected with all beings. We see that the self does not really exist. It is like a dream, a phantom, a bubble, a shadow, a drop of dew, or a flash of lightning, as the *Diamond Sutra* says. The self is in its self-being empty. So, we need to forget the self. Even the self that is studying the Buddha Way should be forgotten. The self forgets the self in studying the self. This is what we do in our zazen by opening the hand of thought. We let go of whatever thoughts, feelings, or emotions come up from our selves in zazen. Letting go is complete negation of everything coming up from egocentric karmic self. We let go not only of selfish ideas but also our understanding of the Dharma. Just sitting—shikantaza—is the complete negation of the self. And at the same time, in letting go everything is accepted. Nothing is negated. Everything is just as it is. Letting go of thought is not killing the thought. Thoughts are coming up moment by moment, but we just let go. Thoughts are there, but in our zazen we don't think. We just sit. Within just sitting everything is just as it is. Nothing is negated and nothing is affirmed. This just sitting is the *prajna* (wisdom) which sees emptiness without separation of subject and object. Zazen is not a kind of contemplation as a "method" through which "I" (subject) can see "emptiness" as object. Practice of just sitting is itself prajna. This is why Dogen Zenji said in the *Shobogenzo*, "Zanmai-o-zanmai": "Sitting is itself Buddha Dharma." In the *Shobogenzo* "Zuimonki" Dogen Zenji said, "Sitting is itself the true form of the self."

"To forget the self is to be verified by all things." "To be verified by all things" is the same as "all things coming and carrying out practice/enlightenment through the self." By totally just sitting, we put our whole being on the ground of interdependent origination. We do nothing but "just sitting" with whole body and mind. Dogen Zenji's zazen (shikantaza) is a unique practice even within different kinds of meditation practices in the various forms of Buddhism. We don't meditate. Meditation is done by our mind. But in zazen, we don't do anything with our mind. We don't count breath. We don't watch breath. We don't chant mantra. We don't contemplate anything. We don't try to concentrate our mind on any particular object. We have no techniques. We really just sit with both body and mind. We sit in an upright posture, breathe through the nose quietly, deeply, and smoothly from our abdomen. We keep our eyes open. Even when we sit in this posture, our mind is functioning. Our heart is beating; our stomach is digesting food. Each and every organ in our body continues to function. There is no reason that our brain stops working in our zazen. The function of our brain is to secrete thoughts. Thoughts well up in our mind moment by moment. But we refrain from doing anything with our thoughts. We just let everything come up freely and go away freely. We don't grasp anything. We don't try to control anything. We just sit.

This is such a simple practice. To be simple does not mean to be easy. It is very difficult and it is very deep practice. In zazen, we accomplish nothing. As Sawaki Roshi said, zazen is good for nothing. But zazen is itself Buddha Dharma. Refraining from doing anything, the self is illuminated and verified by all things. Just sitting is not our personal practice. But we let go of our karmic self that always wants to be satisfied.

"To be verified by all things is to let the body and mind of the self, and body and mind of others, drop off." Dropping off body and mind is a translation of *shinjin datsuraku*. This is one of the key words in Dogen

Zenji's teachings. Originally this is the expression used by Dogen's teacher [Tendo] Nyojo (Tiantong Rujing). In the *Hokyoki*, Dogen Zenji recorded his conversations with Ju-ching while he was practicing at the T'ien-t'ung (Tiantong) Monastery. This expression, shinjin datsuraku, was one of the topics Dogen Zenji discussed with his teacher repeatedly.

Nyojo said, "Sanzen is dropping off body and mind. We don't use incense burning, prostration, *nembutsu*, practice of repentance, reading sutras. We only just sit (shikantaza)."

Dogen asked, "What is dropping off body and mind?" Nyojo said, "Dropping off body and mind is zazen. When we just practice zazen, we part from the five desires and get rid of the five coverings." Dogen asked, "If we part from the five desires and get rid of the five coverings, that is the same as the teaching taught in the teaching schools. Thus we are the same as the practitioners of Mahayana and Hinayana."

Nyojo said, "The descendants of the Ancestor (Bodhidharma) should not dislike the teachings taught by Mahayana and Hinayana. If a practitioner is against the sacred teachings of the Tathagata, how can such a person be the descendant of the buddhas and ancestors?" Dogen asked, "In recent times, some skeptical people say that the three poisonous minds are themselves Buddha Dharma and the five desires are themselves the way of the ancestors. If we get rid of them, it is nothing other than like and dislike. Such practice is the same as the Hinayana."

Nyojo said, "If we don't get rid of the three poisonous minds and the five desires, we are the same as the non-Buddhists in the country of the King Bimbisara and his son Ajatasattu (at the time of Shakyamuni Buddha). For the descendants of buddhas and ancestors, if we get rid of even one covering or one desire, that is the great benefit. That is the time we meet the buddhas and ancestors."

Nyojo Zenji said that sanzen is dropping off body and mind and dropping off body and mind is zazen. He also said that dropping off body and mind is being free from the five desires and getting rid of the five coverings. The five desires are caused in our mind by contacting the objects of the five sense organs. When we see, hear, smell, taste, and touch some pleasurable objects, we enjoy them, we attach ourselves to them, and we want them more and more. Or if the objects are not pleasurable, we dislike them and try to keep away from them. But they often come toward us, so we hate them and become angry. Greed and anger are caused by the five desires.

The five coverings refer to hindrances that cover our mind and prevent it from functioning in a healthy way. Those are coverings of greed, anger or hatred, sleepiness or dullness, distraction, and doubt about the principle of causes and conditions. These five desires and five coverings are discussed originally in the *Daichidoron* (a commentary on the *Prajnaparamita Sutra* by Nagarjuna) as obstacles in meditation practice. And Tendai Chigi, the great philosopher of the Chinese Tiantai (Tendai) School, mentioned them in the manual of meditation practice, the *Makashikan (Larger Book of Shamatha and Vipashyana)*. Chigi said that a practitioner should part from the five desires and get rid of the five coverings in the meditation practice called shikan (shamatha and vipashyana). Dogen Zenji was originally ordained as a Tendai monk in Japan and was familiar with the teachings and meditation practice in the Tendai tradition. Dogen was not satisfied by Tendai practice and began to practice Zen. That was why Dogen asked Nyojo if he should part from the five desires and the five coverings. Until then, Dogen Zenji was looking for something that is different from the teachings he learned in the teaching school. But Nyojo said that our practice of zazen should not be different from the Buddha's teachings recorded in the sutras and systematized in philosophical teaching schools. The next conversation on the same topic between Dogen and Nyojo was as follows.

Nyojo said, "The descendants of the buddhas and ancestors should first get rid of the five coverings and then the six coverings. Adding the covering of ignorance to the five coverings makes six coverings. Even if a practitioner only gets rid of the covering of ignorance, that makes the practitioner free from the five coverings. Even if a practitioner gets rid of the five coverings, if ignorance is not gotten rid of, the practitioner has not yet reached the practice of the buddhas and ancestors."

Dogen immediately made a prostration and expressed gratitude for the teaching. He put his hands in *shashu* position and said, "Until today, I have not heard of such an instruction as that which you have given me now, teacher. Elders, experienced teachers, monks and Dharma brothers here do not know at all. They have never spoken like this. Today, fortunately, specially I have received your great compassion and have heard what I have not heard before. This is fortunate for me, because of the Dharma connection from the previous lives. And yet, is there any secret method to get rid of the five or six coverings?"

The teacher smiled and said, "Where have you been putting your whole energy? That is practicing nothing other than the Dharma to part from the six coverings. The buddhas and ancestors have not set up any classification in practice. They directly point out and singularly transmit the way of departing from the five desires and six coverings and getting free from the five desires. Making effort in just sitting and dropping off body and mind is the method to depart from the five coverings and the five desires. Besides this, there is nothing at all. Absolutely, there is nothing else. How can it fall into two or three?"

This is Tendo Nyojo Zenji's explanation of dropping off body and mind. Since Nyojo was the original person who used this expression we should understand it based on Nyojo's teaching. To drop off body and mind is to be free from the six coverings, the three poisonous minds that are the causes of samsara. In just sitting zazen, we let go of the three poisonous minds. That is why Dogen Zenji said zazen is not a practice of human beings but the practice of buddhas.

Dogen and Nyojo talked about dropping off body and mind one more time in the *Hokyoki*, as follows:

Nyojo said:

The zazen of *arhats* and *pratyekabuddhas* does not have attachment and yet lacks great compassion. Therefore it is different from the zazen of buddhas and ancestors in which they put primary importance on great compassion and the vow to save all living beings. The non-Buddhist practitioners in India also practice zazen. And yet, non-Buddhists have three sicknesses. That is, attachment, mistaken views, and arrogance. Therefore, their zazen is different from buddhas' and ancestors' zazen. *Shravakas* also practice zazen, and yet their compassion is weak. They don't penetrate the true reality of all beings with wisdom. They try to improve only themselves and cut off the seeds of Buddha. Therefore, their zazen is different from buddhas' and ancestors' zazen.

In buddhas' and ancestors' zazen, they wish to gather all buddha-dharma from the time they first arouse bodhi-mind. Within zazen, they don't forget living beings. They offer a compassionate heart even to an insect. They vow to save all living beings and they dedicate all merits to all living beings. Therefore, buddhas and ancestors practice zazen within the world of desire. Even within the world of desire, they have the best connection with this realm. They practice many virtues generation after generation and allow their mind to be flexible.

Dogen made a prostration and said, "What do you mean by allowing the mind to be flexible?"

Nyojo said, "Affirming buddhas' and ancestors' dropping off body and mind is the flexible mind. This is called the mind-seal of buddhas and ancestors." Dogen prostrated six more times.

What does shinjin datsuraku mean in our practice? The literal meaning of the Chinese character *datsu* means "to take off," or "slough off," and *raku* means "to drop off," "cast off," or "fall down." Carl Bielefeldt translates this expression as "slough off body and mind." This translation puts emphasis on the first half of the compound, "datsu." "Dropping or casting off" puts emphasis on the second half, "raku."

We always wear clothing from the time of our birth to the time of our death. Clothing indicates the class or occupation of a person in society. Monks wear a monk's robe. An emperor wears an emperor's garment. Soldiers wear a soldier's uniform, depending upon their position. Farmers wear farmers' clothes. Rich people wear luxurious garments. Poor people wear cheap clothes. Clothing also shows the national, cultural or religious background of a person. Chinese wear Chinese clothes. Japanese wear Japanese clothes. Americans wear American clothes. When we see people's clothing, we see who people are in society.

It is not only clothes that we put on to cover ourselves. We wear costumes that show us as rich, poor, or middle class. Occupations such as a doctor, lawyer, mechanic, priest, student, and teacher are also a kind of clothing. But when we sit facing the wall, and let go of thought and association with others, we take off all the clothing. When we just sit facing the wall, and let go of thought and association, at that time I am not a Japanese Buddhist priest. We are neither Japanese nor American. We are neither rich nor poor. We are neither Buddhist nor Christian. We are Japanese or American, Buddhist or Christian, man or woman, only when we compare ourselves with others. When I compare myself with Americans, I am a Japanese. Until I knew that there are some people who are not Japanese, I didn't know that I was a Japanese. When we just sit, we are neither deluded living beings nor enlightened buddhas. We are neither alive nor dead. We are just as we are. That's it. We take off all the clothes and become a naked being in zazen.

Since our birth, we have had many different experiences. In the process of experiencing billions of things, we create a self-image, such as we are capable or not; we are superior or inferior; we are rich or poor; we are honest or not. This is how we define ourselves. And we grasp ourselves as, for example, a rich, superior, capable person or a poor, inferior, stupid person. These are the selves created by karma. When we sit in zazen and let go, all these self images are ungrasped. When we open our hands, all these concepts drop off. Our body and mind are released from karmic hands. This is what datsuraku means.

As Nyojo Zenji said, when we just sit and let go of thought, we are released from the five desires and six coverings. We are not pulled by objects. We are released from the three poisonous minds that bind us within samsara. This just sitting zazen is itself the practice of nirvana.

I am a Buddhist priest. I am my wife's husband. I am my children's father. When I am with my family, I am a father. So, I try to play a role of a father at home. When I give a lecture, I am a teacher. So, I try to do my best to talk on Dogen Zenji's teachings in the most understandable way, though I don't know whether I am successful or not. These are the costumes I put on in each situation. And I define myself as a father or a teacher, and I try to do my best to play the role in each situation. But when I sit facing the wall, I am not a father. I am not a Buddhist priest. I am nothing. I am empty. I am just who I am. This is liberation from my karmic life.

"To be verified by all things is to let the body and mind of the self and the body and mind of others drop off." This means that the separation between self and others is dropped off. Zazen reveals the total reality of interdependent origination. When we let go of thought, we put our whole being in the reality of interpenetrating reality. This is how we are verified by all beings.

"There is a trace of realization that cannot be grasped." The original expression Dogen Zenji uses for "cannot be grasped" is *kyukatsu*. *Kyu* means "to be in rest." It is not working, not in action. *Katsu* means "to stop." Trace of realization and kyukatsu are contradicted. Kyukatsu means "to be traceless." Trace of enlightenment is to rest and stop being. This sentence means that there is a traceless trace of realization. Dogen is saying, "there is" and "there is not" at the same time. As soon as we grasp it we miss it. We just keep going on practicing without grasping the trace of realization. When we think, "Now I am verified by all things," we already miss it. Just practice, then the trace is there and yet it isn't. This trace is like the trace of birds flying. It is there but we cannot see it. When we try to grasp it, we miss it. When we open our hands, it is there.

"We endlessly keep expressing the ungraspable trace of realization." In our practice of zazen and the activities of our daily lives, we try to express this traceless trace of realization. We need to make an effort to find how we can express the reality of interdependent origination. This is the point of Dogen Zenji's teaching in "Genjokoan." When we actually practice in this way we can truly see that practice and realization are one. Without practice there is no such thing called enlightenment. We usually think practice is one thing and enlightenment is another; that practice is the means and enlightenment is the reward. This is not correct. In truth, realization is within the process of moment by moment practice.

On "Silent Illumination"

Sheng-yen

THE STYLE OF MEDITATION called "silent illumination" is one of the great practices of the Chan (Zen) tradition. Silent illumination originated around the eleventh century, and its greatest advocate was Master Hung-chih Cheng-chueh (Hongzhi Zhengjue) of the Ts'ao-tung (Caodong) sect, which became the Soto sect in Japan. In Tibet, the *mahamudra* practice is very similar. The practice originated in India, where it was called *shamatha-vipashyana*, or serenity-insight. The aim of this practice is a mind unburdened with thoughts. This leads the mind to profound awareness about its own state.

Silently and serenely one forgets all words,
Clearly and vividly it appears before you.

First there is silence, then comes illumination. Ordinary people express themselves through a never-ending succession of words and images. This is moving away from serenity. On retreat we have the rule of no talking. Even so, is your mind ever without thoughts or words? In interviews, people tell me that their biggest problem is that they can't stop thinking. Even when you're sitting there, wordless and silent, you may be conversing with mental objects all the time. After fast-walking meditation today, I asked you to relax and put down all thoughts. Had you been able to do this, you would have achieved a state of silence and serenity, and you would be practicing at an advanced level.

Silent illumination is a very peaceful style of meditation in which there is not one thought, yet your mind is extremely clear. I use three phrases to describe this state: first, "bright and open"; second, "no scattered thoughts"; and third, "not one thought."

When the mind drops all use of words, it becomes bright and open; this is the first characteristic. Next, "no scattered thoughts" refers to single-mindedness—total concentration on the method. But when you finally forget the method itself, and no one thought remains, that is genuine serenity. Ultimately, Silent Illumination is the method of no method. Counting and following the breath are methods of collecting the scattered mind, and kung-an (koan) is the method of applying great pressure to achieve a sudden breakthrough. Silent illumination is just dropping all thoughts and words and going directly to the state of Chan.

I do not recommend this method to people too often. First, you must have a firm practice to really benefit from it; you must be at a stage where there's no problem becoming settled, when you can sit with unbroken concentration, with almost no outside thoughts. The other reason is that it is hard to tell whether your mind is truly "bright and open," or just blank. You can be just idling, having very subtle thoughts, and believe you are practicing Silent Illumination. You can be silent without illuminating anything.

The key is in the line, "Clearly and vividly it appears before you." What are you to be clear and vivid about? About everything in your mind, which, though motionless, reflects everything, like a mirror.

When one realizes it, time has no limits.
When experienced, your surroundings come to life.

When silence is achieved, time has no duration. It is only because thoughts come and go that we are aware of time. When there are no thoughts, neither is there time. Time is limitless, beyond measure. One night, when Great Master T'ai-hsü (Daixu) was meditating, he heard the evening bells. Immediately afterwards, he heard the morning bells. Because he was in samadhi, a whole night had passed during which he had no sense of time.

The next line refers to space, a clear and vivid sense of the environment. When your mind is moving, your awareness is narrowly focused by your thoughts. If you could see and hear without using your mind, and be very attentive at the same time, you would sense limitless space. But this is not an especially high state. Higher yet is the state of "not one thought." In this state distinctions of vast or small just don't exist.

There is a saying that all the buddhas of the past, present, and future are turning the Dharma Wheel on the point of a fine hair. When you can empty your mind of all thoughts, the mind becomes all-inclusive and sees no difference between the infinitesimally small and the infinitely large.

Singularly illuminating is the bright awareness,
Full of wonder is the pure illumination.

The bright awareness that illuminates is that of a Buddha who sees sentient beings in their perfection, unlike ordinary awareness, which is confused, and sees the world as dark. This brightness throws its light on all things, and they take on the aspect of wonder. This is like the songs of Milarepa, which reveal the harmony between all things great and small. It is the wonder of the *Avatamsaka Sutra,* where everything is seen in such detail, from every point of view. A mind so illuminated could see the cosmos in a grain of sand. This is the realm perceived by wisdom arising from samadhi.

The moon's appearance, a river of stars,
Snow-clad pines, clouds hovering on mountain peaks.

The state of Silent Illumination is like the moon unobscured by clouds—clear, soft, and cool. The moon rather than the sun symbolizes enlightenment, because the moon is cool and serene, while the sun is hot and active. "A river of stars" refers to the Milky Way where the dense stars form a river of light. "Snow-clad pines...." All these are images of brightness and openness.

Have you ever seen clouds move freely through up-thrusting mountain peaks? This symbolizes the liberated mind which, even when it encounters obstructions, is not bound by them.

In darkness, they glow with brightness.
In shadows, they shine with a splendid light.

These lines contrast the mind of wisdom, which shines even in the dark in the midst of vexation, and the mind of foolishness, which remains in the dark. Wise persons, although perhaps appearing foolish, prefer obscurity. Yet they express their power in everything they do.

Like the dreaming of a crane flying in empty space,
Like the clear, still water of an autumn pool,
Endless eons dissolve into nothingness,
Each indistinguishable from the other.

The mind of Silent Illumination is broad, high, and deep. It is like the crane in flight, feeling the vastness of empty space, unaware of its own existence, silently floating in a timeless dream. The autumn pool, despite its great depth, is so still that the bottom is clearly seen. In autumn the pool is not thriving with life as it is in summer. The active elements have settled, and with settling there comes a clarity, and the depths can finally be seen.

Into the sky of the crane's dream and the depths of the autumn pool, eons of time dissolve into nothing. We term it "nothing" because our sense of time comes from the endless succession of thoughts and images passing through our minds. This flow of experience also gives rise to a sense of a separate self. If you could cease the march of thoughts through your mind, and fix on just one constant thought of Silent Illumination, time would freeze. If you could then forget even that thought, time would dissolve.

Can you fix your mind on one thought for even a minute? Is it dangerous to stop a plane in midair? Of course. But you must be determined to stop your thoughts, and not be afraid of dying. If you panic, you will be filled with thoughts. You must more than ever drop everything and concentrate on just the practice, abandoning all thoughts of life, body, fears, desires, everything but the method.

In this illumination all striving is forgotten.
Where does this wonder exist?

There are many wonders to discover in Silent Illumination. But the mind of practice cannot be the seeking mind, even if the goal is enlightenment. For while thoughts exist they are obstacles. "All striving is forgotten" means that nothing exists except illumination itself; there is no thought of losing or gaining anything. The wonder is in abandoning confusion and with a clear, bright mind, just dedicating yourself to practice.

Brightness and clarity dispel confusion
On the path of Silent Illumination,
The origin of the infinitesimal.

When we are practicing the method, vexation and ignorance diminish, wisdom and compassion increase. When vexation and ignorance reach the extreme of smallness, they vanish; when wisdom and compassion reach the extreme of largeness, they too vanish. Therefore, for all sentient beings, Bodhisattvas, and Buddhas, the path aims at lessening vexation and increasing wisdom. But at the stage of Buddhahood, neither vexation nor wisdom exist.

They penetrate the extremely small,
There is the gold shuttle on a loom of jade.

The gold shuttle and jade loom are used to weave the clothing of the devas, or heavenly beings, and symbolize the wisdom which harmonizes the realms of existence. With wisdom, the nature of the least of things can be directly perceived.

Subject and object influence each other.
Light and darkness are mutually dependent.

These lines refute the dualisms of ordinary thinking. Subject and object are mutually dependent, like light and darkness. Silent Illumination dispels the idea that wisdom is simply the absence of vexation. During this retreat, one student came to me in a very emotional state, saying that her compassion had been moved powerfully, that she felt pity for suffering people and wanted to help them. From her point of view this seemed like a very good experience to have, but I scolded her, saying, "You're just fooling around in sentimentality. This is not wisdom. In the mind of wisdom, there is no such thing as people needing to be pitied." Compassion is not simple sentimentality; it is just a natural response to help people.

There is neither mind nor world to rely on,
Yet do the two interact, mutually.

When the distinction between self and others is dropped, when there is no sense of self or outside world, inner and outer become one, and even that one will disappear. When you are practicing poorly, you can't even connect two successive thoughts, much less dissolve the boundary between inner and outer.

The previous lines describe the serene, internal aspect of Silent Illumination. The following lines deal with functioning in the world.

Drink the medicine of correct views.
Beat the poison-smeared drum.

To drink the medicine of correct views is to infuse yourself with the Dharma; to beat the poison-smeared drum is to help sentient beings kill delusion and vexation. (In Indian mythology, a drum smeared with a certain poison could kill enemies who heard the drum, even from a great distance.) Yet, while compassion and helping exist, there is no sense of saving sentient beings. You must rely on three pillars of practice—precepts, samadhi, and wisdom. Of these, samadhi produces concrete results the most easily. Someone who has had their self-centered point of view demolished even for a short time can understand Silent Illumination. But ultimately the essence of this practice is simply to sit, just sit, and keep on sitting. It is like letting the impurities in a murky pond settle until the water is so clear you can see to the bottom.

When Silence and Illumination are complete,
Killing and bringing to life are choices I make.

The spirit of the Bodhisattva is this: the path of delivering oneself from suffering lies in relieving the suffering of others. Even with this ideal, if your practice is weak, your most sincere actions cannot help. But when your practice reaches the level described in this poem, your power to help flows spontaneously, even in ways that seem unconventional. "Killing and bringing to life" means that the Bodhisattva applies any skillful means, even increasing a disciple's vexation, to bring him to realization. We kill vexations to give life to wisdom; we give life to vexations to exercise wisdom.

At last, through the door, one emerges.
The fruit has ripened on the branch.

When practice is fulfilled, the meditator passes through the door of samsara—the cycle of birth and death—and emerges on the path of wisdom. Having labored long and hard, his practice has ripened. The fruit of the Bodhi tree, the Buddha's tree of awakening, is ready for picking. In Chan practice, this "door" is described as consisting of three thresholds one must pass. The first threshold is called *ch'u ch'an (chuchan)*, or "initial Chan." By investigating Chan, and smashing through the wall of great doubt, you cross this threshold to see your self-nature, or Buddha nature. This is the first taste of the fruit, a glimpse of enlightenment, but not final liberation, for vexation is still deeply ingrained.

On the darkest of nights, moonless and starless, a bolt of lightning splits the sky; for an instant you see everything with stunning clarity, then darkness again. But having seen it once, your faith is increased, and you will never totally lose your practice.

The second threshold is in fact many thresholds. It is called *t'seng kuan (zenguan)*, the "multilayered pass." This is like a mountain range with ever-ascending peaks, which you must pass, one by one. The peaks are your own obstructions and vexations. This stage takes a long time, but with every peak crossed, your strength grows. As vexations get lighter, the peaks seem less high.

The third and last threshold is called *lao kuan (laoguan)*, the "prison pass," so-called because one merges from it into final liberation from the wheel of *samsara*—the temporal realms of past, present, and future. This liberation is called *nirvana*. At this stage, the Bodhisattva's capacity to help sentient beings is vast and unhindered.

> *Only this Silence is the ultimate teaching.*
> *Only this Illumination, the universal response.*

Silence is the ultimate teaching. After a billion words are uttered, they are still not the Dharma. No description of enlightenment can approach the direct experience. Silence is itself the teaching that transcends words. Illumination is perfect wisdom. Only with perfect wisdom can you respond to all sentient beings.

> *The response is without effort.*
> *The teaching, not heard with the ears.*

Illumination is without effort because there is no serenity through striving. The effortless response is the way of the Bodhisattva. While others see in him great compassion, he sees himself as ordinary.

> *Throughout the universe all things*
> *Emit light and speak the Dharma.*

It is said that green bamboo and yellow flowers are the Buddha speaking the Dharma. But is there anything that is not a manifestation of Buddha Dharma? There is a story that Master Tao-Sheng (Daosheng) spoke to a pile of rocks because nobody attended his lectures. According to the account, when he was finished, the rocks nodded in appreciation. But, in fact, everything is the Dharma body of the Buddha, and the illumined mind simply sees the world bright and full of vitality.

> *They testify to each other*
> *Answering each other's questions.*

Mutually answering and testifying,
Responding in perfect harmony.

In this conversation between all things, when everything speaks the Dharma, the response is always on the mark. The illuminated mind includes all. In it, all things are friendly and harmonious, without lack, without excess. It is a perfect conversation—the perfect answer to the perfect question; all without words.

When illumination is without serenity,
Then will distinctions be seen.
Mutually testifying and answering,
Giving rise to disharmony.

When there is illumination without silence, thoughts intrude and distinctions are made. Things lose their quality of being "just this." The dialogue between things is discordant—the wrong answers to the wrong questions.

If within serenity illumination is lost,
All will become wasteful and secondary.

In the previous lines the poet speaks of illumination without silence. Here, as earlier, he speaks of silence without illumination. Neither state by itself is complete; neither is the goal of practice.

When Silent Illumination is complete,
The lotus will blossom, the dreamer will awaken.

These lines say clearly that the proper practice of Silent Illumination can lead to enlightenment. Silent Illumination is complete when serenity and illumination are both present. Much hard work and persistence are needed to get to this point. Ultimately, the Buddha lotus inherent in you will blossom, and you will awaken from the deep dream of samsara, the dream of vexation.

The hundred rivers flow to the ocean,
The thousand mountains face the loftiest peak.

The hundred rivers are like sentient beings who are attached to thinking and suffer vexations. Each river, following its own course, flows into the great ocean of wisdom where it loses its sense of self and becomes one with the ocean. The thousand mountains suggest discriminating minds that see themselves as separate, but each one ultimately gazes upon the lofty peak of wisdom, which sees only the one great mountain of all sentient beings.

Like the goose preferring milk to water,
Like a busy bee gathering pollen,
When Silent Illumination reaches the ultimate,
I carry on the original tradition of my sect.

The goose choosing nutritious milk over water and the bee busily gathering pollen are both expressing natural intelligence; you might say animal wisdom. When practicing Silent Illumination you are doing the same, completing the natural process of attaining wisdom. Just as the bee does not waste time looking for pollen in a dead flower, the wise practitioner does not waste time just sitting with a blank mind. Just as the bee is untiring in its efforts, the serious practitioner works until he tastes the honey of wisdom. When the poet has brought his practice to fruition, he is transmitting and honoring the tradition of his sect. But fundamentally, what is he transmitting, and whom is he honoring? He is really transmitting the method discovered by the Buddhas, and he is honoring the Buddha nature that is intrinsic in all sentient beings.

This practice is called Silent Illumination.
It penetrates from the deepest to the highest.

These lines speak of faith—faith in a tradition of practice that has been handed down without interruption from the Buddha on through countless generations. Is there anyone who can practice it and not find in it all of the Buddha Dharma, from the deepest to the highest?

John Daido Loori

MASTER DOGEN'S 300 KOAN SHOBOGENZO, CASE 8

Main Case

ZEN MASTER MAZU DAOYI was an attendant to Nanyue and personally received the mind-seal from him, exceeding his peers. Before that, he lived in Kaiyuan Monastery and did zazen all day long. Knowing that Mazu was a Dharma vessel, Nanyue went to him and asked, "Great monastic, what do you intend by doing zazen?" (1)

Mazu said, "I am intending to be a buddha." (2)

Nanyue picked up a brick and started polishing it. (3)

Mazu said, "What are you doing?" (4)

Nanyue said, "I am trying to make a mirror." (5)

Mazu said, "How can you make a mirror by polishing a brick?" (6)

Nanyue said, "How can you become a buddha by doing zazen?" (7)

Mazu said, "What do you mean by that?" (8)

Nanyue said, "Think about driving a cart. When it stops moving, do you whip the cart or the horse?"

Mazu said nothing.

Nanyue said, "Do you want to practice sitting Zen or sitting Buddha? If you understand sitting Zen, you will know that Zen is not about sitting or lying down. (9) If you want to learn sitting Buddha, know that sitting Buddha is without any fixed form. (10) Do not use discrimination in the nonabiding Dharma. If you practice sitting as Buddha, you must kill Buddha. (11) If you are attached to the sitting form, you are not yet mastering the essential principle." (12)

Mazu heard this admonition and felt as if he had tasted sweet nectar.

Commentary

You should understand that zazen is not meditation or contemplation; it is not about quieting the mind, focusing the mind, or studying the mind; it is not mindfulness or mindlessness. If you want to really understand zazen, then know that zazen is not about sitting or lying down. Zazen is zazen; it is undefiled.

With regard to "sitting as Buddha," you should understand that the very moment of "sitting Buddha" is the killing of Buddha. Thus, sitting Buddha is beyond any set form and has no abode. Therefore, when the brick is a mirror, Mazu is Buddha. When Mazu is Buddha, Mazu is at once Mazu. When Mazu is Mazu, his zazen is immediately zazen. Each thing is not transformed into the other but is, in fact, originally the other. Practice is its unfoldment.

The truth of the universe fills your body and mind; yet it is not manifest without practice; nor is it realized without enlightenment. Unless you are prepared to move forward and take risks, the truth of your life and that of the universe is never realized as this very life itself.

All this notwithstanding, what is the truth of the universe that fills your body and mind? Don't tell me—show me.

Capping Verse

On the tips of ten thousand grasses
each and every dewdrop contains the light of the moon.
Since the beginning of time,
not a single droplet has been forgotten.
Although this is so,
some may realize it, and some may not.

Additional Pointers

1. Is this a real dragon or an imitation?
2. Can Buddha become Buddha?
3. What exists is not just what appears before our eyes.
4. He wants to understand.
5. What is he saying, really?
6. Indeed!
7. Indeed!
8. He understands polishing the brick, but does he understand the mirror?
9. Then what is it?
10. Nor any abode.
11. The virtue of realizing Buddha reveals killing Buddha.
12. It simply makes it two.

This is a very famous koan. It's referred to often in Zen practice, and it's included in one of the most important fascicles of Dogen's *Shobogenzo*, called "Zazenshin." *Za* means sitting. *Zen* is derived from the Chinese word *Chan*, which in turn is derived from the Sanskrit word *dhyana*, which means meditation. *Shin* is a bamboo needle used for acupuncture in ancient China. Carl Bielefeldt, a scholar and expert on Dogen, translates this fascicle as "Lancet of Seated Meditation." It's an interesting and accurate analogy: zazen functioning like an acupuncture needle that heals the body and mind. Originally in Buddhism the term "zazenshin" referred to something that had the power to cure a human being of physical or mental pain. Yet healing did not mean transforming sickness into health. Rather, it was a return to a natural, inherent state of health.

In the context of Zen practice, "shin" is the name for a short verse used in the teaching of important points in Zen training. Just as with healing, zazen is understood as a process for returning to our original self, a self that is originally perfect and complete, lacking nothing. This perfection is not something to attain; it's something that we are all born with, and that we die with, whether we realize it or not. We may go through life suffering from illness, but our original healthy nature is there, hidden. Sickness is no different from the delusion at the source of our suffering, and the reason we suffer is because we don't understand the true nature of the universe or ourselves.

Master Nanyue is addressing this delusion with Mazu. To me, one of the interesting things is that Nanyue, who was a successor of the Sixth Ancestor, went after the student. Mazu didn't come to him to ask him about becoming Buddha. Nanyue approached him because he was aware that Mazu was "a great Dharma vessel"—and indeed he was. He turned out to be one of the greatest masters in the history of Zen. He had eighty-four enlightened disciples, all of whom were also exceptional. His lineage continues down to the present day as Rinzai Zen.

Nanyue went to him [Mazu] and asked, "Great monastic, what do you intend by doing zazen?" In other words, "What's the point of your zazen?" *Mazu said, "I am intending to be a buddha." Nanyue picked up a brick and started polishing it. Mazu said, "What are you doing?" Nanyue said, "I am trying to make a mirror." Mazu said, "How can you make a mirror by polishing a brick?" Nanyue said, "How can you become a buddha by doing zazen?" Mazu said, "What do you mean by that?"* He didn't get it. *Nanyue said, "Think about driving a cart. When it stops moving, do you whip the cart or the horse?" Mazu said nothing. Nanyue said, "Do you want to practice sitting Zen or sitting Buddha? If you understand sitting Zen, you will know that Zen is not about sitting or lying down. If you want to learn sitting Buddha, know that sitting Buddha is without any fixed form. Do not use discrimination in the nonabiding Dharma."* He's saying, don't separate zazen.

Zazen is zazen; it's undefiled. In it, there is nothing extra. It's not a process to go from A to B. We tend to interpret everything in terms of process and goal, and so we separate them and let ourselves be driven by those goals. We don't understand that the process *is* the goal. It's not a method that takes us to the goal, but is the goal itself. Zazen is Buddha; zazen is enlightenment. Practice is also enlightenment. It's not just a convenient tool to realize yourself.

Nanyue then says, *"If you practice sitting as Buddha, you must kill Buddha."* Indeed. If you meet the Buddha, kill the Buddha, which is the same as saying, don't put another head on top of the one you already have. This koan is full of the same questions Dogen grappled with in the early years of his practice. The Buddha said, "All sentient beings are per-

fect and complete, lacking nothing." As a young monk, Dogen wanted
to know, if this is so, then why must we practice? Why isn't our perfection obvious from the beginning?

Practice is a continuum—it's ceaseless. Realization and actualization
are a continuum. They're undefiled, just like zazen. There are no impurities. Dogen said we should not take our own viewpoint to be definitive.
We need to study alternate interpretations in order to develop unified
understanding. We tend to see everything from one perspective, which
is usually self-centered. When we say, "When you meet the Buddha,
kill the Buddha," that's the self that has no abode. That's the sitting
Buddha. Having no abode means having no fixed form. Having no fixed
form is wisdom, and its activity is compassion. That's why compassion
is even possible. That's why the ten thousand hands and eyes of Avalo-
kiteshvara Bodhisattva are manifested according to circumstances,
because she has no fixed form. Her abode is determined by the imperative of the moment. Such is the case of all buddhas.

Nanyue said, "How can you become a buddha by doing zazen?"
Dogen says, "Know without doubt the principle that one does not become
Buddha by doing zazen, and the point that becoming Buddha has no relationship to zazen." *Mazu said, "What do you mean by that?"* Nanyue
responds to him by asking him about whipping the cart or the horse.

The commentary says we should understand that "zazen is not meditation or contemplation; it is not about quieting the mind, focusing the
mind, or studying the mind; it is not mindfulness or mindlessness." We
hear an awful lot about meditation these days. For most people, it's a
generic thing that has to do with awareness, or quieting or focusing the
mind. All of these are true of meditation, but not of zazen. "If you really
want to understand zazen, then know that zazen is not about sitting or
lying down. Zazen is zazen; it is undefiled." With regard to sitting as a
buddha, we should understand that "the very moment of 'sitting
Buddha' is killing Buddha." That is, we kill the notion of separateness,
of having some place to go. Yet, instead of killing the self we kill our lives
because of our goals. We're constantly scuffling and struggling and asking, Where am I now? How far have I advanced?

The commentary continues, "Thus, sitting Buddha is beyond any set
form, and has no abode." That's true for each one of us. That's what it

means to realize the self. That's what it means to forget the self. Because sitting Buddha is beyond any set form, "when the brick is a mirror, Mazu is Buddha. When Mazu is Buddha, Mazu is at once Mazu. When Mazu is Mazu, his zazen is immediately zazen. Each thing is not transformed into the other, but is in fact originally the other, and practice is its unfoldment." The lancet of acupuncture does not transform someone from unhealthy to healthy; healthy is originally there. Zazen does not transform one from a deluded being into an enlightened being. Enlightenment is originally present.

The truth of the universe fills the body and mind of each of us, the text says, "yet it is not manifest without practice, nor is it realized without enlightenment. Unless you are prepared to move forward and take risks, the truth of your life and that of the universe is never realized as this very life itself.... What is the truth of the universe that fills your body and mind? Don't tell me—show me." Most people who have read even a little about Buddhism can explain this truth, but explaining it doesn't reach it. There's a big difference between the words and ideas that describe a reality, and the manifestation of that reality.

Dogen says that foolish people mistakenly believe that the divine light of the Buddha is like the light radiated by the sun and the moon, or the beams reflected by bright gems. Sun and moonlight are nothing more than pale beams in the six worlds of *samsara* and cannot be compared to the brilliant divine light of the Buddha. The "divine light of Buddha" is an expression we must receive and pay attention to, a dharma we must maintain and protect. It is the direct transmission of zazen. If that divine light does not shine on us, we cannot preserve the tradition or keep the faith. That is why Dogen says, "[Throughout history] there have been few who understood seated meditation as seated meditation. And at the present, in the [Chan] mountains of the great Sung, many of those who are heads of the principal monasteries do not understand, and do not study, seated meditation. There may be some who have clearly understood it but not many. Of course, the monasteries have fixed periods for seated meditation; the monks, from the abbot down, take seated meditation as their basic task and, in leading their students, [the teachers] encourage its practice. Nevertheless, there are few abbots who understand it." That's been true all through the history of Zen. Zazen is very deceiving. Once you sit on your cushion and fold your legs, only you know what you're doing with your mind. If you're not willing to practice the edge, to thoroughly examine what it is that you're doing, to doubt and question it—and at the same time trust the process—you'll never get to the practice of sitting Buddha. You'll never have the opportunity to kill Buddha.

Practicing superficially or half-heartedly is where many of us stick. We come into a workshop or a training period, receive some basic instructions in zazen, and then figure we don't need to look any further. Zen offers us numerous opportunities to deepen our practice. That's why we have the other seven gates of training: the teacher-student relationship, liturgy, body practice, art practice, academic study, work practice, the precepts, as well as the ten thousand things that we do in our lives. They're all part of the process of manifesting sitting Buddha.

Dogen also points out that we need to appreciate the fact that there are times when we see Buddha without realizing Buddha, or we see water without realizing that it's water, see mountains without realizing that they are mountains. What exists is not just the phenomena that appear directly before our eyes, so we shouldn't limit our understanding. That's not the way to study Buddhism. That's not the way to study the self.

The capping verse says, *On the tips of ten thousand grasses each and every dewdrop contains the light of the moon. Since the beginning of time, not a single droplet has been forgotten. Although this is so, some may realize it, and some may not.* "The tips of ten thousand grasses" refers to the myriad forms, the whole phenomenal universe, and on the tip of each blade of grass is a dewdrop. The light of the moon is a metaphor for enlightenment, realization, so each drop is not illuminated by the moon but actually contains the moon. But more than just a metaphor, this is actually so. If you look at a dewdrop in the light of the moon, you'll see the moon in the dewdrop. And if there are ten thousand dewdrops, all of them equally contain and reflect the moon. *Since the beginning of time, not a single droplet has been forgotten.* There's not a single thing that's not so endowed. No matter how dull you may be, no matter how deep your stupor may be, nonetheless that inherent perfection resides in your body, in your mind.

The last lines of the poem say, *Although this is so, some may realize it, some may not.* It ultimately brings it home to each one of us. It's up to you, whether you realize it or not. You have the potential; you're fully equipped. There's no handicap to realization. It has no form, it has no abode, but whether you do it or not depends on the way you practice your life. We read about zazen, we talk about it, we practice it for days on end from dawn to dusk, but have we really penetrated its depths, or are we still dealing with the surface—quieting the mind, focusing the mind, calming the mind? It's time to stop picking daisies and start digging. It's only then that you get the opportunity to kill the Buddha, and when you kill the Buddha, you free yourself. You realize personally the inherent freedom that is our birthright. That is no small thing.

Yaoshan's Non-Thinking

John Daido Loori

Master Dogen's 300 Koan Shobogenzo
Case 129

Main Case

When Yaoshan was sitting in meditation, (1) a monk asked, (2) "What do you think about, sitting in steadfast composure?" (3)

Yaoshan said, "I think not-thinking." (4)

The monk said, "How do you think not-thinking?" (5)

Yaoshan said, "Non-thinking." (6)

Commentary

Abide in neither thinking nor not-thinking. Thinking is linear and sequential, a separation from the reality that is the subject of thought, and thus is an abstraction rather than the reality itself. Not-thinking is suppressive. It cuts away thoughts the moment they arise, making the mind into a great impenetrable mountain—dead, unresponsive. Non-thinking has no such edges. It is the boundless mind of samadhi that neither holds on to, nor lets go of, thoughts. It is the manifestation of the buddha-mind in which the dualism of self and other, thinking and not thinking, dissolves. This is the dharma of thusness that is the right thought of all the buddhas in the ten directions.

Capping Verse

When the dharma wheel turns
it always goes in both directions.
The still point is its hub, and from here,
all of our myriad activities emerge.
Rather than give solace to the body,
give solace to the mind.
When both body and mind are at peace,
all things appear as they are:
perfect, complete, lacking nothing.

Additional Pointers

1. What is he doing? Even Kasho Buddha didn't attain it with hundreds of kalpas of zazen.
2. Why doesn't he leave the old man alone?
3. Huh? What are you thinking, venerable monk, in asking such a question?
4. He's much too kind. It really can't be explained; he's just setting the monk to thinking.
5. Now they're both in the same hole. Just shut up and sit.
6. How kind. But say, what does it mean?

There are many kinds of meditation, and in Buddhism different schools use various forms to develop concentration and insight: the breath, visual images, sounds, or gestures. In Zen Buddhism, the form we use to see directly into the nature of the self is zazen, sitting meditation.

At Zen Mountain Monastery we engage two methods of zazen: koan study and shikantaza. Koan introspection is a directed and focused kind of meditation. In it students use *joriki*, the power of concentration developed in zazen, to penetrate the koan which is the object of attention during meditation. Shikantaza—just sitting—is less pointed than koan study. It is zazen based fundamentally on faith—faith in the Buddha's enlightenment, faith in one's own buddha nature, faith in the process of practice itself. Most students in the Soto lineage of Zen sit shikantaza.

Though the process is different, both forms address the same thing: the study and realization of the true nature of the self.

It's remarkable that in all the literature on Zen, there is very little about how to actually do zazen. I remember when I first started sitting I couldn't find any specific instructions. Everybody talked about how wonderful zazen was and how important it was, and how everybody should do it, but there was very little to be found on how to actually do it.

Among those masters who did write about shikantaza, the first one to focus on it in his writings was the twelfth-century Chinese master Hongzhi. In the thirteenth century, Master Dogen used many of Hongzhi's beautiful poetic descriptions of silent illumination—as he called shikantaza—to elaborate on this form of sitting. Unfortunately, for many years after that, shikantaza became identified exclusively with the Soto School, while koans were thought to be used only by those in the Rinzai School of Zen. This simplistic view, however, can be easily refuted by the fact that Hongzhi was also the compiler of the *Book of Equanimity*, a collection of one hundred koans used for training in the Soto lineage, while Dogen himself collected three hundred koans in his Chinese *Shobogenzo*. His successor, Keizan Zenji, not only wrote the *Zazen Yojinki*, a manual for zazen, but also put together the *Transmission of the Light*, a volume of koans based on the enlightenment experiences of teachers in the Soto lineage. Furthermore, after students finish koan study, they then take up the practice of shikantaza. So it is obvious that practitioners in either one of these schools make use of both sitting techniques during the course of their training.

Whether students are working with koans or the silent illumination that Hongzhi wrote about, the ultimate purpose of both is realization, but that realization can't be separated from our own inherent being, our immediate moment-to-moment awareness. As Dogen points out over and over again, practice and enlightenment are one reality. On the one hand, koans harness doubt so we can smash through our conditioned way of thinking. On the other hand, shikantaza is based on our own faith that practice and enlightenment are one. Koans can be seen and passed through, but shikantaza cannot be gauged by any standard. Students who do shikantaza and ask, "Where am I? How far am I from realization?" miss the vital point of shikantaza. In a sangha like ours where some people work on shikantaza and others sit with koans, people inevitably compare themselves with others. For students working on koans, breakthrough is pivotal. I need to speak about kensho to let them know that it's possible; to encourage them. But when I mention breakthrough, all the shikantaza people say, "When am I going to see it?" Shikantaza can't be measured the same way, but this doesn't mean that one technique is better than the other.

As with anything else, both approaches have their shortcomings. Koan practitioners get stuck with results and accomplishments. Passing koans becomes some sort of race, and the process is forgotten. In shikantaza it is very easy for students to get lulled into a state of complacency, believing that "Since I'm already enlightened, I don't have to do anything." People who think this end up sitting with no awareness and no effort, never appreciating what no-effort in shikantaza really is. What is the effort of no-effort?

When I was a kid, Charles Atlas came up with a form of exercising and body building that he called "dynamic tension." His advertisements showed him beating up bullies on a beach. He was a skinny weakling who, through this method of working out, developed an impressive physique and a worldwide following. Interestingly, the method did not depend on the use of weights. It simply relied on generating and maintaining effort against effort, muscle group against muscle group—just resisting yourself. Evidently it worked, and it developed a unique kind of body type. It wasn't a bulky form with huge muscles, but a nicely toned body with remarkable strength.

When you're doing shikantaza you don't try to focus on anything specifically, or to make thoughts go away. You simply allow everything to be just the way it is. Thoughts come, thoughts go, and you simply watch them, you keep your awareness on them. It takes a lot of energy and persistence to sit shikantaza, to not get caught up in daydreaming. But little by little, thoughts begin to slow down, and finally they cease to arise. When the thought disappears, the thinker disappears. This is the samadhi of falling away of body and mind.

Whether we work on the breath, with a koan, or shikantaza, zazen eventually leads to samadhi. The first indication is usually an off-sensation of the body. This happens most frequently during sesshin because of the long periods of sitting. When you sit for a while without moving the body, it stops receiving information about its edges through the senses, such as the friction of your clothing, or an itch on your leg. So, although you know the body is there, you don't feel it. Some people get frightened at this point and involuntarily their body twitches and defines its edges. Then they slowly move to that place again, and gradually they learn to trust it and they begin to go a little bit further each time. Next comes the off-sensation of the mind. The mind is dependent upon thoughts, but when the thoughts disappear, the mind disappears, the self disappears. That constant reflex action that says, "I'm here, I'm here, I'm here" is the ego manifesting itself. This is when we realize that we are constantly re-creating ourselves.

Sometimes during sitting people have what we call *makyo:* a vision or hallucination. Other times it's a smell or a sound. Students often think this means they're enlightened—particularly if the image is related to Zen, like the Buddha sitting on a golden lotus—and they immediately run off to *dokusan* to get it confirmed. The teacher will usually listen and then say something like, "Maybe you're not sitting straight. Sit straight. Don't worry, it will go away." It doesn't matter whether we attach to a regular thought, or to the thought of enlightenment. Whatever it is, it is still attachment.

There's a famous koan of an ancient master who was a hermit. He had been practicing many, many years, living isolated in the mountains. One day he was cooking soup and in the steam Manjushri Bodhisattva appeared and in his deep, resonant voice proclaimed the dharma to him. The old hermit immediately picked up the ladle and started beating him with it. "Get out of here!" he said. "Get out of here!" In other words, don't put another head on top of the one you already have. Anything that we hold on to along the way—anything—is a dead end, because the minute we attach, we create two things: the "attachee" and the "attachor." That is not the intimacy of samadhi; it is not the intimacy of shikantaza.

One of Dogen's fascicles concerned with shikantaza is titled "Zazen-shin." It is usually translated as "Admonishments for Zazen," but Carl Bielefeldt translated it as "Lancet of Seated Meditation," which is a beautiful image for shikantaza. A lancet is a scalpel: a precise, very sharp surgical instrument that's used to cut away all the extra material. That's what happens in shikantaza. We cut away all the stuff that we hold on to. Thoughts continuously arise, but our attention dissolves them.

In his fascicle called "Learning through the Body and Mind," Dogen says, "The stage of non-thinking is beyond egocentric cognition. If you reach the state of non-thinking, you will realize the true luminous nature of mind. Non-thinking must become the eye through which you view phenomena. The activity of every buddha is based on non-thinking." So what is this non-thinking? In "The Thirty-Seven Conditions Favorable to Enlightenment" Dogen quotes: "An ancient buddha (Yaoshan) said, 'Think non-thinking. How? By using nonthinking.' This is right thought; sitting until the cushion is worn away is also right thought." He very clearly distinguishes non-thinking from not thinking. So what is Dogen referring to when he talks about right thought?

In this koan it says, *When Yaoshan was sitting in meditation.* Yaoshan was a successor of Shitou and the teacher of Yunyan, who in turn was the teacher of Dongshan, one of the founders of the Caodong (Soto) school. Yaoshan's practice of sitting in steadfast composure is the tradition of Buddhism correctly transmitted to him down through thirty-six generations beginning with Shakyamuni Buddha. But what does it mean to sit in steadfast composure?

I added some notes to clarify the koan. The note to the first line says, "What is he doing? Even Kasho Buddha didn't attain it with hundreds of kalpas of zazen." The next line says, *A monk asked,* and the note says, "Why doesn't he leave the old man alone?"

"What do you think about, sitting in steadfast composure?" The note says, "Huh? What are you thinking, venerable monk, in asking such a question?" The next line says, *Yaoshan said, "I think not-thinking."* The note says, "He's much too kind. It really can't be explained; he's just setting the monk to thinking." That's what happens with koans. Students read the question and when they don't immediately understand it, they begin to think about it because that's the way we've all been taught to solve problems. That's the way we've earned our little gold stars in elementary school and our A's in college—through good old, linear, sequential thought. But thinking doesn't help in seeing a koan. A whole other aspect of consciousness needs to open up. We need to exhaust that

process of linear thinking, and when the mind finally stops functioning, out of the blue the realization of the koan appears. It is like a quantum leap. It's a very different way of using the mind. It is nonthinking that is neither intellectual nor based on the subconscious.

In the next line the monk asks, *"How do you think not-thinking?"* The note says, "Now they're both in the same hole. Just shut up and sit." That's ultimately what you're going to be left with—just sitting. There is no handbook that tells you how to go beyond thinking and not-thinking. You just have to sit, and it's through the process of sitting that you will realize Yaoshan's non-thinking. The next line says, *Yaoshan said, "Non-thinking."* The note says, "How kind. But say, what does it mean?" Indeed, what does it mean?

In the commentary it says "Abide in neither thinking nor not think-ing." Thinking is one side. It's linear, sequential. On the other side you have not-thinking, which is blank consciousness. We call this state "eyes staring out of the coffin" or "making a living in a ghost cave" or "being stuck on top of the mountain." Dogen's Zen and Yaoshan's Zen and the Zen of the great masters wasn't about leaving the world; it was about manifesting the dharma in our everyday activities. Thinking falls on one side, not thinking falls on the other side. How do we leap clear of these two extremes? Yaoshan says, by non-thinking. Non-thinking has no such edges. It's the boundless mind of samadhi that neither holds on to, nor lets go of, thoughts. But this doesn't mean suppressing thoughts, either.

In my years of practice I've seen a lot of western students trying to forcibly quiet the mind by making it a big barrier that keeps things out. I've run into students who have been working on Mu for ten or more years who are like boiler factories about ready to explode because they've been suppressing stuff that needs to come up and be let go of. There's no way that you're going to see Mu if you're suppressing or holding on to anything. The mind must truly be emptied out before you can be Mu. When the mind is finally empty, all the dualistic ways of looking at things disappear: thinking, not-thinking; holding on, let-ting go; being, non-being; existence, non-existence. All gone. This is the dharma of the Middle Way; it's the practice of just sitting.

I remember when I went to my very first dokusan with Soen Nakagawa Roshi and I said to him, "Please teach me." He said, "Have you sat before?" I said, "No." I had actually been sitting for a number of years but I wanted to get his instruction as a total beginner. I was doing a mixture of all kinds of things. I had no idea what meditation was really about. He said to me, "Put your mind in the hara." And he took his long stick, the *kyosaku*, and poked me in the hara at a spot two inches below the navel. Then he said, "Put your mind in the hara and chant." He had a deep, guttural, beautiful chanting voice. He went first, "*Namu dai bosa*. Do you understand?" I said, "Yes." He said, "Now you do it." And in a squeaky voice I said, "*Namu dai bosa*." He said, "No, no, no. Hara." Poked again. "*Namu dai bosa*." I chanted, "*Namu dai bosa*." He said, "Ah, good enough. Day and night, *Namu dai bosa*" and he rang the bell. I took it literally and chanted *Namu dai bosa* day and night. I would wake up in the morning, go to sleep: *Namu dai bosa*. In the beginning I had no idea what it meant to put your mind in the hara, but I worked on it. Years of sitting went by and then it began: a feeling of warmth in a spot two inches below the navel, a feeling of buoyancy. That's when my sitting began to change. It went much, much deeper. I began to recognize from my own experience that the hara was the spiritual center of the body, and later I found proof of it being the physical center as well.

Recently I read a very interesting article in the *New York Times* with the headline: "Complex and Hidden Brain in the Gut Makes Stomachaches and Butterflies." It said,

The gut has a mind of its own—the enteric nervous system—just like the larger brain in the head, researchers say. This system sends and receives impulses, records experiences, responds to emotions; its nerve cells are influenced by the same neurotransmitter. The gut can upset the brain just as the brain can upset the gut.... It's considered a single entity; it's a network of neurons, neurotransmitters, and proteins that zap messages between neuron support cells like those found in the brain. The brain proper and complex circuitry enables it to act independently, learn, remember, and as the saying goes, "produce gut feelings." The brain and the gut play a major role in human happiness and misery. But few people know that it exists.

Included in the article they had a picture of the gut, and lo and behold! It was the hara. Yet you don't need scientific proof to experience the fact that by simply putting your attention in the hara your body becomes settled and your mind quiets down.

The capping verse begins: *When the dharma wheel turns it always goes in both directions. The still point is its hub, and from here, all of our myriad activities emerge.* The turning of the dharma wheel in both directions simultaneously is the merging of the differences: good/bad, thinking/not thinking, up/down, self/other, on the mountain/in the world, monk practice/lay practice, and on and on. Our minds are dualistic and our tendency is always to look at things in terms of that dualism. In the "Sandokai," "The Identity of Relative and Absolute," we chant, "The absolute and the relative fit like a box and its lid.... It's like the foot before and the foot behind in walking. Within darkness there is light, but do not look for that light. Within light there is darkness, but do not try to understand that darkness." These are concepts that are hard to understand, but that can be experienced once the mind stops moving. "When the dharma wheel turns it always goes in both directions" refers to the Fifth Rank of Master Dongshan where unity is attained, where absolute and relative, self and other, this and that, thinking and non-thinking become unified.

Rather than give solace to the body, give solace to the mind. When both body and mind are at peace, all things appear as they are: perfect, complete, lacking nothing. If we can get out of the way and trust things as they are, the dharma of thusness is manifested. People who sit deeply, whether they're working on koans or shikantaza, always manifest this reality. It shows in the way they interact with others; it shows in the way they live their lives. Ultimately, it all boils down to zazen. Just sitting.

Please take up this practice of zazen. You don't need any special props to do it. You don't need complex instructions or monasteries and teachers. You just need a quiet corner to settle your body, settle your mind, and taste your breath. Then just let the breath breathe itself. Think of non-thinking. This is the dharma of thusness that is the right thought of all the buddhas in the ten directions. It is Shakyamuni's realization at the moment of his enlightenment: all sentient beings are perfect and complete, lacking nothing. You are perfect and complete, lacking nothing. Trust that. Trust the process of zazen. If you were to live for a hundred thousand years, you would never find in this life anything more powerful, more healing, more empowering, than the simple practice of zazen. Please don't take it lightly. It's an incredible gift.

SUZUKI ROSHI'S PRACTICE OF SHIKANTAZA

Sojun Mel Weitsman

I REMEMBER reading a description of shikantaza by a contemporary Japanese Zen master. He described shikantaza as a very special kind of practice in which you sit zazen so hard the sweat pours out of your body. You can sit for only about half an hour because it's so intense. And when I read that I thought, "Boy, that's not the shikantaza that I know anything about or ever heard anything about from Suzuki Roshi!"

I wasn't thinking that such intense zazen is a wrong practice of shikantaza. But it does seem to me that this is elitist shikantaza or Olympic-style shikantaza: trying to accomplish some great feat. Suzuki Roshi always talked about shikantaza as one's day-to-day, moment-to-moment life of selflessness.

One of the main themes of Suzuki Roshi was "Don't be selfish." At Sokoji, when we were in the middle of a sesshin—maybe my first or second one—for some reason or another he said, "You people don't know how selfish you are." And I thought, "Is that the right word? Maybe he means *selfless*." So that was a turning word for me, too, because I really understood that the central teaching of Suzuki Roshi was not to be selfish.

It's a very simple phrase. It's something that our mother always tells us, right? "Don't be selfish." But in Buddhism we learn to be *selfless*—no self. "Be selfless." But Suzuki Roshi said *selfish*, which has a connotation that is a little more personal and is one that we don't like so much.

Suzuki Roshi's simple day-to-day activities—the way he would sit down and stand up, eat his dinner, walk, put on his sandals—this was his expression of shikantaza. Everyday activity with no selfishness—just doing the thing for the thing—this was his shikantaza. We usually say that shikantaza means "just sitting." And that's true. Just putting on your shoes too. But this "just" has a special meaning. It means "without going any further" or "without adding anything extra."

When we go about our daily activities we always have a purpose. If I go to the store, I want to buy something. So I have a purpose. And that purpose motivates me to go to the store. But while going to the store, I'm living my life step by step. It has something to do with going to the store and the motivation to do so, but it's totally separate at the same time. It's just this step, this step, this step, totally living the life of walking within walking.

We're always doing something, making up a story about our life. And making up this story about our life today is okay. This is our dream. We've been talking about the dream. Everybody has a dream. We have a dream of going to the store. Every thought is a dream. But the shikantaza, or the "just doing," is the selfless activity of just doing *within* the dream. In other words, we move and then we rest. We move and then we rest. Life is a movement and a rest. But in our practice we move and rest at the same time. Within our movement is perfect stillness. Stillness and movement are the two aspects of this life.

I think about shikantaza as a state in which our thought and our activity have no gap. When an athlete is skiing in the Olympics and performing an outstanding feat, body and mind have no gap. Thought and activity are one. The athlete isn't thinking *about* something. The thought is the activity and the activity is the thought.

But shikantaza doesn't require a highly motivated spectacular event like Olympic skiing. It should be our day-to-day, moment-to-moment activity. The simplest activity. And this is what we recognized in Suzuki Roshi. When we say, "This is what he was like," we mean that his shikantaza was right there for all of us to experience. It was not spectacular, yet there was something so wonderful about it. We couldn't put our finger on it. Just putting on his sandals or the simple act of standing up and sitting down. We all do that, but there was something about putting on his sandals that was exactly the same as skiing in the Olympics. It had exactly the same quality.

Shikantaza is rather indefinable. How do we practice shikantaza? It is the very simple practice of lack of selfishness, of lack of self-centeredness, and of just doing. If you put yourself totally into an activity, the universe meets you and confirms you and there's no gap between you and the universe.

A Coin Lost in the River
Is Found in the River

Zoketsu Norman Fischer

TODAY I WANT TO TALK about zazen, Zen meditation. Here is how Dogen begins his *Fukanzazengi,* his fundamental text on zazen:

> *The Way is basically perfect and all-pervading. How could it be contingent upon practice and realization? The Dharma vehicle is free and untrammeled. What need is there for concentrated effort? Indeed, the whole body is far beyond the world's dust. Who could believe in a means to brush it clean? It is never apart from one, right where one is. What is the use of going off here and there to practice?*

Zazen is fundamentally a useless and pointless activity. A person is devoted to zazen not because it helps anything or is peaceful or interesting or because Buddha tells him to do it—though we may imagine that it helps or is peaceful or interesting—but simply because one is devoted to it. You can't argue for it or justify it or make it into something good. You just do it because you do it. It's not even a question of wanting to or not wanting to. Zazen for zazen's sake. Birds sing, fish swim, and people who are devoted to zazen do zazen with devotion all the time although there is no need for it.

Our life is already fine the way it is. Everything that happens is already a manifestation of our original enlightenment even though we don't know it. We don't need to enter another condition or improve or disprove anything. The gentle rain of the Dharma is falling all the time evenly and freely on everything, and each thing receives that rain and uses it in its own way, each in a different way. The whole world is unfolding in a beautiful and perfect interplay of forces. We may have difficulty appreciating this but after all we are only people and why would we not have difficulty? Our difficulty is this: our minds can't see difference without making comparisons, without making judgments and having preferences. We want either everything to be the same as everything else, which it is although we can't experience it that way, or if things must be different from one another we struggle to rank them.

This kind of difficulty has to do with knowing and thinking, not with our actual being. As far as our actual being is concerned, whether we have difficulty or not we are just fine. What, then, could be more foolish than the idea of religious cultivation, than the thought that we need to change our condition and become more holy, more peaceful, or more wise. In fact, such thoughts only remove us from the holiness, peacefulness, and wisdom that are the actual essence of every moment of our lives. These qualities are with us wherever we are right now. What's the use in making efforts to acquire them? Such efforts can only lead us in the wrong direction. Someone once asked Master Yunmen, "What does 'sitting correctly and contemplating true reality' really mean?" Yunmen said, "A coin lost in the river is found in the river."

We need to appreciate the truth of these things in order to do zazen. If we don't appreciate them our zazen will be very acquisitive. Everything else in our lives is inherently acquisitive because our strong, habitual sense of self always demands that we get some good out of everything we do. We become exhausted by all this activity. But zazen is something different. If we don't appreciate its fundamental uselessness which comes from the fundamental all-rightness of our life we will turn it into something acquisitive and busy, just like everything else we do. Another story from Master Yunmen:

Once a monk asked, "What is my self?" Master Yunmen said, "I, this old monk, enter mud and water for you." The monk said, "Then I should crush my bones and tear my body to pieces in gratitude." The master gave a great shout. He said, "The water of the whole ocean is on your head right now. Speak! Speak!" The monk couldn't say anything. Master Yunmen answered for him, speaking from the monk's standpoint: "I fear that you, Master, don't think I'm genuine."

The problem is that we actually are incapable of seeing zazen as useless because our minds can't accept the fundamental genuineness and all-rightness of our lives. We are actually very resistant to this reality. We hate it because it is too simple and we persistently think we need more. This is not a detail or a quirk of our minds; it is not even a habit really; it is the deep nature of our minds. The Sanskrit word for consciousness is *vijnana*, which means to divide, or to cut. In order for us to have what we call experience we have to divide or cut reality. Genuineness or all-rightness is wholeness, indivisibility, so it can't be an experience. And even if we practice zazen and have an enlightenment experience we immediately confuse ourselves with it. Such an experience can be a promising beginning, but we have to be careful to let go of it, not to define it or to name it, not to make it into a cherished memory, into a hook for identity.

Dogen goes on in the *Fukanzazengi*:

And yet, if there is the slightest discrepancy, the Way is as distant as heaven from earth. If the least like or dislike arises, the Mind is lost in confusion. Suppose one gains pride of understanding and inflates one's own enlightenment, glimpsing the wisdom that runs through all things, attaining the Way and clarifying the Mind, raising an aspiration to assault the very sky. One is making the initial, partial excursions about the frontiers but is still somewhat deficient in the vital way of total emancipation.

He then continues:

You should therefore cease from practice based on intellectual understanding, pursuing words and following after speech, and learn the backward step that turns your light inwardly to illuminate your self. Body and mind of themselves will drop away, and your original face will be manifest. If you want to attain suchness, you should practice suchness without delay.

This "backward step" is a famous saying of Master Dogen. It is the opposite of knowing or experiencing—or rather, "prior to" knowing or experiencing. Not prior to in time, but in depth. In any case all language fails us here because what I am trying to express doesn't have to do with space or time, and all our language is built on metaphors of space and time. One student had a good image for it. He said consciousness is like cutting an onion. The edge of the blade of the knife comes into contact with the skin of the onion and immediately slices it, and the onion is divided. Every moment we divide the world like this, and feel separate and lonely in it, divided from ourselves, divided from everything, in exile, lost. And someone else added—"We cry because of this, just as we cry when we divide the onion and release its juices into the air." The "backward step" is that time when the edge of the blade of the knife touches the skin of the onion. At that precise instant there isn't any division—not even between knife and onion, let alone onion and onion. There's only one thing contacting itself, in touch completely with itself. This is how our life is in the present moment—one thing in touch with itself, not past, not future, and not present either. This is the backward step. Resting in the very beginning of the act of consciousness.

When I say this it sounds as if I mean that we should all carefully analyze our minds and carefully watch every act of consciousness. Although this might be a useful exercise, and an exercise incidentally, that can only be done in the midst of and after careful training in meditation, still, it is a fundamentally futile exercise because it is based on a space-time notion of consciousness. They say in Zen that a fingertip cannot touch itself, and that a knife cannot cut itself. In fact that first undivided moment of consciousness cannot be formed in isolation; it pervades the whole of consciousness. The whole act of slicing the onion, even the tears, is the beginning.

In Zen practice we do two things: We just do zazen and pay attention to our lives. We sit with a spirit of the uselessness of sitting, entering it not as our self but as someone who is bigger than ourselves and includes ourselves. We try not to assume anything about anything. Just sit, as Dogen says, "upright in correct bodily posture, neither inclining to the left nor to the right, neither leaning forward nor backward." Just be determined to be there without any idea of up or down, inside or outside, self or other, until the bell rings or you drop dead, whichever comes first. And then when you get up and resume your life just be aware and simple. Know all the time, as you will have discovered laboriously in zazen, that what is going on in your mind is just what is going on in your mind, that thoughts and feelings are simply thoughts and feelings. What is actually also going on, events that the thoughts and feelings seem to refer to and define, are in reality unknown. Don't forget that and when you do forget it remind yourself many many times. Be sure to keep your sense of humor. Don't get too tangled up in what happens because while you are tangled up something else is happening that you miss. So move through things as much as you can, just straight ahead, without too much deliberation.

When we sit in zazen we take care of our posture and try to pay attention to our breathing. When we breathe in we know this is breathing in and when we breathe out we know this is breathing out. We give ourselves with great devotion, creativity, and love to our breath and we let everything else go without denying anything or burying anything. When we forget we remind ourselves and come back. But we don't make the breath into something and we don't make the fact of our doing zazen into something. There are no big deals in Zen or in zazen because everything in our whole life and in the whole wide world is a big deal—so how could anything be special? If everything is a big deal there is no such thing as a big deal. What we mean by big deal is that something is important and something else is not. So we don't worry about our zazen and we don't think we are doing it right or doing it wrong. We just do it. My favorite Zen dialogue about zazen, which I quote whenever I have an excuse, is the saying of Master Chao Jo (Zhaoruo). When a student asked him, "What is zazen?" he replied, "It is non-zazen." The student said, "How can zazen be non-zazen?" Chao Jo replied, "It's alive!"

In *Fukanzazengi* Dogen says,

> *The zazen I speak of is not learning meditation. It is simply the Dharma gate of repose and bliss, the practice-realization of totally culminated enlightenment. It is the manifestation of ultimate reality. Traps and snares can never reach it. Once its heart is grasped, you are like the dragon when he gains the water, like*

the tiger when she enters the mountain. For you must know that just there in zazen the right Dharma is manifesting itself and that, from the first, dullness and distraction are struck aside.

"Ultimate reality" sounds like a pretty exalted idea, but actually where would ultimate reality be? Is it under my zafu? Is it buried deep within my brain? Is it in a cloud or under the ocean? I think it is in all those places and everywhere else as well. So sitting in zazen or not sitting in zazen is not preparation for something else. My zazen, your zazen, and Buddha's zazen are all the same—manifestations of ultimate reality. It's not a question of meditation or non-meditation. It's a wonderful thing because it is the one thing that is incorruptible. Traps and snares can never reach it. Reality is reality no matter what anyone does about it or doesn't do about it. You don't need to understand it—you can't understand it. All you need is confidence in it. Once you sit down and have real confidence in sitting down—not because it is something wonderful but just because it is nothing and useless—supremely useless—then you have real confidence in your life. Things certainly could fall apart tomorrow. You could be disgraced and humiliated and lose your job or your reputation, your husband or wife, or your body. But it would still be ultimate reality, it would still be real and genuine life and you would be able to bear it and be with it and see deeply into it for what it is.

We are living in a historical period in which we understand that it is necessary for all of us to be conscious and active in our world. None of us can ignore this call to action. And yet, if we do not practice zazen, whether we call it zazen or whatever we call it and however we do it, we cannot act in any accurate way. There has been plenty of action—too much action. What we need is not more action, we need enlightened action. And this means letting go of action.

JUST SITTING

Tenshin Reb Anderson

THE TEACHING OF THUSNESS has been intimately communicated by buddhas and ancestors. The meaning of this practice of suchness is not in words, and yet it responds to our energy, it responds to our effort. It comes forth and meets us. We sit here and the blue jays sing it to us, the stream sings it to us, because we come and listen. This is our practice of sitting, just sitting. It is a themeless meditation, a seamless meditation. It has no form, no beginning, and no end, and it pervades everything completely. It leaves no traces, and if I try to trace it, it's not that I trace it, but that it generously and compassionately responds to my tracing, to my speaking, and to your listening.

Shakyamuni Buddha transmitted the teaching of thusness. He said the following:

> Please train yourselves thus. In the seen, there will be just the seen. In the heard, there will be just the heard. In the sensed, there will be just the sensed. In the cognized, there will be just the cognized. When for you, in the seen there is just the seen, in the heard just the heard, in the sensed just the sensed, in the cognized just the cognized, then you will not identify with the seen, and so on. And if you do not identify with them, you will not be located in them; if you are not located in them, there will be no here, no there, or in-between. And this will be the end of suffering.

This is themeless meditation. It is seamless meditation. There is no seam between you and the heard: there is just the heard. No seam: only the heard and the seen and the imagined. This is having no object of thought.

Shakyamuni Buddha also said, "If you approach the five *skandhas*, if you approach colors or sounds, or if they approach you, this is misery."

Approaching colors is not just the colors being the colors, but you approaching them. This is misery. Approaching feelings, approaching perceptions, approaching emotions, approaching consciousness, making these approaches, or being approached by these phenomena: this is misery. But if we do not approach these phenomena, if there is no seam between them and us, then these very same skandhas, these very same colors and sounds, are bliss. We can see the roots of the Zen tradition of objectless meditation in this teaching of Buddha.

When the twenty-first ancestor Vasubandhu was talking to Jayata, the ancestor Jayata said,

I don't seek enlightenment, nor am I deluded. I don't worship Buddha, nor am I disrespectful. I don't sit for long periods, nor am I lazy. I don't eat only once a day, nor am I a glutton. I am not contented, nor am I greedy. When the mind does not seek anything, this is called the Way.

Hearing this, Vasubandhu realized the undefiled knowledge. "Hearing this." Now those words are gone. What were they about? Can you hear the spirit of enlightenment, can you smell and taste the spirit of enlightenment in those words? Does it sound familiar? Does it sound like your school song?

After Vasubandhu had realized the undefiled knowledge, he taught his successor, Manorhita. Manorhita asked Vasubandhu, "What is the enlightenment of the buddhas?" Vasubandhu said, "It is the original nature of mind." Manorhita said, "What is the original nature of mind?"

Vasubandhu said, "The emptiness of the sense organs, the sense consciousness, and the sense fields." Hearing this, Manorhita was enlightened. What are you hearing?

The realization of just conception is the truth, the teaching, the enlightenment of the sages. For the mind to stop on just conception is the way Buddha functions. Vasubandhu does not deny a level of perceptual experience where there is no sense of self or self-clinging. However, this level is unknown to you in your daily life. The level of your normal experience, where you know things clearly, is concepts. In the practice of sitting, of awareness of body and breath, what you are aware of at the level of knowing is a concept, or a beautiful string of concepts, of the body. If the mind can realize just the concept of body, your work is done. There is direct and immediate bodily experience, and it is from this immediate bodily experience that the conceptual experience of the body is created. Just sitting practice is just the mind terminating on the concept of sitting, on the concept of the body and the mind and the breath, sitting.

In the term shikantaza, the word *shikan* is sometimes translated as "just," or "only." *Ta* means "hit," and *za* means "sit." It literally means "hit sitting," but the ta really intensifies "sitting." So it means "sitting." *Shikan* means "just," but it also means "by all means do it," or "get on with it." In English, *just* also means "valid within the law, legitimate, suitable, or fitting." It means "sound, well-founded." It means "exact, accurate." It means "upright before God, righteous, upright before the truth."

Live "just." Just concept, just sitting, just the heard in the heard, just the seen in the seen. Upright hearing, righteous hearing, exact hearing, accurate hearing, sound hearing, hearing in accordance with the law, honorable hearing. Just is a big word in Buddhism. It's all over the place, everywhere fitting just exactly right with what's happening. That's the sitting we do: perfectly settled right on itself.

A friend of mine was waiting for the Fillmore bus in San Francisco, and an old man was also there waiting for the bus. My friend got into a conversation with him, and he told her that he was one hundred years old. Of course she asked him, "How did you get to be so old?" He quoted from the Bible: "'Not a thing will I withhold from you if you stand upright before me.'"

You do your part: you put the "just sitting" out there. That's your job. You just sit. That's your energy, coming right down on your energy; precisely, exactly, honorably you, upright you, being your experience.

And you will get a response called enlightenment. It's already there, completely pervading you already: you just have to put a little energy forward in order to realize it. But it's not exactly a little energy, or a lot of energy, but just the energy of this moment, whatever it is. That's why you don't need anything else but what you've got. You don't need to be more awake or less awake. You don't need to have more food or less food than you already have. You just need to be just this. This is your upright, honorable self that you have right here. You've got to celebrate it, you've got to be there for it.

What I'm saying here is just reminding you of what you already know, what you already intend. Mostly, what I will be doing besides reminding you will be simply adjusting you, just "justing" you. That's all. That's all I can do. I'm not correcting you, I'm adjusting you. Of course, I can't really adjust you: you're already adjusted. But sometimes I may feel that you'd look a little more "just" if you sat like this, rather than like that. If I see your mudra over here, I may think, "You'd be a little bit more just if it were over there." Of course, this way is just, too, but still, I may adjust it over there. It's just my aesthetic opinion. It's just my personal adjustment for you.

I try to steer clear of any kind of judgment in the adjustment: I just adjust. And then it's for you not to think about being judged, but rather whether you feel more just after the adjustment. At first, you may feel sometimes, "Gee, this is wacko. I feel kind of off. I thought I was sitting upright, but now I feel like I'm leaning somewhat." Maybe in that doubt that you feel after a postural adjustment or after a verbal adjustment, in the reorientation that you experience at that point, even though it may be sort of a surprise and you may wonder what's going on, you will be reminded of something that you heard before about the buddha way. As Vasubandhu said, "I don't seek enlightenment, nor am I deluded." I'm not right or wrong. I'm in some place that's beyond hearing and seeing. So if you are in the realm of hearing and seeing, and you get adjusted into the space that's beyond hearing and seeing, there may be a slight disorientation for a while. Suddenly, you're living someplace where you can't get a hold of anything.

When you're just sitting, you can't get a hold of anything, because you're just sitting. You're not sitting and getting a hold of something.

You're just sitting: you're earnestly doing just that. When you lose that something else that may have given you some orientation—of being here or there or in between—at first you may wonder what's going on. But you might trust that new space, that space where you don't know exactly what's happening. At least, trust it for a little while.

It was like this for Bodhidharma. He didn't have any special teachings for his disciple Huike. He just said, "Outside, have no involvements." That's it! No involvements. "Inside, have no sighing or coughing. With your mind like a wall, thus you enter the way." With your mind like a wall: in other words, just. With your mind just, or your mind thus. Thus you enter the way.

He didn't say much, but that's the teaching for a lifetime, right there. That's all you need: "Outside, have no involvements. Inside, have no sighing or coughing." No sighing, no shrinking away from exactly just this. Inside, no shrinking violet: "I can't live up to this experience, it's too much for me! It's too fast, it's too intense, it's too yucky!" None of that! Also, no coughing or scoffing. Such as, "This is beneath me. I've got better things to do than think this way. There are better birds than blue jays to listen to. Now, woodpeckers are different. They're really interesting." No coughing in the mind, and also no shrinking away. Don't get rid of it, don't shrink away from it. Just, inside, let it be thus: let your experience be like a wall.

We have a traditional meal ritual in Soto Zen. The set of bowls that we use for this ritual is called *oryoki*. Oryoki means "just enough equipment," or "bowls that are just enough" to support our lives. At the end of the meal, we lean forward to wash these bowls. This is a time when being tall might be difficult. Somebody who is quite tall is many feet away from his bowl. If you're tall and you wear glasses and you don't have them on, you can't even see your bowl down there, right? So you may have the impulse to get your eyes closer to look: "Say, what's happening down there?" There are some bowls and food and all kinds of stuff! It's okay if you want to get your face way down there; but keep your back straight. If you bend over, bend over with a straight back. Don't hunch over. It's another "just" type of thing. In other words, be aware of your back. It makes quite a difference, and it's good exercise for your back, too, incidentally. Most of these things happen to be good exercise.

Also, try not to put your elbows on your knees to hold yourself up. Use your back. Leaning on your elbows is kind of friendly, it's true. "Well, here I am, I'm working on my bowls, and, you know, what's the problem?" It's not really a bad thing to do. But a straight back is very precise. It's more present. When you hunch your back, your consciousness goes. I don't know what happens to it. You can get bent way over without noticing that you're doing it. These little things such as keeping your back straight and being on time, these are about justness, too.

There's a poem called "Love," by George Herbert, which I think is about justness. It's about uncertainty, our lack of faith as to whether we can really be just, in all the meanings of just.

Love

Love bade me welcome: yet my soul drew back,
Guilty of dust and sin.
But quick-eyed Love, observing me grow slack
From my first entrance in,
Drew nearer to me, sweetly questioning
If I lacked anything.

"A guest," I answered, "worthy to be here":
Love said, "You shall be he."
"I, the unkind, ungrateful? Ah, my dear,
I cannot look on thee."
Love took my hand, and smiling did reply,
"Who made the eyes but I?"
"Truth, Lord; but I have marred them; let my shame
Go where it doth deserve."
"And know you not," said Love, "who bore the blame?"
"My dear, then I will serve."
"You must sit down," said Love, "and taste my meat."
So I did sit and eat.

WILL YOU SIT WITH ME?

Bonnie Myotai Treace

ONE NIGHT, around one or two o'clock, I got a phone call from a student in a hospital. The words between us were few, though the call lasted nearly an hour. His voice was so faint, but strong somehow, like hearing water running underground. He asked, "Will you sit with me?" and we began just breathing together. During my visit a week earlier, it had been obvious that he was close to the end of his life. He seemed paler than the sheets around him; there was that mild, acrid smell that circulates in hospitals, and uneaten food from several meals sat on the bed table. It was good last night to sit with him, until he was able to let go, and turn to sleep.

The week before he had been troubled, and was working hard to live or die "correctly." Then he'd made a shift, like the one we have to make over and over again in zazen: knowing something, then having what we know fall apart, and tumbling into ourselves, finding that we've tumbled into a luminous and trustworthy moment. And then knowing arises again, and there's the tumbling, and the trusting. Someone had told the student that when one passed away, it was preferable to leave the body unmoved for three days and to have friends and family sit with the corpse for that period of time. He was really worried because he wasn't sure what the hospital regulations were concerning this, and whether the administration was going to allow it to happen. He had to take up the question "what is the nature of three days, of time itself?" The Buddha's teachings say "One moment, ten thousand years. Ten thousand years, one moment." Just like in a period of zazen, the clock can seem to slow or speed up, to forgive or punish, until the watching stops, the watcher retires. My friend shifted his way of seeing time and now, whatever happens with the hospital, he communicates a sense that nothing is wrong, that the time will be sufficient. His ease with it has relaxed the air around him, and everyone feels it. His practice is serving deeply. He's practicing dying, and his practice has become an unwitting teaching in intimate life.

Master Dogen begins "The Sound of the Valley, Color of the Mountain" chapter of the *Shobogenzo:*

> There are many examples of the various methods used to transmit the incomparable Buddhist Way from master to disciple. All of these stories tell us to practice diligently, to do our best and make a strong effort.

The simple reminder—put your life on the line, don't wait, don't defer, give it all—is the repeated tone of story after story in the Zen tradition. Why is it so hard to let that in, to let it shake us to the bone? We force such a redundancy on those who would help us awaken, and yet the freshness can't be killed. Kind of amazing, isn't it?

Huike, the second ancestor in China, practiced diligently and cut off his arm to demonstrate his full-bodied commitment. His story is upsetting; when we discern that we've made the same commitment, we get a little worried about what might be required of our limbs should we proceed.... But of course Buddhism is not about harm, and doesn't exalt self-mortification. The Buddha saw through that, and the tradition he inspired continued that clarity. So, Huike's example of not holding on, of being willing to offer oneself completely, is offered to teach us about offering, about *dana*, true giving. His giving was not giving to a religion, but to what is real, to the reality that supports us so completely there is no need to protect our own agenda. Huike was challenged by Bodhidharma, who implied, "You could be dissuaded by the merest breeze." And Huike met the challenge by letting the worst blow through him, letting the weather in. That's the diligence of practice, its unconditional offering. It is the diligence of profound love, and it doesn't wait for any reward or reciprocation. It is the practice we cultivate and realize so that we're not limited to comfortable situations, to living out our anxieties.

It is the practice that takes a chance, that gives itself away for all sentient beings. We'll study this all our lives and still find more to study. This is the lineage transmitted from master to disciple: the great mystery of our own hearts and minds in the midst of this giving. We should diligently study this.

Dogen says: "When Shakyamuni was still a bodhisattva in a previous incarnation, he showed his resolve to his teacher by bending over until his hair touched the ground, splashing himself with muddy water." Like the gentlemen in the Victorian stories who lay out their coats for the young ladies, the Buddha spreads out his hair over the water to allow his teacher to walk safely across. There is nothing to protect, and so he doesn't protect himself; he just takes care of what needs taking care of. The long, thick hair spread across the mud shows itself in so many gestures: the unmeasured nights of a parent tending to a sleepless child, the fireman walking into the fire everyone else is running away from. It is in the sitting period when the logic of why the pain in your legs shouldn't be your only imperative is realized. It is showing up at the boring meeting with the assembly of arrogant and irritating townspeople, after a long day at a hard job, to take care of community issues. The ten thousand gestures of the bodhisattva: always the challenge of practice is to not separate ourselves from them, moment after moment.

There was one August sesshin years ago when I was so miserable with a prickly rash all I wanted was to get in the river and stay there. It was murder, and my mind was just hating everything for days. Then in the peak of the heat one afternoon Daido arrived to give a dharma talk and somehow through the steamed malaise of my brain the thought, "He doesn't need to do this; he's doing this for me," made its way into my consciousness, and it seemed like everything just opened up. I felt the reality of that "hair on the mud" and that it was for me. I still can't remember anything about the talk that day, only that I felt flooded with how astonishing the whole thing is, and so humbled by how I'd spent days not noticing it, not feeling it.

Dogen continues: "If we consider these examples, we can't practice with complacency." We focus on the legacy of the lineage not so much to have a sound Buddhist history under our belt, but because something happens in hearing these stories about ancient practitioners and teachers. We remember in ourselves what is possible in a human life. In that remembering, there is energy. That energy manifests: we gather together and ring the bell and go through the absurd activity of saying we're going to "practice." We're going to "realize." We begin with a particular form and say, "We'll wake up in this form." Among all the myriad forms, of all the myriad possibilities, with each and every one expressing itself perfectly, we take up one completely, and vow to practice and realize it. How deep can it go? That's the rush of any commitment, whether it's marriage or a cause or a kid. Each day it's new. The bell rings to end the period, and Dogen warns us not to get complacent: once the arm has been offered, once the hair is placed over the muddy passage—then what? Always, then what?

"When seekers gain freedom, escape from the obstacles of illusion and self-ego, and achieve detachment from their limited viewpoints, their real nature—enlightenment—emerges. It actualizes itself without us realizing it. No one knows or expects it. Even the eye of Buddha can't penetrate it so how can it be recognized by human beings?" Enlightenment is not a thing. Perhaps nothing is. "It's not what you think it is," the teachings tell us, "and neither is it otherwise." I remember an old friend catching me in the middle of an attempt to be "better" (I was sure I would single-handedly destroy the monastery because I was such a lousy example of whatever at the time I'd decided I should be an example of)—he just winked at me as I was straining so hard to be something, and said, "Hey, don't be enlightened; just practice." Letting go of the idea can be such hard and subtle work. Half the time we don't even notice that we're acting out some idea of being something: a man, a woman, a parent, a leader, whatever. Sangha makes the work easier, because sangha has no other purpose than intimacy.

There is story about a layman named So Toba, a very famous Chinese essayist. He lived during the Sung Dynasty, when there was a great sparking of dharma activity. It must have been an extraordinary time to live. Layman Toba is said to have had "a profound understanding of the vast ocean of Buddhism" and to have been "a dragon in the sea of letters." He was able to use words to illuminate clarity, to give a sense of the basis and scope of movement and possibility. Hearing the sound of a stream in a mountain valley, he wrote:

The sound of the valley stream
is his great tongue,
The colors of the mountains
are his pure body.
In the night,
I have heard eighty-four thousand hymns,
But how to tell it to people
the next day?

Eighty-four thousand was said to be the number of atoms in the human body and was also used to indicate the number of emanations, or manifestations of the Buddha of infinite light. Eighty-four thousand hymns, every cell in the body a hymn, and suddenly Layman Toba heard them. But then what? "How to tell it to people the next day?" When I first read this, I asked Roshi about it: "Isn't this the same thing as what everyone does when they want to share their supposedly superior insight? Is he just figuring out how to package his insight? You know that uncomfortable moment when we recognize we're going to be delivered someone's great insight? It's worse than hearing unprocessed dreams." Roshi offered the so-obvious observation, "Maybe you're not understanding the last line. Maybe he's not saying, 'How can I share?' Maybe he's saying, 'How can I serve?'" Dogen says:

Master Toba's insight enabled him to receive enlightenment when he heard the valley stream. It's a pity that from ancient times up to the present there are people who don't realize that the universe is proclaiming the actual body of Buddha. These people are miserable. What do they see when they look at a mountain? What do they hear when they listen to a valley stream? Do they hear only one sound instead of eighty-four thousand hymns? It's regrettable that many only appreciate the superficial aspects of sound or color. They can neither perceive nor experience Buddha's shape, form, and voice in a landscape. They never have the opportunity to see the wonderful Buddhist Way: mountains and rivers ceaselessly proclaiming the truth!

The brightest pain, the dullest ride home on the subway: just mountains and rivers proclaiming the awakening Way. Nothing excluded. What is the body of truth? What is the tongue, the voice, the sheer expression of reality?

From the beginning, spring and fall, mountains and rivers have never been separated. Absolute and relative: never separated. Life and death: never separated. You and I: never separated. Yet we perceive each thing, each moment, independently. "Time cannot be separated from mountains and rivers. Seekers of the Buddhist Way should study the verse: 'The mountain flows, the river sits.'" That study is zazen: one position, not apart from and revealing the position of no-position. That study is face-to-face teaching: two minds distinct yet inexorably one. It is the study of what moves in moving, and what is still in stillness. To present this koan directly is inevitably the work not just of formal koan students, but of every one of us. Doesn't each moment ask for the presentation of our life? Each moment we can waste our time asking for a different koan, or we can, as my friend advised, "just practice." Being intimate with our lives, perhaps we begin to realize the koan.

"Should we not appreciate it? The bright streams' colors and brilliance are boundless. Color after color, in every scintillation of light, are the merit of the whole universe. Could anything ever snatch them away?" This is not a moment for explanation. Sometimes in the night a dying friend asks, "Will you sit with me?" The light is flickering, our heart feels broken, and we recognize with a jolt that the whole universe asks when he asks. Let's vow to appreciate it. Let's vow to respond.

YANGSHAN'S STATE OF MIND

Dharma Talk by Geoffrey Shugen Arnold, Sensei

BOOK OF SERENITY, CASE 32

Pointer to the Assembly

THE OCEAN IS THE REALM of the dragon—it sinks and emerges with tranquil sport. Heaven is the home of the crane—it flies and calls in perfect freedom. Why does an agonized fish remain in the shallows, or a stupid bird live among the reeds? Is there any measure of gain or loss to be made of this?

Main Case

Attention! Yangshan asked a monastic, "Where were you born?"
    The monastic replied, "Yu province."
    Yangshan said, "Do you think of it?"
    The monastic replied, "I think of it always."
    Yangshan said, "Subjective thought is mind; objective thought is surroundings. In that are such things as mountains, rivers, the great earth, towers and buildings, people and animals. Reflect upon the mind that thinks. Isn't something there?"
    The monastic said, "As for that, I don't see anything at all."
    Yangshan said, "As a belief, that's all right; as a person, that's not all right."
    The monastic asked, "Master, do you have any particular instruction?"

Yangshan replied, "To say I have something particular or not misses the mark. As for your view, it obtains only one mystery. In taking a seat and wearing robes, observe it for yourself later on."

Appreciatory Verse

Retain without separation; fly without impediment.
Gate and fence tower high, barrier and chain weigh heavily.
When drinking has reached a high, let the guest go to sleep;
(Some) bellies are full, but the farmers are destitute.
Shooting into the vast sky, the wind flaps the Garuda bird's wings.
Stamping waves in the blue sea, thunder sends off the sporting
     dragon.

"Do you think of it?" "I think of it always." "Subjective thought is mind; objective thought is surroundings." What is subjective thought? What is surroundings? We can say that subjective thought—mind—is the creator, and surroundings—environment—is the created; it's also true that environment is the creator, mind is the created. We are forever thinking about our environment: places, objects, people, activities, pleasures, things we have done and hope to do in our lives. Yet how often do we consider the thinker? If we shine the light upon ourselves, we can easily turn the thinker into an environment as well. We look at this thinker from the point of view of our likes and dislikes, as something to be controlled and managed, fixed, identified and enhanced.

Yangshan is asking us to go beyond this customary way of looking at the thinker, which is binding and, ultimately, destructive. Why is this? Consider our relationships with our perceived environments. In order to show the world that we exist—to say, "Here I am—we often want to leave our mark, to alter or "improve" upon what we see because it somehow always seems inadequate, never sufficient unto itself. We do this with our physical surroundings: mountains, lakes, rivers, and valleys. We do it with our homes, careers, and loved ones. Naturally, we also do this with ourselves; we become the object that is incomplete.

Yangshan says, *"Reflect upon the mind that thinks."* And then he asks, *"Isn't something there?"* What do you see when you shine the light upon yourself? Can the mind think of itself? Can the eye see itself? In "Zazenshin," a chapter in *Shobogenzo,* Master Dogen begins with a koan: *"Once when the Great Master Yaoshan was sitting, a monastic asked him, 'What are you thinking, sitting there so fixedly?' The master answered, 'I'm thinking of not thinking.' The monastic asked, 'How do you think of not thinking?' The master answered, 'Non-thinking.'"* Dogen goes on to comment on this, *"The monastic asked, 'How do you think of not thinking?'* Indeed, though the notion of not thinking may be old, here it is the question, *how* do you think of it? that is being taken up." Dogen says, "Could there be no thinking in sitting fixedly? In sitting fixedly, how could we fail to penetrate this? If we are not the sort of fool that despises what is near, we ought to have the strength—and the thinking—to question sitting fixedly."

Dogen concentrates on the question, *"How do you think of not thinking?"* Yaoshan's response was "Non-thinking." Dogen says, "Although the employment of non-thinking is crystal clear, when we think of not thinking, we always use non-thinking. There is someone in non-thinking, and this someone maintains us. Although it is we who are sitting fixedly, our sitting is not merely thinking: it presents itself as sitting fixedly. Although sitting fixedly is sitting fixedly, how could it think of sitting fixedly? Therefore, sitting fixedly is not the measure of the Buddha, not the measure of awakening, not the measure of comprehension." In the footnote the translator mentions that the character for "fixedly" could also be "toweringly," which is a nice way of expressing it.

A scholar, critiquing Dogen's elaboration, says, "Unfortunately, Dogen's brief commentary following this story is not very helpful in interpreting the master's conversation, let alone in determining just how one might go about this non-thinking." He says, "Given the topic of these comments, perhaps we should not think that Dogen owes us something more substantial to think about here, but clearly he has no interest in demystifying what he calls the essential art of zazen. On the contrary, it is precisely the unthinkable mystery of non-thinking and the orthodox transmission of fixed sitting that seems to attract him." The key to sitting fixedly is to think non-thinking, yet how are we to do this? This scholar laments that Dogen does not give us better instruction. Yet, when Dogen says to "think not thinking," this is direct pointing.

"Think of not thinking." "Reverse your thought to think of the thinking mind." Are these different, or the same? What kind of thinking is this? When the whole universe is nothing but an eye, when undefiled awareness swallows heaven and earth, what kind of seeing and awareness is this? When one thought contains every thought, every difference without distinction, this is sitting fixedly. It is not static or fixed, it is not lifeless or rigid. It is sitting fixedly, one body of space that reaches throughout the ten directions. There is no comparison, nothing to measure with or against. How could this sitting fixedly be the "measure of the Buddha, the measure of awakening?" This is the intimacy of the buddhas and ancestors. Dogen says, "If we are not the sort of fool that despises what is near, we ought to have the strength—and the thinking—to question sitting fixedly." How near do we have to be to experience this intimacy? Not until near and far have both been extinguished will we understand.

Yangshan says, *"Reflect upon the mind that thinks. Isn't something there?"* What is it to turn your awareness upon yourself? Is Yangshan just instructing us to watch our thoughts? When Dogen speaks of sitting fixedly, is he referring to a physical posture? Dogen describes zazen as the "the dharma gate of ease and joy." It is the effort of no effort: to cease all striving, controlling, managing, and maneuvering, to neither push away nor hold on. What remains, then? If we're not actively creating, what is left?

To appreciate this is to understand what makes practice so difficult. This is our struggle; this is *why* we struggle. Our constant desire to change, manipulate, and correct our environment—both internally and externally—means that we are forever working in opposition to the way things are. That's why the simple practice of leaving no traces is so difficult. What is the Middle Way? When we really begin to see how busy we've been overlaying one version of reality with another, we see just how radical the Middle Way is as a spiritual practice and a path for living one's life.

Zazen is to sit toweringly in suchness, in things as they are. To neither add nor take away; to sit down and turn our awareness around to see, but not meddle or correct. The tendency is to do with our zazen what we do with everything else, which is often to go from one extreme to another. We go from banging our heads against the wall, against our-selves, against our breath, against our mind and barriers, to being inert, passive, or uncaring. It's important to recognize the same patterns that we bring to our relationships and daily work as they appear in our zazen.

In my own practice, there was a time when I became aware of the way in which I was practicing and had always practiced, the way I had done almost everything in my life. I had always been a "hard worker" and had never questioned this, mostly because I was rewarded for it. Working hard seemed to bring me results, even through the beginning of my formal Zen practice. When I received my Buddhist name Shugen, which means "rigorous practice," I took this as further confirmation that pushing in this way was good. Yet, at a certain point I began to see clearly, and painfully, that my "hard work" was precisely the thing pre-venting me from really giving up my self-clinging. Around this time I was ordained and received the name Kodo, which means "way of light." This was very hard for me; I couldn't practice this, because I was afraid and didn't have trust. I was fearful of giving up the familiar mode of being that I thought I needed to get somewhere. To explore another kind of effort felt like I was dead, like I wasn't trying or had given up. It was so hard! And I began to sense that this was an edge, a real barrier. It was like a wall that I couldn't get over. Of course, the heart of my clinging was to my sense of myself.

Yangshan says, "*Reflect upon the mind that thinks. Isn't something there?*" The monastic answers, "*As for that, I don't see anything at all.*" Yangshan responds by saying, "*As a belief, that's all right; as a person, that's not all right.*" For this monastic, there is not a single thing—everything washed clean by the non-discriminating eye. This is the place where the exhausted fish and the sluggish bird stop to rest. While this may be sufficient for gaining entry to the Way, to bring true peace to our world, we must enter "the stage of person." In other words, we must come home, which is the same as coming to life; having once died to the illusory nature of who we think we are, we must come back to life.

The monastic presses Yangshan, saying, "*Master, do you have any particular instruction?*" He clearly doesn't hear what Yangshan is offer-ing him, so Yangshan says, "*To say I have something particular or not misses the mark."* And then he finishes with him, saying, *"As for your view, it obtains only one mystery. In taking a seat and wearing robes, observe it for yourself later on."* He doesn't get caught in this monastic's place of no existence. Instead, he urges him to go straight ahead, to leave the shoals and reeds and claim his true birthright, "the stage of person." It is this, being the true person, that is the merging of mind and environment, self and other, practice and verification.

In his poem Hongzhi begins, *Retain without separation; fly without impediment.* Isn't this sitting toweringly? There is a story of a master who, while traveling with his attendant, stopped overnight at a countryside inn. The master was practicing zazen in his room, sitting with Master Zhaozhou's koan "Cypress tree in the garden." Before retiring for the night, the attendant knocked on his teacher's door to check on him. Hearing no response, he opened the door and peeked in. All he saw was a massive tree firmly rooted in the center of the room. At such a time, how can there be any obstruction? When this great body is undivided, there can be no hindrance, and so, nothing to pass through. Thus, *Gate and fence tower high, barrier and chain weigh heavily.*

Yet, *When drinking has reached a high, let the guest go to sleep; (Some) bellies are full, but the farmers are destitute.* Grasping at anything leads to ruin. Attachment to knowledge, Dharma, or emptiness itself creates anew our sense of a separate self. This is the radical nature of the Middle Way, given our deep propensity for clinging to extremes, any extreme. Thus, even though our attachment may be debilitating us, it creates a false sense of security or safety simply because within this clinging there is knowing. In this we can deceive ourselves into believing that we know who, where, and what we are.

Yet, there is another way. *Shooting into the vast sky, the wind flaps the Garuda bird's wings. Stamping waves in the blue sea, thunder sends off the sporting dragon.* That's why dragons roam freely in the ocean and cranes find their home in the sky. When we let go of either side, of any extreme, of all positions, this is the freedom of being complete and natural in one's native realm. So, where is our home? Where is the place where we can be free?

Dogen says:

If you grasp the point of this practice, the four elements of the body will become light and at ease, the spirit will be fresh and sharp, thoughts will be correct and clear, the flavor of the Dharma will sustain the spirit, and you will be calm, pure, and joyful. Your daily life will be the expression of your true natural state. Once you achieve clarification of the truth, you may be likened to the dragon gaining the water or the tiger taking to the mountains. You should realize that when right thought is present, dullness and agitation cannot intrude.

This true natural state is not something that can ever be created. So what are we to do? Stop creating. What we experience of ourselves in this very moment is the product of all our creation; it is the product of our efforts. So enter into the profound practice of not doing, regardless of what your practice is. If it's the breath then be the breath through and through, sitting fixedly. Where is the effort? If it is the koan, then be the koan; sit toweringly. Where is the effort? If your zazen is shikantaza, then think non-thinking. Where is the effort? Once we achieve this clarification of the truth, then the dragon rides the clouds and the Buddha joyfully appears in the world—which is nothing other than our own awakening.

APPENDIX:
FOUNDATIONAL TEXTS

Satipatthana Sutta: The Foundations of Mindfulness

Shakyamuni Buddha

Translated by Bhikkhu Nanamoli,
edited by Bhikkhu Bodhi

Thus have I heard. On one occasion the Blessed One was living in the Kuru country at a town of the Kurus named Kammasadhamma. There he addressed the bhikkhus thus: "Bhikkhus." "Venerable sir," they replied. The Blessed One said this:

"Bhikkhus, this is the direct path for the purification of beings, for the surmounting of sorrow and lamentation, for the disappearance of pain and grief, for the attainment of the true way, for the realization of Nibbana—namely, the four foundations of mindfulness.

"What are the four? Here, bhikkhus, a bhikkhu abides contemplating the body as a body, ardent, fully aware, and mindful, having put away covetousness and grief for the world. He abides contemplating feelings as feelings, ardent, fully aware, and mindful, having put away covetousness and grief for the world. He abides contemplating mind as mind, ardent, fully aware, and mindful, having put away covetousness and grief for the world.He abides contemplating mind-objects as mind-objects, ardent, fully aware, and mindful, having put away covetousness and grief for the world.

"And how, bhikkhus, does a bhikkhu abide contemplating the body as a body? Here a bhikkhu, gone to the forest or to the root of a tree or to an empty hut, sits down; having folded his legs crosswise, set his body erect, and established mindfulness in front of him, ever mindful he breathes in, mindful he breathes out. Breathing in long, he understands: 'I breathe in long'; or breathing out long, he understands: 'I breathe out long.' Breathing in short, he understands: 'I breathe in short'; or breathing out short, he understands; 'I breathe out short.' He trains thus: 'I shall breathe in experiencing the whole body [of breath]'; he trains thus: 'I shall breathe out experiencing the whole body [of breath].' He trains thus: 'I shall breathe in tranquilizing the bodily formation'; he trains thus: 'I shall breathe out tranquilizing the bodily formation.' Just as a skilled turner or his apprentice, when making a long turn, understands: 'I make a long turn'; or, when making a short turn, understands: 'I make a short turn'; so too, breathing in long, a bhikkhu understands: 'I breathe in long,'… He trains thus: 'I shall breathe out tranquillizing the bodily formation.'

"In this way he abides contemplating the body as a body internally, or he abides contemplating the body as a body externally, or he abides contemplating the body as a body both internally and externally. Or else he abides contemplating in the body its arising factors, or he abides contemplating in the body its vanishing factors, or he abides contemplating in the body both its arising and vanishing factors. Or else mindfulness that 'there is a body' is simply established in him to the extent necessary for bare knowledge and mindfulness. And he abides independent *(sic)*, not clinging to anything in the world. That is how a bhikkhu abides contemplating the body as a body.

"Again, bhikkhus, when walking, a bhikkhu understands: 'I am walking'; when standing, he understands: 'I am standing'; when sitting, he understands: 'I am sitting'; when lying down he understands: 'I am lying down'; or he understands accordingly however his body is disposed.

"In this way he abides contemplating the body as a body internally, externally, and both internally and externally…. And he abides independent, not clinging to anything in the world. That too is how a bhikkhu abides contemplating the body as a body.

"Again, bhikkhus, a bhikkhu is one who acts in full awareness when going forward and returning; who acts in full awareness when looking ahead and looking away; who acts in full awareness when flexing and extending his limbs; who acts in full awareness when wearing his robes and carrying his outer robe and bowl; who acts in full awareness when eating, drinking, consuming food, and tasting; who acts in full awareness when defecating and urinating; who acts in full awareness when walking, standing, sitting, falling asleep, waking up, talking, and keeping silent.

"In this way he abides contemplating the body as a body internally, externally, and both internally and externally.... And he abides independent, not clinging to anything in the world. That too is how a bhikkhu abides contemplating the body as a body.

"Again, bhikkhus, a bhikkhu reviews this same body up from the soles of the feet and down from the top of the hair, bounded by skin, as full of many kinds of impurity thus: 'In this body there are head-hairs, body-hairs, nails, teeth, skin, flesh, sinews, bones, bone-marrow, kidneys, heart, liver, diaphragm, spleen, lungs, large intestines, small intestines, contents of the stomach, feces, bile, phlegm, pus, blood, sweat, fat, tears, grease, spittle, snot, oil of the joints, and urine.' Just as though there were a bag with an opening at both ends full of many sorts of grain, such as hill rice, red rice, beans, peas, millet, and white rice, and a man with good eyes were to open it and review it thus: 'This is hill rice, this is red rice, these are beans, these are peas, this is millet, this is white rice'; so too, a bhikkhu reviews this same body...as full of many kinds of impurity thus: 'In this body there are head-hairs...and urine.'

"In this way he abides contemplating the body as a body internally, externally, and both internally and externally.... And he abides independent, not clinging to anything in the world. That too is how a bhikkhu abides contemplating the body as a body.

"Again, bhikkhus, a bhikkhu reviews this same body, however it is placed, however disposed, as consisting of elements thus: 'In this body there are the earth element, the water element, the fire element, and the air element.' Just as though a skilled butcher or his apprentice had killed a cow and was seated at the crossroads with it cut up into pieces; so too, a bhikkhu reviews this same body...as consisting of elements thus: 'In this body there are the earth element, the water element, the fire element, and the air element.'

"In this way he abides contemplating the body as a body internally, externally, and both internally and externally.... And he abides independent, not clinging to anything in the world. That too is how a bhikkhu abides contemplating the body as a body.

"Again, bhikkhus, as though he were to see a corpse thrown aside in a charnel ground, one, two, or three days dead, bloated, livid, and oozing matter, a bhikkhu compares this same body with it thus: 'This body too is of the same nature, it will be like that, it is not exempt from that fate.'

"In this way he abides contemplating the body as a body internally, externally, and both internally and externally.... And he abides independent, not clinging to anything in the world. That too is how a bhikkhu abides contemplating the body as a body.

"Again, as though he were to see a corpse thrown aside in a charnel ground, being devoured by crows, hawks, vultures, dogs, jackals, or various kinds of worms, a bhikkhu compares this same body with it thus: 'This body too is of the same nature, it will be like that, it is not exempt from that fate.'

"...That too is how a bhikkhu abides contemplating the body as a body.

"Again, as though he were to see a corpse thrown aside in a charnel ground, a skeleton with flesh and blood, held together with sinews...a fleshless skeleton smeared with blood, held together with sinews...a skeleton without flesh and blood, held together with sinews... disconnected bones scattered in all directions—here a hand-bone, there a foot-bone, here a shin-bone, there a thigh-bone, here a hip-bone, there a back-bone, here a rib-bone, there a breast-bone, here an arm-bone, there a shoulder-bone, here a neck-bone, there a jaw-bone, here a tooth, there the skull—a bhikkhu compares this same body with it thus: 'This body too is of the same nature, it will be like that, it is not exempt from that fate.'

"...That too is how a bhikkhu abides contemplating the body as a body.

"Again, as though he were to see a corpse thrown aside in a charnel ground, bones bleached white, the color of shells...bones heaped up, more than a year old...bones rotted and crumbled to dust, a bhikkhu compares this same body with it thus: 'This body too is of the same nature, it will be like that, it is not exempt from that fate.'

"In this way he abides contemplating the body as a body internally, or he abides contemplating the body externally, or he abides contemplating the body as a body both internally and externally. Or else he abides contemplating in the body its arising factors, or he abides contemplating in the body its vanishing factors, or he abides contemplating in the body both its arising and vanishing factors. Or else mindfulness that 'there is a body' is simply established in him to the extent necessary for the bare knowledge and mindfulness. And he abides independent, not clinging to anything in the world. That too is how a bhikkhu abides contemplating the body as a body.

"And how, bhikkhus, does a bhikkhu abide contemplating feelings as feelings? Here, when feeling a pleasant feeling, a bhikkhu understands: 'I feel a pleasant feeling'; when feeling a painful feeling, he understands: 'I feel a painful feeling'; when feeling a neither-painful-nor-pleasant feeling, he understands: 'I feel a neither-painful-nor-pleasant feeling.' When feeling a worldly pleasant feeling, he understands: 'I feel a worldly pleasant feeling'; when feeling an unworldly pleasant feeling, he understands: 'I feel an unworldly pleasant feeling'; when feeling a worldly painful feeling, he understands: 'I feel a worldly painful feeling'; when feeling an unworldly painful feeling, he understands: 'I feel an unworldly painful feeling'; when feeling a worldly neither-painful-nor-pleasant feeling, he understands: 'I feel a worldly neither-painful-nor-pleasant feeling'; when feeling an unworldly neither-painful-nor-pleasant feeling, he understands: 'I feel an unworldly neither-painful-nor-pleasant feeling.'

"In this way he abides contemplating feelings as feelings internally, or he abides contemplating feelings as feelings externally, or he abides contemplating feelings as feelings both internally and externally. Or else he abides contemplating in feelings their arising factors, or he abides contemplating in feelings their vanishing factors, or he abides contemplating in feelings both their arising and vanishing factors. Or else mindfulness that 'there is feeling' is simply established in him to the extent necessary for bare knowledge and mindfulness. And he abides independent, not clinging to anything in the world. That is how a bhikkhu abides contemplating feelings as feelings.

"And how, bhikkhus, does a bhikkhu abide contemplating mind as mind? Here a bhikkhu understands mind affected by lust as mind affected by lust, and mind unaffected by lust as mind unaffected by lust. He understands mind affected by hate as mind affected by hate, and mind unaffected by hate as mind unaffected by hate. He understands mind affected by delusion as mind affected by delusion, and mind unaffected by delusion as mind unaffected by delusion. He understands contracted mind as contracted mind, and distracted mind as distracted mind.

He understands exalted mind as exalted mind, and unexalted mind as unexalted mind. He understands surpassed mind as surpassed mind, and unsurpassed mind as unsurpassed mind. He understands concentrated mind as concentrated mind, and unconcentrated mind as unconcentrated mind. He understands liberated mind as liberated mind, and unliberated mind as unliberated mind.

"In this way he abides contemplating mind as mind internally, or he abides contemplating mind as mind externally, or he abides contemplating mind as mind both internally and externally. Or else he abides contemplating in mind its arising factors, or he abides contemplating in mind its vanishing factors, or he abides contemplating in mind both its arising and vanishing factors. Or else mindfulness that 'there is mind' is simply established in him to the extent necessary for bare knowledge and mindfulness. And he abides independent, not clinging to anything in the world. That is how a bhikkhu abides contemplating mind as mind.

"And how, bhikkhus, does a bhikkhu abide contemplating mind-objects as mind-objects? Here a bhikkhu abides contemplating mind-objects as mind-objects in terms of the five hindrances. And how does a bhikkhu abide contemplating mind-objects as mind-objects in terms of the five hindrances? Here, there being sensual desire in him, a bhikkhu understands: 'There is sensual desire in me'; or there being no sensual desire in him, he understands: 'There is no sensual desire in me'; and he also understands how there comes to be the arising of unarisen sensual desire, and how there comes to be the abandoning of arisen sensual desire, and how there comes to be the future non-arising of abandoned sensual desire.'

"There being ill will in him…. There being sloth and torpor in him…. There being restlessness and remorse in him…. There being doubt in him, a bhikkhu understands: 'There is doubt in me'; or there being no doubt in him, he understands: 'There is no doubt in me'; and he understands how there comes to be the arising of unarisen doubt, and how there comes to be the abandoning of arisen doubt, and how there comes to be the future non-arising of abandoned doubt.

"In this way he abides contemplating mind-objects as mind-objects internally, or he abides contemplating mind-objects as mind-objects externally, or he abides contemplating mind-objects as mind-objects both internally and externally. Or else he abides contemplating in mind-objects their arising factors, or he abides contemplating in mind-objects their vanishing factors, or he abides contemplating in mind-objects both their arising and vanishing factors. Or else mindfulness that 'there are mind-objects' is simply established in him to the extent necessary for bare knowledge and mindfulness. And he abides independent, not clinging to anything in the world. That is how a bhikkhu abides contemplating mind-objects as mind-objects in terms of the five hindrances.

"Again, bhikkhus, a bhikkhu abides contemplating mind-objects as mind-objects in terms of the five aggregates affected by clinging. And how does a bhikkhu abide contemplating the mind-objects as mind-objects in terms of the five aggregates affected by clinging? Here a bhikkhu understands: 'Such is material form, such its origin, such its disappearance; such is feeling, such its origin, such its disappearance; such is perception, such its origin, such its disappearance; such are the formations, such their origin, such their disappearance; such is consciousness; such its origin, such its disappearance.'

"In this way he abides contemplating mind-objects as mind-objects internally, externally, and both internally and externally…. And he abides independent, not clinging to anything in the world. That is how a bhikkhu abides contemplating mind-objects as mind-objects in terms of the five aggregates affected by clinging.

"Again, bhikkhus, a bhikkhu abides contemplating mind-objects as mind-objects in terms of the six internal and external bases. And how does a bhikkhu abide contemplating mind-objects as mind-objects in terms of the six internal and external bases? Here a bhikkhu understands the eye, he understands forms, and he understands the fetter that arises dependent on both; and he also understands how there comes to be the arising of the unarisen fetter, and how there comes to be the abandoning of the arisen fetter, and how there comes to be the future non-arising of the abandoned fetter.

"He understands the ear, he understands sounds…. He understands the nose, he understands odors…. He understands the tongue, he understands flavors…. He understands the body, he understands tangibles…. He understands the mind, he understands mind-objects, and he understands the fetter that arises dependent on both; and he also understands how there comes to be the arising of the unarisen fetter, and how there comes to be the abandoning of the arisen fetter, and how there comes to be the future non-arising of the abandoned fetter.

"In this way he abides contemplating mind-objects as mind-objects internally, externally, and both internally and externally.... And he abides independent, not clinging to anything in the world. That is how a bhikkhu abides contemplating mind-objects as mind-objects in terms of the six internal and external bases.

"Again, bhikkhus, a bhikkhu abides contemplating mind-objects as mind-objects in terms of the seven enlightenment factors. And how does a bhikkhu abide contemplating mind-objects as mind-objects in terms of the seven enlightenment factors? Here, there being the mindfulness enlightenment factor in him, a bhikkhu understands: 'There is the mindfulness enlightenment factor in me'; or there being no mindfulness enlightenment factor in him, he understands: 'There is no mindfulness enlightenment factor in me'; and he also understands how there comes to be the arising of the unarisen mindfulness enlightenment factor, and how the arisen mindfulness enlightenment factor comes to fulfillment by development.

"There being the investigation-of-states enlightenment factor in him.... There being the energy enlightenment factor in him.... There being the rapture enlightenment factor in him.... There being the tranquillity enlightenment factor in him.... There being the concentration enlightenment factor in him.... There being the equanimity enlightenment factor in him, a bhikkhu understands: 'There is the equanimity enlightenment factor in me'; or there being no equanimity enlightenment factor in him, he understands: 'There is no equanimity enlightenment factor in me'; and he also understands how there comes to be the arising of the unarisen equanimity enlightenment factor, and how the arisen equanimity enlightenment factor comes to fulfillment by development.

"In this way he abides contemplating mind-objects as mind-objects internally, externally, both internally and externally.... And he abides independent, not clinging to anything in the world. That is how a bhikkhu abides contemplating mind-objects as mind-objects in terms of the seven enlightenment factors.

"Again, bhikkhus, a bhikkhu abides contemplating mind-objects as mind-objects in terms of the Four Noble Truths. And how does a bhikkhu abide contemplating mind-objects as mind-objects in terms of the Four Noble Truths? Here a bhikkhu understands as it actually is: 'This is suffering'; he understands as it actually is: 'This is the origin of suffering'; he understands as it actually is: 'This is the cessation of suffering'; he understands as it actually is: 'This is the way leading to the cessation of suffering.'

"In this way he abides contemplating mind-objects as mind-objects internally, or he abides contemplating mind-objects externally, or he abides contemplating mind-objects as mind-objects both internally and externally. Or else he abides contemplating in mind-objects their arising factors, or he abides contemplating in mind-objects their vanishing factors, or he abides contemplating in mind-objects both their arising and vanishing factors. Or else mindfulness that 'there are mind-objects' is simply established in him to the extent necessary for bare knowledge and mindfulness. And he abides independent, not clinging to anything in the world. That is how a bhikkhu abides contemplating mind-objects as mind-objects in terms of the Four Noble Truths.

"Bhikkhus, if anyone should develop these four foundations of mindfulness in such a way for seven years, one of two fruits could be expected for him: either final knowledge here and now, or if there is trace of clinging left, non-return.

"Let alone seven years, bhikkhus. If anyone should develop these four foundations of mindfulness in such way for six years…for five years…for four years…for three years…for two years…for one year, one of two fruits could be expected from him: either final knowledge here and now, or if there is a trace of clinging left, non-return.

"Let alone one year, bhikkhus. If anyone should develop these four foundations of mindfulness in such a way for seven months…for six months…for five months…for four months…for three months…for two months…for one month…for half a month, one of two fruits could be expected for him: either final knowledge here and now, or if there is trace of clinging left, non-return.

"Let alone half a month, bhikkhus. If anyone should develop these four foundations of mindfulness in such way for seven days, one of two fruits could be expected for him: either final knowledge here and now, or if there is a trace of clinging left, non-return.

"So it was with reference to this that it was said: 'Bhikkhus, this is the direct path for the purification of beings, for the surmounting of sorrow and lamentation, for the disappearance of pain and grief, for the attainment of the true way, for the realization of Nibbana—namely, the four foundations of mindfulness.'"

That is what the Blessed One said. The bhikkhus were satisfied and delighted in the Blessed One's words.

Bloodstream Sermon

Bodhidharma

Translated by Red Pine

EVERYTHING THAT APPEARS in the three realms comes from the mind. Hence buddhas of the past and future teach mind to mind without bothering about definitions.

But if they don't define it, what do they mean by mind?

You ask. That's your mind. I answer. That's my mind. If I had no mind, how could I answer? If you had no mind, how could you ask? That which asks is your mind. Through endless kalpas without beginning, whatever you do, wherever you are, that's your real mind, that's your real buddha. *This mind is the buddha* says the same thing. Beyond this mind you'll never find another buddha. To search for enlightenment or nirvana beyond this mind is impossible. The reality of your own self-nature, the absence of cause and effect, is what's meant by mind. Your mind is nirvana. You might think you can find a buddha or enlightenment somewhere beyond the mind, but such a place doesn't exist.

Trying to find a buddha or enlightenment is like trying to grab space. Space has a name but no form. It's not something you can pick up or put down. And you certainly can't grab it. Beyond this mind you'll never see a buddha. The buddha is a product of your mind. Why look for a buddha beyond this mind?

Buddhas of the past and future only talk about this mind. The mind is the buddha, and the buddha is the mind. Beyond the mind there's no buddha, and beyond the buddha there's no mind. If you think there's a buddha beyond the mind, where is he? There's no buddha beyond the mind, so why envision one? You can't know your real mind as long as you deceive yourself. As long as you're enthralled by a lifeless form, you're not free. If you don't believe me, deceiving yourself won't help. It's not the buddha's fault. People, though, are deluded. They're unaware that their own mind is the buddha. Otherwise they wouldn't look for a buddha outside the mind.

Buddhas don't save buddhas. If you use your mind to look for a buddha, you won't see the buddha. As long as you look for a buddha somewhere else, you'll never see that your own mind is the buddha. Don't use a buddha to worship a buddha. And don't use the mind to invoke a buddha. Buddhas don't recite sutras. Buddhas don't keep precepts. And buddhas don't break precepts. Buddhas don't keep or break anything. Buddhas don't do good or evil.

To find a buddha, you have to see your nature. Whoever sees his nature is a buddha. If you don't see your nature, invoking buddhas, reciting sutras, making offerings, and keeping precepts are all useless. Invoking buddhas results in good karma, reciting sutras results in a good memory; keeping precepts results in a good birth, and making offerings results in future blessings—but no buddha.

If you don't understand by yourself, you'll have to find a teacher to get to the bottom of life and death. But unless he sees his nature, such a person isn't a teacher. Even if he can recite the Twelvefold Canon, he can't escape the Wheel of Birth and Death. He suffers in the three realms without hope of release.

Long ago, the monk Good Star was able to recite the entire canon. But he didn't escape the Wheel, because he didn't see his nature. If this was the case with Good Star, then people nowadays who recite a few sutras or shastras and think it's the Dharma are fools. Unless you see your mind, reciting so much prose is useless.

To find a buddha all you have to do is see your nature. Your nature is the buddha. And the buddha is the person who's free: free of plans, free of cares. If you don't see your nature and run around all day looking somewhere else, you'll never find a buddha. The truth is, there's nothing to find. But to reach such an understanding you need a teacher and you need to struggle to make yourself understand. Life and death are important. Don't suffer them in vain. There's no advantage in deceiving yourself. Even if you have mountains of jewels and as many servants as there are grains of sand along the Ganges, you see them when your eyes are open. But what about when your eyes are shut? You should realize then that everything you see is like a dream or illusion.

The Fundamental Expedient Teachings for Calming the Mind That Attains Enlightenment

Ta-I Tao-hsin (Dayi Daoxin)

Translated by David W. Chappell

THE FUNDAMENTAL TEACHINGS of mind are: (1) the mind of all the Buddhas is the First Principle, based on the *Lankavatara Sutra,* and (2) *I-hsing san-mei* means that the mind that is aware of the Buddha *is* the Buddha, whereas [the mind that] does false thinking is the ordinary person, based on the *Wen shu shuo po jo ching.*

The *Wen shu shuo po jo ching* says:

Manjushri asked the World Honored One the meaning of i-hsing san-mei. The Buddha replied: "Ultimate reality has a unified form. Fixing your awareness on ultimate reality is called i-hsing san-mei. If sons and daughters of noble families want to enter i-hsing san-mei, they should first listen to the Perfection of Wisdom [teaching] and cultivate their practice in terms of what it says. Later they will be able to enter i-hsing san-mei, and their awareness will be like ultimate reality: free from retrogression, indestructible, inconceivable, lacking obstructions, and without form. Sons and daughters of noble families who want to enter into i-hsing san-mei [but cannot], should stay in an enclosure empty [of distractions], and give up all chaotic thoughts. Without grasping onto outward appearances, they should concentrate their minds on a particular Buddha and exclusively recite his name. By properly facing in the direction of the Buddha, having an upright body, and being able to continuously think on one Buddha thought after thought, means that in this contemplation they are able to see all the Buddhas of the past, present, and future. Why?

"Contemplating the measurelessness and boundlessness of the merit of one Buddha is the same as the merit of countless Buddhas [since] they are nondualistic and inconceivable. The Buddha's Dharma is without distinctions. Everything conforms to the One True Suchness to achieve the most perfect realization. [Therefore,] everyone will attain unlimited merit and unlimited abilities [by contemplating the merits of one Buddha]. Those who enter i-hsing san-mei in this way exhaustively know ultimate reality and the undifferentiated forms of Buddhas as numerous as the sands of the Ganges."

Every aspect of the mind and body, [even] lifting your foot and putting it down, always is the place of enlightenment. All of your behavior and actions are enlightenment.

The *P'u hsien kuan ching* says: "The sea of all karmic hindrances totally arises from false thinking. Those who desire to repent should sit upright and contemplate true reality." This is called Repentance according to the First Principle, which eradicates the mind of the three poisons, the grasping mind, and the conceptualizing mind. If one continuously meditates on Buddha thought after thought, suddenly there will be clarity and serenity, and still further not even an object of thought. The *Ta p'in ching* says: "No object of thought means to be thinking on Buddha."

[…] The mind that is "thinking on Buddha" is called thinking on no object. Apart from mind there is no Buddha at all. Apart from Buddha there is no mind at all. Thinking on Buddha is identical to the thinking mind. To seek the mind means to seek for the Buddha.

Why is this? Consciousness is without form. The Buddha lacks any outer appearance. When you understand this truth, it is identical to calming the mind. If you always are thinking on Buddha, grasping [onto externals] does not arise, [and everything] disappears and is without form, and thinking is impartial without [false] discrimination. To enter into this state, the mind that is thinking on Buddha disappears, and further it is not even necessary to indicate [the mind as Buddha]. When you see this, your mind is none other than the body of the real and true nature of the Tathagata. It is also called the True Dharma; it is also called Buddha nature; it is also called the Real Nature or Real Ultimate of the various dharmas; it is also called the Pure Land; it is also called enlightenment, the diamond *samadhi,* and original enlightenment; it is also called the realm of nirvana and wisdom *(prajna).* Although the names are innumerable they are all the same One Essence, and do not mean a subject of contemplation nor an object of contemplation.

When the mind is impartial like this, without fail it is made clear and pure and always appears in front of you so that the various conditions are not able to become obstructive. Why is this? Because all these phenomena are the body of the One Dharma of the Tathagata. When one stays in this unified mind, all bondage and illusion spontaneously disappear. Within a single speck of dust are all innumerable realms. Innumerable realms are collected on the tip of a single hair. Because their original nature is suchness (emptiness), there is not any mutual interference. The *Hua yen ching [The Flower Garland Scripture]* says: "There is one volume of scripture [explaining that] 'in a single speck of dust one can see the phenomena of three thousand chiliocosms [universes].'" As briefly pointed out, it is impossible to exhaust everything when it comes to [describing the methods for] calming the mind. In this, skillfulness comes from the heart.

Question: What kind of a person is a Chan master?
Tao-hsin replies: Someone who is not disturbed either by chaos or serenity is a person with the know-how of good Chan practice. When one always dwells in tranquility, the mind perishes. But if you are always in a state of discernment, then the mind scatters chaotically. The *Lotus Sutra* says: "The Buddha himself dwells in the Great Vehicle (Mahayana). The power of meditation and of wisdom gives remarkable splendor to the dharmas that he has acquired. These he uses to save all beings."

Question: How can we be enlightened to the nature of things and our minds attain lucid purity?
Tao-hsin replies: Neither by [trying to] meditate on the Buddha, nor by [trying to] grab hold of the mind, nor by seeing the mind, nor by analyzing the mind, nor by reflection, nor by discernment, nor by dispersing

confusion, but through identification with the natural rhythms of things. Don't force anything to go. Don't force anything to stay. Finally abiding in the one sole purity, the mind spontaneously becomes lucid and pure.

Some people can see clearly that the mind is lucid and pure like a bright mirror. Some need a year [of practice] and then the mind becomes lucid and pure. Others need three or five years and then the mind is lucid and pure. Or some can attain enlightenment without ever being taught by someone else. The *Nirvana Sutra* says: "The nature of the mind of beings is like a pearl that falls into the water. The water is muddy so the pearl becomes hidden. When the water is pure, the pearl is revealed."

Beings do not awaken to the true nature of their minds, which are originally and everlastingly pure because the Three Jewels [the Buddha, the Dharma, and the Sangha] are slandered, because the unity of the Sangha is broken, and because of the defilements of various wrong views and illusions and the stain of covetousness, anger, and delusions. Because the ways in which students attain enlightenment differ, there are distinctions like these [we have listed]. Therefore, we have now briefly pointed out the differences in capacities and conditions [for enlightenment]. Those who are teachers of the people must be very conscious of these differences.

The *Hua yen ching* says: "The form of the body of Samantabhadra is like empty space. [His actions] are based on Suchness, not on the Buddha Land." When you are enlightened the Buddha Lands are all Suchness (emptiness). This means that you do not rely either on suchness or on the Lands. The *Nirvana Sutra* says: "The length of the body of Bodhisattva Wu-pien-shen is like space." It also says: "Because it is very radiant, it is like the summer sun." It also says: "Because the body is boundless, it is like Nirvana." It also says: "The nature of Great Nirvana is broad and vast."

Therefore, we should know that there are four kinds of students [of Buddhism]. Those who do practice, have understanding, and attain enlightenment are the highest group. Those who do not practice but have understanding and attain enlightenment are the middle-upper group. Those who do practice and have understanding but have not

attained enlightenment are in the middle-lower group. Those who neither practice nor have understanding nor have attained enlightenment
are in the lowest group.

*Question: The moment we are going to begin practice, how should we
contemplate?*
Tao-hsin replies: "We must identify with the natural rhythms of
things."

It was also asked: "Should we face toward the West or not?"

Tao-hsin replies: If we know our original mind neither is born nor
dies but is ultimately pure and is identical to the pure Buddha Land,
then it is not necessary to face toward the West. The *Hua yen ching*
says: "Unlimited kalpas of time are contained in a single moment. A
single moment contains unlimited kalpas." Therefore you should know
that a single place [contains] an unlimited quantity of places, and an
unlimited quantity of places is in one place.

The Buddha causes beings who have dull capacities to face toward the
West, but he does not teach people with keen abilities to do so. Bodhisattvas who have profound practice enter [the stream of] birth and death
(samsara) in order to save beings, and yet do not [drown in] desire. If
you have the view that "beings are in samsara and I am able to save
them, and these beings are capable of being saved," then you are not to
be called a Bodhisattva. "Saving beings" is similar to "saving the empty
sky." How could [the sky] ever have come or gone!

The *Diamond Sutra* says: "As for an infinite number of beings who
have been saved, in fact there are no beings who have been saved." As a
whole, Bodhisattvas of the First Stage at the beginning have the realization that all things are empty. Later on they obtain the realization
that all things are not empty, which is identical to the "wisdom of non-
discrimination." [The *Heart Sutra* says:] "Form is identical to emptiness." It is not because form is eliminated and then there is emptiness.
"The nature of form is emptiness."

All Bodhisattvas think that studying emptiness is identical to
enlightenment. Those who have just begun to practice [Buddhism]
immediately understand emptiness, but this is only a view of emptiness
and is not true emptiness. Those who obtain true emptiness through

cultivating the Way, do not see either emptiness nor non-emptiness. They do not have any views at all. You should by all means thoroughly understand the idea that form is emptiness. The activity of the mind of those who are really proficient [in emptiness] will definitely be lucid and pure.

When you are awakened to the fundamental nature of things, when you completely understand and are clearly discerning, then later on you yourselves will be considered as masters! Furthermore, inner thoughts and outward behavior must coincide, and there must be no disparity between truth and practice. You should sever relationships with written works and spoken explanations. In pursuing the sacred Way [toward enlightenment], by staying alone in a place of tranquility you can realize by yourself the attainment of the Way.

Again there are some people who have not yet understood the ultimate truth, and yet for the sake of fame and wealth guide others. Although they do not know the relative keenness or dullness in the capacities [of their followers], if it appears to them that there is something exceptional [in their followers] they always give the seal of approval. Alas, alas! What a great calamity! Or seeing that the mental activities [of their followers] appear to be lucid and pure, they give their seal of approval. These people bring great destruction to the Buddha's Dharma. They are deceiving themselves and cheat others. Those who are proficient in practice [consider] that having such exceptional attainments as these is just an outer appearance but that [true] mindfulness has not yet been attained.

Those who have truly attained mindfulness are aware and discerning by themselves. Much later their Dharma-eye will open spontaneously and they can skillfully distinguish nonsubstantiality from artificiality [that is, true reality from false appearances]. Some people conclude that the body is empty and the nature of the mind also disappears. These people have nihilistic views. They are the same as heretics and are not disciples of the Buddha. Some consider that the nature of the mind is indestructible. These are people with eternalistic views, and are the same as heretics.

Now we shall describe the disciples of the Buddha. They do not conclude that the nature of the mind is destroyed. Although they are constantly bringing beings to enlightenment, they do not generate emotional attachment. They constantly cultivate insight, so that stupidity and wisdom are equalized [for them]. They constantly dwell in meditation, so that there is no difference between clarity and chaos [for them]. They constantly view sentient beings [whom bodhisattvas have vowed to save], and yet they know the beings have never had permanent existence and ultimately neither come into existence nor pass away. [True disciples] everywhere manifest form that is neither seen nor heard. Completely understanding all things, they have never grasped or rejected anything. They have never transformed themselves [into other bodily forms], and yet their bodies are everywhere in Ultimate Reality.

In former times, the meditation master Chih-ming (Jiming) advised:

> The dharma for cultivating the Way must by all means have understanding and practice mutually supporting each other. First you should understand the source of the mind and the various essences and functions [of things], and then the truth will be seen lucidly and purely with complete understanding and discernment without any doubts. Then afterwards meritorious work can be accomplished. A thousand things comply if you understand but once, whereas a single deception [brings] ten thousand doubts. To miss by the slightest hair-breadth is to err by a thousand li.

These are not empty words.

The *[Kuan] Wu liang shou ching* says: "The Ultimate Dimension *(dharmakaya)* of the various Buddhas penetrates the thoughts of every being. The mind and the Buddha are identical. This mind creates Buddha." You should know that the Buddha is identical to your mind, and that there is no other Buddha outside of your mind.

Briefly, I suggest that overall there are five principles:

(1) Know the essence of the mind. The essential nature is pure. The essence is the same as the Buddha.

(2) Know the function of the mind. It functions to give rise to the jewel of the Dharma. It is always productive but constantly tranquil. The ten thousand delusions are all like this (that is, are all suchness).

(3) Constant awakening is unceasing. The awakening mind is always present. The teaching of this awakening is without form.

(4) Always view the body as empty and tranquil. Inside and outside [of yourself] are transparent to each other. Your body enters into the center of Ultimate Reality. There never have been any obstacles.

(5) Maintain unified mindfulness without deviation. Both movement and stillness constantly remain. Those practitioners are able to clearly see their Buddha Nature and enter into the gate of meditation without delay.

When you consider the great many kinds of meditation methods in the various scriptures, it was only Layman Fu who advocated "maintain unified mindfulness without deviation." First you cultivate the body and take the body as the basis for close scrutiny. This body is a unity of the four elements [of earth, water, fire, and air] and the five skandhas [of form, sensations, perception, impulse, and consciousness] to which it finally returns since it lacks any permanency and does not have independent existence. Although it has not yet decayed and disappeared, ultimately it is nonsubstantial. The *Vimalakirti Sutra* says: "The body is like a drifting cloud that changes and disappears in an instant."

Also, constantly contemplate that your own body is sheer empty space, like a shadow that you can see but can't grasp. Wisdom arises from the shadow, and ultimately is without location, unmoving and yet responsive to things, changing endlessly. The six sense organs are born in nonsubstantiality. If the six sense organs are nonsubstantial, then the six corresponding sense objects are to be understood as a dream. Just as when the eye sees something, there is nothing in the eye.

It is like a mirror that reflects the image of your face, that you understand fully and most distinctly. In the emptiness [of the mirror] appears the shadow of a form [since] not a single thing exists in the mirror. You should know that the face of a person does not come and enter into the mirror, nor does the mirror go and enter the face of a person.

In this detailed way, we know that the mirror as well as one's face inherently do not go out nor enter in, do not come nor go, but are identical to the meaning of the Tathagata. Thus, by analyzing this thoroughly, [we see that] it is inherently always nonsubstantial and tranquil in the eye and in the mirror. The mirror reflecting and the eye seeing are both the same.

For this reason, if we take the nose or tongue or another sense organ for comparison, the idea will again be like this. Knowing that the eye is inherently nonsubstantial, one should understand that all form which the eye sees is "objectified form." When the ear hears a sound, know that this is "objectified sound." When the nose smells a fragrance, know that this is an "objectified fragrance." When the tongue distinguishes a flavor, know that this is an "objectified flavor." When the mind considers a thought, know that this is an "objectified thought." When the body senses a touch, know that this is an "objectified touch." In the same way, when one practices contemplation, know that this is to contemplate non-substantiality (emptiness) and tranquility, so that when you see form, understand that this is not a sensation you receive. Not to receive the sensation of a form [means that] form is identical to nonsubstantiality. Nonsubstantiality is identical to formlessness and formlessness is identical to non-[ambitious] action. This is the gate of liberation. For practitioners who obtain liberation, the customary use of the various sense organs is like this.

Again, weigh carefully the words I speak. Always contemplate the nonsubstantiality of the six sense organs, which are as serene as if there was no hearing nor seeing. The *I chiao ching* says: "At that time in the middle of the night it was serenely quiet without a sound." You should know that the teaching of the Tathagata always takes nonsubstantiality (emptiness) and tranquility as the basis. Always meditate on the non-substantiality and tranquility of the six sense organs as if they were constantly like [the stillness of] the middle of the night. Whatever is seen or heard during the day are phenomena external to the body, while in the body it always is empty (nonsubstantial) and pure.

Those who "maintain unified mindfulness without deviation" use the eye that is empty and pure to fix the mind on seeing one thing constantly day and night without interruption, exclusively and zealously without moving. When the mind is about to gallop off, a quick hand still gathers it in, like a cord tied to the foot of a bird still controls and holds onto it when it wants to fly. Throughout the whole day seeing has not been abandoned, [disturbance] is eliminated, and the mind itself is settled. The *Vimalakirti Sutra* says: "The mind that is collected is the place of enlightenment." This is the method of collecting the mind.

The *Lotus Sutra* says: "For innumerable kalpas of time up to now, through eliminating drowsiness and always collecting your thoughts, and by using all the various merits, you are able to attain various meditative states...." The *I chiao ching* says: "Consider the mind as the lord of the other five sense organs...fixing it in one place and there is nothing you cannot do." That's it!

The five items spoken of above are all true principles of the Great Vehicle (Mahayana Buddhism). All are based on that which is stated in the scriptures and commentaries and none are false teachings contrary to the truth. This is not the activity of illusion but is the ultimate truth.

Transcending the shravaka stage, one immediately advances quickly along the path of a bodhisattva. Those who hear [these teachings] should practice and not have any doubts. Like a man who is studying archery, first he shoots with great license, but then he hits the bull's-eye with a small leeway [of error]. First he hits something big, next he hits something small, then he hits a hair, and then he divides a hair into one hundred parts and hits one hundredth of a hair.

Next, the last arrow hits the end of the previous arrow [shot into the air]. A succession of arrows do not allow the [previous] arrows to drop [to the ground]. It is like a man who practices the Way. Moment after moment he dwells in his mind. Thought after thought continuously without even a short interval in awareness he practices correct awareness without interruption and correct awareness in the present.

As the [*Prajnaparamita*] *Sutra* says: "Use the arrow of wisdom to hit the three gates of liberation and by a regular succession of arrows do not allow them to fall to the ground."

Also, like fire produced by friction, before it is hot [one gets tired] and stops. Although one wants to start a fire, the fire is difficult to get.

It is also like the wish-granting jewel that a family had. There was nothing that they wanted that they didn't get but suddenly their heritage (that is, the gem) was lost. [Thus,] there never was an instant when their thoughts forgot about it.

It is like a poisoned arrow piercing the flesh. The shaft is out, but the barb is deep inside. In this manner you receive severe pain and there is no instant when you can forget it. Moment after moment it is on your mind. Your state [of contemplation] is to be considered just like this.

This teaching is profound and significant. I do not transmit it to unsuitable people. It is not because I am miserly about the Dharma that I do not transmit it to them, but only for fear that the above-mentioned people will not believe but will fall into the error of slandering the Dharma. One must select people in order to avoid taking a chance of speaking hastily [to the wrong persons]. Be careful! Be careful!

Although the sea of the Dharma is unlimited, in actual practice it is contained in a single word. When you get the idea, you can dispense with words, for then even one word is useless. When you understand completely in this way, you have obtained the mind of the Buddha.

When you are first beginning to practice sitting meditation, dwell in a quiet place and directly contemplate your body and mind. You should contemplate the four elements and the five skandhas, [the six sense organs,] the eye, ear, nose, tongue, body, and mind, and [the three poisons of] desire, anger, and delusion, whether they are good or evil, whether they are enemies or allies, whether they are profane or sacred, and so on through all the various items [of existence]. From the very beginning they are nonsubstantial and tranquil, neither arising nor disappearing, being equal and nondual. From the very beginning they have never existed, but ultimately are utterly tranquil. From the very beginning they are totally pure and free.

Without any interval both day and night, whether walking, staying, sitting, or lying down, always practice this contemplation. Then instantly you will understand that your own body is like the moon [reflected] in the water, or like an image in a mirror, or like the air shimmering in the hot summer, or like an echo in an empty valley. If you say these exist, everywhere you look you are not able to see them. If you say these do not exist, then you completely understand that they always are in front of your eyes. The Dharma body of all the various Buddhas is just like this. This means you should understand that your own body from an unlimited number of ages (kalpas) ago ultimately has never been born, and from the present and forever, there is absolutely nobody who dies.

If you are able to constantly practice this contemplation, then this is repentance in accord with true reality. The most extreme forms of evil karma [accumulated during] a thousand or ten thousand kalpas are utterly destroyed spontaneously. Only those with doubt who are not able to develop faith are excluded and are not able to achieve enlightenment. If one develops faith based on this practice, there is no one who cannot achieve entrance into the uncreated correct truth [of reality].

And again, if your mind attaches itself to devious phenomena [when sitting in meditation], the moment when you realize this occurring then immediately concentrate on [the fact that] the place where it arises ultimately does not come into being. When this mind does begin to attach itself, it does not come from [any place in] the ten directions and when it goes there is no place at which it arrives. Constantly watch any clinging to objectified phenomena, or any conceptualizing, or any false consciousness, or [false] thinking, or scattered ideas. If this chaotic mind does not arise, it means that you calm down those coarse mental activities. If you achieve a calm mind and do not have the mind that clings to objectified phenomena, then your mind gradually becomes tranquil and stable and step by step eliminates the various passions. Therefore, you finally do not create new [illusions], and it can be said that you are free. When you notice that your mind is becoming tied up with passions or sad and depressed and falling into a mental stupor, then you should immediately shake this off and readjust yourself. Very slowly things will become orderly. Now, having attained this, the mind spontaneously becomes calm and pure, but you must be fiercely alert as if to save your life (literally, your head). Don't be negligent. Work hard! Work hard!

When you first begin practicing sitting meditation (zazen) and viewing the mind, go off by yourself and sit in one place. First make your body erect and sit correctly. Make your clothes roomy and loosen your belt. Relax your body and loosen your limbs. Massage yourself seven or eight times. Expel completely the air in your belly. Through the natural flow you will obtain your true nature, clear and empty [of desire], quiet and pure. The body and mind being harmonized, the spirit is able to be peaceful. Then obscure and mysterious, the inner breath is clear and cool. Slowly, slowly, you collect the mind and your spiritual path becomes clear and keen.

The state of the mind is lucid and pure. As contemplation becomes increasingly lucid, and inner and outer become empty and pure, the nature of your mind becomes utterly tranquil. The manifestation of the awakened mind is utterly tranquil just like this.

Although the nature [of your awakened mind] has no form, inner constancy always exists. The mysterious spiritual power is never exhausted but always shines clearly. This is called your Buddha Nature. Those who see their Buddha Nature are forever free from [the stream of] birth and death, and are called "people who have transcended the world." The *Vimalakirti Sutra* says: "Suddenly you regain the original mind." Believe these words!

Those who awaken to their Buddha Nature are called Bodhisattvas. They are also called "people awakened to the Way," "people conscious of the truth," people who have arrived," and "people who have obtained their true nature." Therefore the scripture says that "The succession of time is endless for the spirit that becomes colored by a single [true] phrase." This is an expedient aid *(upaya)* for those who are just beginning to practice. Therefore, you should know that the cultivation of the Way involves [using] expedient aids and that this is the very place for the awakened mind [to be manifest].

Generally, in the practice of giving up attachment to your self, you should first of all calm and empty your mind in order to cause your mental phenomena to become tranquil and pure. When thinking is cast into a settled state, it is mysterious and tranquil and causes the mind not to deviate. When the nature of the mind is tranquil and settled, clinging to conditioned phenomena is immediately cut off. Being elusive and hidden, the completely pure mind is vacant, so that there is a still and peaceful calm. As the breath is exhausted in death [of this present life], you receive no further rebirths but dwell in the utterly pure body of ultimate reality *(dharmakaya)*. But if you produce a mind that loses mindfulness, rebirth is unavoidable. The method [of attaining] the mental state prior to *samadhi* that we have just described should be like this.

This is our method of cultivation. The basis of our method is no-method. The method of no-method was from the beginning called the method. This method, therefore, is not to be cultivated. Thus, the method of noncultivation is the method of true reality. This is based on the scripture which says: "Nonsubstantiality, noncultivation, nonvowing and nonform are true liberation." Therefore, based on this interpretation the real method is not produced by cultivation.

As for the method of giving up [attachment to] yourself, it means that while temporarily imagining there is a [real] body, you see the lucid state of your mental condition, and then use this spiritual lucidity to determine things.

TREATISE ON THE ESSENTIALS OF CULTIVATING THE MIND

Daman Hongren

Translated by John R. McRae

TREATISE ON THE ESSENTIALS OF CULTIVATING THE MIND, in one fascicle, [written by] Preceptor [Hong]ren of Qizhou [in order to] lead ordinary people to sagehood and to an understanding of the basic principle of emancipation.

If you do not take care of [this text], then all the [other] practitioners will be unable to see it. Please understand that in copying it, you should take care to make no mistakes or omissions, which might mislead those who follow.

The essence of cultivating the path is to discern that one's own body/mind is inherently pure, [not subject to the laws of] generation and extinction, and without discrimination. Perfect and complete in its self-nature, the pure mind is the fundamental teacher. [Meditating on it] is superior to reflecting on the Buddhas of the ten directions.

Question: How do you know that one's own mind is inherently pure?
Answer: The *Treatise on the [Sutra of the] Ten Stages* says: There is an adamantine Buddha-nature within the bodies of sentient beings. Like the sun, it is essentially bright, perfect, and complete. Although vast and limitless, it is merely covered by the layered clouds of the five skandhas. Like a lamp inside a jar, its light cannot shine. Further, to use the bright sun as a metaphor, it is as if the clouds and mists of this world were to arise together in [all] the eight directions, so that the world would become dark. How could the sun ever be extinguished?

Question: [Without the sun being extinguished,] why would there be no light?
Answer: The sun's light is not destroyed, but merely deflected by the clouds and mists. The pure mind possessed by all sentient beings is also like this, in simply being covered by the layered clouds of discriminative thinking, false thoughts, and ascriptive views. If one can just distinctly maintain [awareness of] the mind and not produce false thoughts, then the Dharma sun of nirvana will be naturally manifested. Therefore, it is known that one's own mind is inherently pure.

Question: How do you know that one's own mind is inherently not subject to the laws of generation and extinction?
Answer: The *Vimalakirti Sutra* says: "Suchness is without generation; suchness is without extinction. " The term *suchness* refers to the such-like Buddha-nature, the mind which is the source [of all dharmas] and pure in its self-nature. Suchness is fundamentally existent and is not conditionally produced. [The *Vimalakirti Sutra*] also says: "Sentient beings all [embody] suchness. The sages and wise men also [embody] suchness." "Sentient beings" means us (i.e., ordinary people), and "sages and wise men" means the Buddhas. Although the names and character-istics of [sentient beings and the Buddhas]˙ are different, the essential reality of the suchness contained within the bodies of each is identical and is not subject to the laws of generation and extinction. Hence [the sutra] says "all [embody] suchness." Therefore, it is known that one's own mind is inherently not subject to the laws of generation and extinction.

Question: Why do you call the mind the fundamental teacher?
Answer: The true mind exists of itself and does not come from outside [oneself. As teacher] it does not even require any tuition fee! Nothing in all the three periods of time is more dear [to a person] than one's mind. If you discern the suchness [inherent in the mind] and maintain awareness of it, you will reach the other shore [of nirvana]. The deluded forsake it and fall into the three lower modes of existence (i.e., animals, hungry ghosts, and residents of the hells). Therefore, it is known that the Buddhas of the three periods of time take their own true mind as teacher.

Hence the treatise says: "The existence of sentient beings is dependent on the waves of false consciousness, the essence of which is illusory. By clearly maintaining awareness of the mind, the false mind will not be activated, and you will reach the state of birthlessness (i.e., nirvana). Therefore, it is known that the mind is the fundamental teacher.

Question: Why is the mind of ordinary people superior to the mind of the Buddhas?
Answer: You cannot escape birth and death by constantly reflecting on Buddhas divorced from yourself, but you will reach the other shore of nirvana by maintaining awareness of your own fundamental mind. Therefore, [the Buddha] says in the *Diamond Sutra:* "Anyone who views me in terms of form and seeks me by sound is practicing a heretic path and is unable to see the Tathagata. Therefore, it is known that maintaining awareness of the true mind is superior to reflecting on Buddhas divorced from oneself. In addition, the word "superior" is only used as a word of encouragement in the context of religious practice. In reality, the essence of the ultimate fruit [of nirvana] is uniformly "same" and without duality.

Question: If the true essence of sentient beings and the Buddhas is the same, then why is it that the Buddhas are not subject to the laws of generation and extinction, but receive incalculable pleasures and are autonomous and unhindered [in their activities], while we sentient beings have fallen into the realm of birth and death and are subject to various kinds of suffering?
Answer: All the Buddhas of the ten directions are enlightened to the Dharma-nature and distinctly illuminate the mind that is the source [of all individual dharmas]. They do not generate false thoughts, never fail in correct mindfulness and extinguish the illusion of personal possession. Because of this, they are not subject to birth and death. Since they are not subject to birth and death, they [have achieved] the ultimate state of serene extinction (i.e., nirvana). Since they [have achieved] serene extinction, the myriad pleasures naturally accrue to them.

Sentient beings, [on the other hand,] are all deluded as to the true nature and do not discern the fundamental mind. Because they cognize the various [dharmas] falsely, they do not cultivate correct mindfulness. Since they do not have correct mindfulness, thoughts of revulsion and attraction are activated [in them]. Because of [these thoughts of] revulsion and attraction, the vessel of the mind becomes defiled (lit., "broken and leaky"). Since the [vessel of] the mind is defiled, [sentient beings] are subject to birth and death. Because of birth and death, all the [various kinds of] suffering naturally appear. The *Sutra of Mind-King [Bodhisattva]* says: "The suchlike Buddha-nature is concealed by knowledge based on the senses. [Sentient beings] are drowning in birth and death within the seas of the six consciousnesses and do not achieve emancipation."

Make effort! If you can maintain awareness of the true mind without generating false thoughts or the illusion of personal possession, then you will automatically be equal to the Buddhas.

Question: [You say that] the suchlike Dharma-nature [is embodied by both sentient beings and the Buddhas] identically and without duality. Therefore, if [one group] is deluded, both should be deluded. If [one group] is enlightened, both should be enlightened. Why are only the Buddhas enlightened, while sentient beings are deluded?
Answer: At this point we enter the inconceivable portion [of this teaching], which cannot be understood by the ordinary mind. One becomes enlightened by discerning the mind; one is deluded because of losing [awareness of the true] nature. If the conditions [necessary for you to understand this] occur, then they occur—it cannot be definitively explained. Simply rely on the ultimate truth and maintain awareness of your own true mind.

Therefore, the *Vimalakirti Sutra* says: "[Dharmas] have no self-nature and no other-nature. Dharmas were fundamentally not generated [in the first place] and are not now extinguished." Enlightenment is to transcend the two extremes and enter into nondiscriminating wisdom. If you understand this doctrine, then during all your activities you should simply maintain awareness of your fundamental pure mind. Do this constantly and fixedly, without generating false thoughts or the illusion of personal possession. Enlightenment will thus occur of itself. If you ask a lot of questions, the number of doctrinal terms will become greater and greater.

If you want to understand the essential point of Buddhism, then [be aware that] maintaining awareness of the mind is paramount. Maintaining awareness of the mind is the fundamental basis of nirvana, the essential gateway for entering the path, the basic principle of the entire Buddhist canon and the patriarch of all the Buddhas of past, present, and future.

Question: Why is maintaining awareness of the mind the fundamental basis of nirvana?
Answer: The essence of what is called nirvana is serene extinction. It is unconditioned and pleasant. When one's mind is true, false thoughts cease. When false thoughts cease, [the result is] correct mindfulness. Having correct mindfulness leads to the generation of the wisdom of serene illumination (i.e., the perfect knowledge or illumination of all things without mental discrimination), which in turn means that one achieves total comprehension of the Dharma-nature. By comprehending the Dharma-nature one achieves nirvana. Therefore, maintaining awareness of the mind is the fundamental basis of nirvana.

Question: Why is maintaining awareness of the mind the essential gateway for entering the path?
Answer: The Buddha teaches that even [actions as seemingly trivial as] raising the fingers of a single hand to draw an image of the Buddha can create merit as great as the sands of the River Ganges. However, this is just [his way of] enticing foolish sentient beings to create superior karmic conditions whereby they will see the Buddha and [become enlightened] in the future. If you wish to achieve buddhahood quickly in your own body, then do nothing except to maintain awareness of the true mind.

The Buddhas of past, present, and future are incalculable and infinite [in number], and every single one of them achieved buddhahood by maintaining awareness of the true mind. Therefore, the sutra says: "When one fixes the mind in a single location, there is nothing it cannot accomplish." Therefore, maintaining awareness of the true mind is the essential [gateway] for entering the path.

Question: Why is maintaining the true mind the basic principle of the entire Buddhist canon?
Answer: Throughout the canon, the Tathagata preaches extensively about all the types of transgression and good fortune, causes and conditions, and rewards and retributions. He also draws upon all the various things [of this world]—mountains, rivers, the earth, plants, trees, etc.—to make innumerable metaphors. He also manifests innumerable supernormal powers and various kinds of transformations. All these are just the Buddha's way of teaching foolish sentient beings. Since they have various kinds of desires and a myriad of psychological differences, the Tathagata draws them into permanent bliss (i.e., nirvana) according to their mental tendencies.

Understand clearly that the Buddha-nature embodied within sentient beings is inherently pure, like a sun underlaid by clouds. By just distinctly maintaining awareness of the true mind, the clouds of false thoughts will go away and the sun of wisdom will appear. Why make any further study of knowledge based on the senses, which [only] leads to the suffering of samsara?

All concepts, as well as the affairs of the three periods of time, [should be understood according to] the metaphor of polishing a mirror: When the dust is gone the nature naturally becomes manifest. That which is learned by the ignorant mind is completely useless. True learning is that which is learned by the inactive (or unconditioned) mind, which never ceases correct mindfulness. Although this is called "true learning," ultimately there is nothing to be learned. Why is this? Because the self and nirvana are both empty, they are neither different nor the same. Therefore, the essential principle of [the words] "nothing to be learned" is true.

One must maintain clear awareness of the true mind without generating false thoughts or the illusion of personal possession. Therefore, the *Nirvana Sutra* says: "To understand that the Buddha does not [actually] preach the Dharma is called having sufficiently listened [to the Buddha's preaching]." Therefore, maintaining awareness of the true mind is the basic principle of the entire Buddhist canon.

Question: Why is maintaining awareness of the mind the patriarch of all the Buddhas of past, present, and future?

Answer: All the Buddhas of past, present, and future are generated within [one's own] consciousness. When you do not generate false thoughts, [the Buddhas] are generated within your consciousness. When your illusions of personal possession have been extinguished, [the Buddhas] are generated within your consciousness. You will only achieve buddhahood by maintaining awareness of the true mind. Therefore, maintaining awareness of the mind is the patriarch of all the Buddhas of past, present, and future.

If one were to expand upon the four previous topics, how could one ever explain them completely? My only desire is that you discern the fundamental mind for yourselves. Therefore, I sincerely tell you: Make effort! Make effort! The thousand sutras and ten thousand treatises say nothing other than that maintaining the true mind is the essential [way to enlightenment]. Make effort! I base [my teaching] on the *Lotus Sutra,* in which [the Buddha] says: "I have presented you with a great cart and a treasury of valuables, including bright jewels and wondrous medicines. Even so, you do not take them. What extreme suffering! Alas! Alas!" If you can cease generating false thoughts and the illusion of personal possession, then all the [various types of] merit will become perfect and complete. Do not try to search outside yourself, which [only] leads to the suffering of samsara. Maintain the same state of mind in every moment of thought, in every phase of mental activity. Do not enjoy the present while planting the seeds of future suffering—[by doing so] you only deceive yourself and others and cannot escape from the realm of birth and death.

Make effort! Make effort! Although it may seem futile now, [your present efforts] constitute the causes for your future [enlightenment]. Do not let time pass in vain while only wasting energy. The sutra says: "[Foolish sentient beings] will reside forever in hell as if pleasantly relaxing in a garden. There are no modes of existence worse than their present state." We sentient beings fit this description. Having no idea how horribly terrifying [this world really] is, we never have the least intention of leaving! How awful!

If you are just beginning to practice sitting meditation, then do so according to the *Sutra of the Contemplation of Amitayus:* Sit properly with the body erect, closing the eyes and mouth. Look straight ahead with the mind, visualizing a sun at an appropriate distance away. Maintain this image continuously without stopping. Regulate your breath so that it does not sound alternately coarse and fine, as this can make one sick.

If you sit [in meditation] at night, you may experience all kinds of good and bad psychological states; enter into any of the blue, yellow, red, and white samadhis; witness your own body producing light; observe the physical characteristics of the Tathagata; or experience various [other] transformations. When you perceive [such things], concentrate the mind and do not become attached to them. They are all empty manifestations of false thinking. The sutra says: "All the countries of the ten directions are [empty,] like space." Also, "The triple realm is an empty apparition that is solely the creation of the individual mind!" Do not worry if you cannot achieve concentration and do not experience the various psychological states. Just constantly maintain clear awareness of the true mind in all your actions.

If you can stop generating false thoughts and the illusion of personal possession, [then you will realize that] all the myriad dharmas are nothing other than [manifestations of your] own mind. The Buddhas only preach extensively using numerous verbal teachings and metaphors because the mental tendencies of sentient beings differ, necessitating a variety of teachings. In actuality, the mind is the basic [subject] of the eighty-four thousand doctrines, the ranking of the three vehicles, and the definitions of the seventy-two [stages of] sages and wise men.

To be able to discern one's own inherent mind and improve [the ability to maintain awareness of it] with every moment of thought is equivalent to constantly making pious offerings to the entire Buddhist canon and to all the Buddhas in the ten directions of space, who are as numerous as the sands of the River Ganges. It is equivalent to constantly turning the wheel of the Dharma with every moment of thought.

He who comprehends the mind that is the source of all dharmas always understands everything. All his wishes are fulfilled and all his religious practices completed. He accomplishes all [that he sets out to do] and will not be reborn again [in the realm of samsara]. If you can stop generating false thoughts and the illusion of personal possession and completely discard [your preoccupation with] the body, then you will certainly achieve birthlessness (i.e., nirvana). How inconceivably [wonderful]!

Make effort! And do not be pretentious! It is difficult to get a chance to hear this essential teaching. Of those who have heard it, not more than one person in a number as great as the sands of the River Ganges is able to practice it. It would be rare for even one person in a million billion eons to practice it to perfection. Calm yourself with care, moderate any sensory activity, and attentively view the mind that is the source of all dharmas. Make it shine distinctly and purely all the time, without ever becoming blank.

Question: What is blankness of mind?
Answer: People who practice mental concentration may inhibit the true mind within themselves by being dependent on sensory perceptions, coarse states of mind, and restricted breathing. Before achieving mental purity, [such people may undertake the] constant practices of concentrating the mind and viewing the mind. Although they do so during all their activities, [such people] cannot achieve [mental] clarity and purity, nor illumine that mind which is the source of all dharmas. This is called blankness [of mind].

[People who possess such a] defiled mind cannot escape the great illness of birth and death. How much more pitiful are those who are completely ignorant of [the practice of] maintaining awareness of the mind! Such people are drowning in the seas of suffering that are concomitant with the realm of samsara—when will they ever be able to escape?

Make effort! The sutra says: If sentient beings are not completely sincere about seeking enlightenment, then not even all the Buddhas of the three periods of time will be able to do anything [for them, even if those Buddhas] are as numerous as the sands of the River Ganges. The sutra says: "Sentient beings discern the mind and cross over [to the other shore of enlightenment] by themselves. The Buddhas cannot make sentient beings cross over [to the other shore]." If the Buddhas were able to make sentient beings cross over [to the other shore of enlightenment], then why—the Buddhas of the past being as incalculable as the sands of the River Ganges—have we sentient beings not yet achieved buddhahood? We are drowning in the seas of suffering simply because we are not completely sincere about seeking enlightenment.

Make effort! One cannot know the transgressions of one's past, and repenting now is of no avail. Now, in this very lifetime, you have had an opportunity to hear [this teaching]. I have related it clearly; it would be well for you to understand what I say. Understand clearly that maintaining awareness of the mind is the highest way. You may be insincere about seeking the achievement of buddhahood and become receptive to the immeasurable pleasures and benefits [that accrue from religious training. You may] go so far as to ostentatiously follow worldly customs and crave [personal] fame and gain. [If you do so you will] eventually fall into hell and become subject to all kinds of suffering. What a plight! Make effort!

One can have success with minimal exertion by merely donning tattered robes, eating coarse food, and clearly maintaining awareness of the mind. The unenlightened people of this world do not understand this truth and undergo great anguish in their ignorance. Hoping to achieve emancipation, they cultivate a broad range of superficial types of goodness—only to fall subject to the suffering concomitant with samsara.

He who, in [mental] clarity, never ceases correct mindfulness while helping sentient beings cross over to the other shore of nirvana is a bodhisattva of great power. I tell you this explicitly: Maintaining awareness of the mind is the ultimate. If you cannot bear suffering during this single present lifetime, you will be subject to misfortune for ten thousand eons to come. I ask you: Which case applies to you?

To remain unmoved by the blowing of the eight winds [of good and ill fortune] is to have a truly special mountain of treasure. If you want to realize the fruit [of nirvana], then just respond to all the myriad different realms of your consciousness by activating transformations as numerous as the sands of the River Ganges. One's discrimination [of each instant] is so skillful it seems to flow. Applying medicine to fit the disease, one is able to stop generating false thoughts and the illusion of personal possession. He who [can do this] has transcended the world and is truly a man of great stature. Ah, the unrestricted freedom of a Tathagata—how could it ever be exhausted!

Having explained these things, I urge you in complete sincerity: Stop generating false thoughts and the illusion of personal possession!

Question: What do you mean by the "illusion of personal possession"?
Answer: When only slightly superior to someone else [in some way], one may think that this [superiority] is due to one's own achievement. To feel this way is to be sick even while in nirvana. The *Nirvana Sutra* says: "This is likened to the realm of space, which contains the myriad things. Space does not think to itself, I am doing this." This is a metaphor for the two teachings of [eradicating the] illness and practicing [the truth, i.e.,] the concept of extinguishing the illusion of personal possession and the "adamantine samadhi."

Question: Even sincere practitioners who seek a perfect and permanent nirvana [may only seek] the crude and impermanent standards of goodness and fail to take pleasure in the ultimate truth. [Such people may] try to have their minds operate according to [Buddhist] doctrines before they have manifested that which is true, permanent, wondrous, and good (i.e., the Buddha-nature). This leads to the activation of discriminative thinking, which constitutes a defiled state of mind. They may try to fix the mind in the locus of non-being. To do so is to be lodged in the darkness of ignorance and is not in accord with the [true] principle. They may grasp emptiness in an improper way, without trying to fix the mind [on a single object of contemplation] according to [Buddhist] doctrines. Although they have received a human body, theirs is the practice of animals. They lack the expedient means of meditation and wisdom and cannot clearly and brightly see the Buddha-nature. This is the predicament of religious practitioners [such as ourselves]. We beseech you to tell us the true teaching by which we can progress toward remainderless nirvana!
Answer: When you are completely in [possession of] the true mind, the achievement of your ultimate wish [is assured].

Gently quiet your mind. I will teach you [how to do this] once again: Make your body and mind pure and peaceful, without any discriminative thinking at all. Sit properly with the body erect. Regulate the breath and concentrate the mind so it is not within you, not outside of you, and not in any intermediate location. Do this carefully and naturally. View your own consciousness tranquilly and attentively, so that you can see how it is always moving, like flowing water or a glittering mirage. After you have perceived this consciousness, simply continue to view it gently and naturally, without [the consciousness assuming any fixed position] inside or outside of yourself. Do this tranquilly and attentively, until its fluctuations dissolve into peaceful stability. This flowing consciousness will disappear like a gust of wind.

When this [flowing] consciousness disappears, [all one's illusions will] disappear along with it, even the [extremely subtle] illusions of bodhisattvas of the tenth stage. When this consciousness and [false cognition of the] body have disappeared, one's mind becomes peacefully stable, simple, and pure. I cannot describe it any further. If you want to know more about it, then follow the "Chapter on the Adamantine Body" of the *Nirvana Sutra* and the "Chapter on the Vision of Aksobhya Buddha" of the *Vimalakirti Sutra*. Think about this carefully, for this is the truth.

Any person who can avoid losing [sight] of this mind during all his actions and in the face of the five desires and the eight winds [of good and ill fortune] has established his pure practice, done that which must be done, and will never again be born into the realm of birth and death. The five desires are [those that arise relative to] form, sound, smell, taste, and touch. The eight winds are success and failure; defamation and praise; honor and abuse; and suffering and pleasure.

While cultivating the Buddha-nature you must never worry about not achieving autonomous [mastery of the supernormal powers, etc.] in this lifetime. The sutra says: "When there is no buddha in the world, then bodhisattvas who have [reached the ten] stages are unable to manifest the functioning [of enlightenment(?)]." You must become emancipated from this retribution body. The abilities of sentient beings [as governed by the factors of the] past differ in ways that cannot be understood. Those of superior [ability can achieve enlightenment] in an instant, while those of inferior [ability take] an incalculable number of eons. When you have the strength, generate the good roots of enlightenment according to [your own] nature (i.e., individual identity) as a sentient being, so that you benefit yourself and others and ornament the path of buddhahood.

You must completely [master] the four dependences and penetrate the true characteristic [of all things]. If you become dependent on words you will lose the true principle. All you monks who have left home (i.e., to become monks) and practice some other form of Buddhism—this is the [true meaning of] "leaving home." "Leaving home" is to leave the home of birth and death. You will achieve success in the cultivation of the path when your [practice of] correct mindfulness is complete. To never fail in correct mindfulness—even when one's body is being torn apart or at the time of death—is to be a Buddha.

My disciples have compiled this treatise [from my oral teachings], so that [the reader] may just use his true mind to grasp the meaning of its words. It is impossible to exhaustively substantiate [every detail] with preaching such as this. If [the teachings contained herein] contradict the sagely truth, I repent and hope for the eradication [of that transgression]. If they correspond to the sagely truth, I transfer [any merit that would result from this effort to all] sentient beings. I want everyone to discern their fundamental minds and achieve buddhahood at once. Those who are listening [now] should make effort, so that you can achieve buddhahood in the future. I now vow to help my followers to cross over [to the other shore of nirvana].

Question: This treatise [teaches] from beginning to end that manifesting one's own mind represents enlightenment. [However, I] do not know whether this is a teaching of the fruit [of nirvana] or one of practice.
Answer: The basic principle of this treatise is the manifestation of the one vehicle. Its ultimate intention is to lead the unenlightened to emancipation, so that they can escape from the realm of birth and death themselves and eventually help others to cross over to the other shore of nirvana. [This treatise] only speaks of benefiting oneself and does not explain how to benefit others. It should be categorized as a teaching of practice. Anyone who practices according to this text will achieve buddhahood immediately. If I am deceiving you, I will fall into the eighteen hells in the future. I point to heaven and earth in making this vow: If [the teachings contained here] are not true, I will be eaten by tigers and wolves for lifetime after lifetime.

THE PLATFORM SUTRA

Ta-chien Hui-neng (Dajian Huineng)

Translated by Philip B. Yampolsky

THE SAMADHI OF ONENESS is straightforward mind at all times, walking, staying, sitting, and lying. The *Ching-ming ching* says: "Straightforward mind is the place of practice; straightforward mind is the Pure Land." Do not with a dishonest mind speak of the straightforwardness of the Dharma. If while speaking of the samadhi of oneness, you fail to practice straightforward mind, you will not be disciples of the Buddha. Only practicing straightforward mind, and in all things having no attachments whatsoever, is called the samadhi of oneness. The deluded man clings to the characteristics of things, adheres to the samadhi of oneness, [thinks] that straightforward mind is sitting without moving and casting aside delusions without letting things arise in the mind. This he considers to be the samadhi of oneness. This kind of practice is the same as insentiency and the cause of obstruction to the Tao (Dao). Tao must be something that circulates freely; why should he impede it? If the mind does not abide in things, the Tao circulates freely; if the mind abides in things, it becomes entangled. If sitting in meditation without moving is good, why did Vimalakirti scold Shariputra for sitting in meditation in the forest?

Good friends, some people teach men to sit viewing the mind and viewing purity, not moving and not activating the mind, and to this they devote their efforts. Deluded people do not realize that this is wrong, cling to this doctrine, and become confused. There are many such people. Those who instruct in this way are, from the outset, greatly mistaken.

Good friends, how then are meditation and wisdom alike? They are like the lamp and the light it gives forth. If there is a lamp there is light; if there is no lamp there is no light. The lamp is the substance of light; the light is the function of the lamp. Thus, although they have two names, in substance they are not two. Meditation and wisdom are also like this.

Good friends, in the Dharma there is no sudden or gradual, but among people some are keen and others dull. The deluded recommend the gradual method, the enlightened practice the sudden teaching. To understand the original mind of yourself is to see into your own original nature. Once enlightened, there is from the outset no distinction between these two methods; those who are not enlightened will for long kalpas be caught in the cycle of transmigration.

Good friends, in this teaching of mine, from ancient times up to the present, all have set up no-thought as the main doctrine, non-form as the substance, and non-abiding as the basis. Non-form is to be separated from form even when associated with form. No-thought is not to think even when involved in thought. Non-abiding is the original nature of man.

Successive thoughts do not stop; prior thoughts, present thoughts, and future thoughts follow one after the other without cessation. If one instant of thought is cut off, the Dharma body separates from the physical body, and in the midst of successive thoughts there will be no place for attachment to anything. If one instant of thought clings, then successive thoughts cling; this is known as being fettered. If in all things successive thoughts do not cling, then you are unfettered. Therefore, non-abiding is made the basis.

Good friends, being outwardly separated from all forms, this is non-form. When you are separated from form, the substance of your nature is pure. Therefore, non-form is made the substance.

To be unstained in all environments is called no-thought. If on the basis of your own thoughts you separate from environment, then, in regard to things, thoughts are not produced. If you stop thinking of the myriad things, and cast aside all thoughts, as soon as one instant of thought is cut off, you will be reborn in another realm. Students, take care! Don't rest in objective things and the subjective mind. [If you do so] it will be bad enough that you yourself are in error, yet how much worse that you encourage others in their mistakes. The deluded man, however, does not himself see and slanders the teachings of the sutras. Therefore, no-thought is established as a doctrine. Because man in his delusion has thoughts in relation to his environment, heterodox ideas stemming from these thoughts arise, and passions and false views are produced from them. Therefore this teaching has established no-thought as a doctrine.

Men of the world, separate yourself from views; do not activate thoughts. If there were no thinking, then no-thought would have no place to exist. "No" is the "no" of what? "Thought" means "thinking" of what? "No" is the separation from the dualism that produces the passions. "Thought" means thinking of the original nature of True Reality. True Reality is the substance of thoughts; thoughts are the function of True Reality. If you give rise to thoughts from your self-nature, then, although you see, hear, perceive, and know, you are not stained by the manifold environments, and are always free. The *Vimalakirti Sutra* says: "Externally, while distinguishing well all the forms of the various dharmas, internally he stands firm within the First Principle."

Good friends, in this teaching from the outset sitting in meditation does not concern the mind nor does it concern purity; we do not talk of steadfastness. If someone speaks of "viewing the mind," [then I would say] that the "mind" is of itself delusion, and as delusions are just like fantasies, there is nothing to be seen. If someone speaks of "viewing purity," [then I would say] that man's nature is of itself pure, but because of false thoughts True Reality is obscured. If you exclude delusions then the original nature reveals its purity. If you activate your mind to view purity without realizing that your own nature is originally pure, delusions of purity will be produced. Since this delusion has no place to exist, then you know that whatever you see is nothing but delusion. Purity has no form, but, nonetheless, some people try to postulate the form of purity and consider this to be Chan practice. People who hold this view obstruct their own original natures and end up being bound by purity. One who practices steadfastness does not see the faults of people everywhere. This is the steadfastness of self-nature. The deluded man, however, even if he doesn't move his own body, will talk of the good and bad of others the moment he opens his mouth, and thus behave in opposition to the Tao. Therefore, both "viewing the mind" and "viewing purity" will cause an obstruction to Tao.

Now that we know that this is so, what is it in this teaching that we call "sitting in meditation" (zazen)? In this teaching "sitting" means without any obstructions anywhere, outwardly and under all circumstances, not to activate thoughts. "Meditation" is internally to see the original nature and not become confused.

And what do we call Chan [Zen] meditation? Outwardly to exclude form is chan; inwardly to be unconfused is meditation. Even though there is form on the outside, when internally the nature is not confused, then, from the outset, you are of yourself pure and of yourself in meditation. The very contact with circumstances itself causes confusion. Separation from form on the outside is Chan; being untouched on the inside is meditation. Being Chan externally and meditation internally, it is known as Chan meditation. The *Vimalakirti Sutra* says: "At once, suddenly, you regain the original mind." The *P'u-sa-chieh* says: "From the outset your own nature is pure."

Good friends, see for yourselves the purity of your own natures, practice and accomplish for yourselves. Your own nature is the *Dharma-kaya* and self-practice is the practice of Buddha; by self-accomplishment you may achieve the Buddha Way for yourselves.

Jewel Mirror of Samadhi

Tung-shan Liang-chieh (Dongshan Liangjie)

Translated by William F. Powell

BECAUSE TS'AO-SHAN (Caoshan) was taking his leave, the Master transmitted this teaching to him. "When I was at Master Yün-yen's (Yunyan) he secretly entrusted me with the *Jewel Mirror of Samadhi*, thoroughly conveying its essence. Now I am giving it to you. It goes as follows:

The Dharma of Suchness, directly transmitted by buddhas and patriarchs,

Today is yours; preserve it carefully.

It is like a silver bowl heaped with snow and the bright moon concealing herons—

When classified they differ, but lumped together their whereabouts is known.

The Mind, not resting in words, accommodates what arises;

Tremble and it becomes a pitfall; missing, one falls into fretful hesitations.

Neither ignore nor confront what is like a great ball of flame.

Giving it literary form immediately defiles it.

Clearly illuminated just at the middle of the night, it does not appear in the morning light;

It is a standard for all beings, used to extricate them from all suffering.

Although it takes no action, it is not without words.

*Like gazing into the jewel mirror, form and reflection view
each other;*

You are not him, but he is clearly you.

Just as in the common infant, the five characteristics are complete;

No going, no coming, no arising, no abiding,

Ba-ba wa-wa, speaking without speaking;

*In the end, things are not gotten at, because the words are
still not correct.*

In the six lines of the doubled li *hexagram, Phenomena and
the Real interact;*

Piled up to become three, each transformed makes five.

Like the taste of the [five-flavored] chih *grass, like the
[five-pronged]* vajra *(diamond);*

Secretly held within the Real, rhythm and song arise together.

Penetration to the source, penetration of the byways,

Grasping the connecting link, grasping the route.

*Acting with circumspection is auspicious; there is no
contradiction.*

*Innately pure, moreover subtle, no connection with delusion
or enlightenment.*

According to time and circumstance, it quietly illuminates.

*Fine enough to penetrate where there is no space, large enough
to transcend its boundaries.*

*Being off by the fraction of a hairsbreadth, the attunement
of major and minor keys is lost.*

*Now there is sudden and gradual because principles and
approaches have been set up;*

With the distinction of principles and approaches, standards arise.

*Even if one penetrates the principle and masters the approach, the
true constant continues as a [defiled] outflow.*

*Externally calm, internally shaking, like a tethered charger
or a hiding rat;*

*The former sages, having compassion for such people, made
a gift of the Dharma.*

In their topsy-turvy state, people take black for white.

*But when their topsy-turvy thinking is destroyed, the acquiescent
mind is self-acknowledged.*

*If you wish to conform with ancient tracks, please consider
the ancients:*

*The Buddha, on the verge of accomplishing the Way, spent
ten kalpas beneath the tree of contemplation;*

*Like the tiger that leaves some remains of its prey, and like
the charger whose left hind leg has whitened.*

*For the benefit of those with inferior ability, there is a jeweled
footrest and brocade robes;*

For the benefit of those capable of wonder, a wildcat or white ox.

*Yı used his skill [as an archer], and there was the bowman who
pierced the target at one hundred paces.*

*Two arrow points meeting head-on—how is such great skill
attained?*

*The wooden man begins to sing, and the stone woman rises
to dance;*

It is not attained in thought or feeling, so why reflect upon it?

A vassal serves his lord, and a child obeys its father;

It is unfilial not to obey, improper not to serve.

*Working unobserved, functioning secretly, appearing dull,
seemingly stupid—*

*If one can simply persist in that, it is called the host's view
of the host.*

Tenshin Reb Anderson is senior dharma teacher and former abbot of San Francisco Zen Center. He began practicing at Zen Center in 1967 and received dharma transmission in 1983. He lives with his family at the Green Gulch Farm practice center near Muir Beach, California.

Geoffrey Shugen Arnold received dharma transmission from Daido Roshi in 1997. He currently works at Zen Mountain Monastery as the Director of Operations, Training Advisor, and head of the National Buddhist Prison Sangha.

Carl Bielefeldt is an Associate Professor of Religious Studies at Stanford University.

Bhikkhu Bodhi was born in 1944 in New York City and became a monk in 1972 in Sri Lanka. He served for many years as the president and editor of the Buddhist Publication Society. His published works include *The Connected Discourses of the Buddha: A New Translation of the Samyutta Nikaya; The Middle Length Discourses of the Buddha: A Translation of the Majjhima Nikaya;* and *Great Disciples of the Buddha: Their Lives, Their Works, Their Legacy.*

Bhikkhu Nanamoli. 1905–1960. Born in England, Bhikkhu Nanamoli became a monk in 1949 in Sri Lanka. He was the translator of many difficult Pali texts, including the *Visuddhimagga.*

Bodhidharma. 470–543(?) C.E. Dharma heir of Prajnadhara and the First Ancestor of Chinese Zen. Regarded as the founder of Zen, which he brought to China from the West (India). He is also well known for the nine years he spent "wall gazing" in meditation at Shaolin Temple.

Dayi Daoxin (also called Shuangfeng). 580–651 C.E. The Fourth Ancestor of Chinese Zen and dharma heir of the Third Ancestor Jianzhi Sengcan. Taught at Mount Huangmei. His posthumous name is Great Master Dayi.

Eihei Dogen. 1200–1253. Considered the most important Japanese Zen master, he brought the teachings of the Soto School from China to Japan. Dogen emphasized the practice of shikantaza as the true form of zazen, at the same time not rejecting a vital, experiential study of koans, as can be seen in his masterwork *Shobogenzo: Treasury of the True Dharma Eye.*

Zoketsu Norman Fischer was installed as abbot of San Francisco Zen Center in 1995. He began practicing at the Center in 1970. He was at Tassajara from 1976 to 1981; from 1981 to the present he has been at Green Gulch Farm. He is also a published poet.

Daman Hongren. 601–674 C.E. The Fifth Ancestor of Chinese Zen. Dharma heir of Fourth Ancestor Dayi Daoxin.

Anzan Hoshin is dharma heir of Yasuda Joshu and the founding abbot of Dainenji, a Soto Zen monastery located in Ottawa, Canada and the White Wind Zen Community, an international association of his students. He has translated over forty fascicles from Eihei Dogen's Shobogenzo, as well as other classic texts such as The Blue Cliff Record (Hekiganroku).

Dajian Huineng. 638–713 C.E. The Sixth Ancestor of Chinese Zen. Dharma heir of Fifth Ancestor Hongren. Taught at Baolin Monastery, Caoxi. His posthumous name is Great Master Dajian.

Keizan Jokin. 1268–1325. Second most important Japanese Zen master. He founded Soji-ji, one of the two main training monasteries of the Japanese Soto School. He was also the author of the *Transmission of the Light (Denkoroku)*, an account of the transmission of the dharma from Shakyamuni Buddha to Koun Ejo, two generations prior to Keizan.

Yasuda Joshu (1895–1979) was an iconoclastic Soto Zen Teacher who left Japan in the early 1930s to wander throughout Asia and Europe. He traveled to Canada in the early 1970s and established a monastery in an old barn on farmland donated by a student. With his dharma heir Anzan Hoshin, he produced many translations of dozens of classical Soto Zen and Chan texts.

Dainin Katagiri came to the United States in 1963 after training at Eiheiji Monastery, then practiced and taught at the Zenshuji Soto Zen Mission in Los Angeles and the San Francisco Zen Center, where he assisted Suzuki Roshi. In 1982 he became the first abbot of the Minnesota Zen Meditation Center in Minneapolis. He died in 1990.

Jiyu Kennett. 1924–1996. A British-born Buddhist master trained in Malaysia and Japan, Reverend Master Kennett came to the United States in 1969. A year later she founded Shasta Abbey, a Buddhist seminary and training monastery in northern California. Master Kennett served as the first Abbess of Shasta Abbey and Head of the Order of Buddhist Contemplatives until her death.

Taigen Dan Leighton is a translator, teacher, and ordained priest in Suzuki Roshi's lineage. He was the head monk at Tassajara Zen Mountain Center, and now teaches at the Graduate Theological Union in Berkeley, at the San Francisco Zen Center, and at the Green Gulch Retreat Center.

Dongshan Liangjie. 807–869 C.E. Dharma heir of Yunyan Tansheng. Author of the *Song of Bright Mirror Samadhi*. Dongshan and Caoshan are regarded as the co-founders of the Caodong (Soto) School, one of the five schools of Chinese Zen.

John Daido Loori was abbot of Zen Mountain Monastery. A successor to Hakuyu Taizan Maezumi Roshi, Daido Roshi trained in rigorous koan Zen and in the subtle teachings of Master Dogen, and is a lineage holder in the Soto and Rinzai schools of Zen. He died in 2009.

John R. McRae, Ph.D. Graduated from Yale University in 1983 and is currently Associate Professor of East Asian Buddhism at Indiana University. His research interests are the ideologies of spiritual cultivation, including the Chinese Chan/Zen and esoteric traditions, as well as multi-disciplinary work on Buddhism and the popular religion of the Bai people of Dali, Yunnan, in southwest China.

Hakuyu Taizan Maezumi. 1931–1995. He was one of the few teachers to receive *inka* (seal of approval) from both the Inzan and Takuju Rinzai lineages, as well as dharma transmission in the Soto School of Zen. He founded the Zen Center of Los Angeles and the Kuroda Institute for the Study of Buddhism and Human Values.

Shohaku Okumura was ordained as a Soto Zen priest under Uchiyama Kosho Roshi in 1970 and trained at Antaiji, Kyoto, Japan. Currently he is the Director of the Soto Zen Education Center and Head Teacher of Sanshin Zen Community.

Red Pine translated *The Collected Songs of Cold Mountain* and *The Diamond Sutra* and its commentaries. He lives and works in Taiwan.

William F. Powell is an Assistant Professor of Chinese Religion at the University of California, Santa Barbara.

Shakyamuni Buddha. 566 or 563–486 or 483 B.C.E. Siddhartha Gautama, the founder of Buddhism, who belonged to the Shakya clan of India.

Sheng-yen was born in 1930 outside Shanghai, and became a monk at the age of thirteen. He studied in Taiwan, did a six-year solitary retreat, then moved to Japan, where he received a doctorate in Buddhist literature. He received transmission in both the Soto and Rinzai Schools, and now lectures in the United States, Europe, and Asia.

Shunryu Suzuki. 1905–1971. Japanese Zen master of the Soto School. He moved to the United States in 1958, where he founded several centers: San Francisco Zen Center and Zen Mountain Center in Tassajara, California, the first Soto Zen Monastery in the West. He is the author of *Zen Mind, Beginner's Mind*.

Kazuaki Tanahashi is a Japanese writer, translator, painter, and activist whose books include *Enlightenment Unfolds, Brush Mind, Moon in a Dewdrop*, and *Penetrating Laughter*. He lives in Berkeley, California.

Bonnie Myotai Treace is Daido Roshi's senior dharma successor. She received dharma transmission in 1996. She now serves as Vice-Abbess of Zen Mountain Monastery and Spiritual Director of Zen Center of New York City (Fire Lotus Temple).

Kosho Uchiyama. 1911–1999. He received an M.A. in Western philosophy and was ordained as a Zen priest in 1937 under Kodo Sawaki Roshi. He became the abbot of Antai-ji in 1965. He was also the author of over twenty books on Zen.

Sojun Mel Weitsman studied with Suzuki Roshi in San Francisco and in 1984 received dharma transmission from Suzuki Roshi's son. In 1985 he was installed as abbot of Berkeley Zen Center, then as co-abbot of San Francisco Zen Center in 1988, where he is a senior dharma teacher.

Philip B. Yampolsky was Professor of East Asian Languages and Cultures at Columbia University until his death in 1996.

Hakuun Yasutani. 1885–1973. A successor of Sogaku Harada Roshi and one of the first authentic Japanese Zen masters who taught in the West. He became known through an introduction to Zen practice edited by one of his students, Phillip Kapleau Roshi, titled *The Three Pillars of Zen*.

Hongzhi Zhengjue. 1091–1157. Chinese Zen master. A graceful stylist, he was the first to use the phrase "silent illumination," a term that in Zen refers to "just sitting."

"To Study the Self," by Shohaku Okumura. Reprinted from *Soto Zen Journal*, September 1999, no. 5: 14–19.

"On 'Silent Illumination' by Hung-chih," from *Getting the Buddha Mind*, by Master Sheng-yen. Elmhurst, NY: Dharma Drum Publications, 1982: 131–38. Reprinted by permission of Dharma Drum Publications.

"Nanyue Polishes a Tile," by John Daido Loori. Unpublished.

"Yaoshan's Non-thinking," by John Daido Loori. Reprinted from *Mountain Record: The Zen Practitioner's Journal*, vol. XVIII, no. 4, Summer 2000: 2–10, by permission of Dharma Communications, Inc.

"Suzuki Roshi's Practice of Shikantaza," by Sojun Mel Weitsman. Reprinted from *Wind Bell*, vol. xxxii, no. 2, Fall/Winter 1998: 29–31, by permission of San Francisco Zen Center.

"Just Sitting" by Reb Tenshin Anderson. Reprinted from *Warm Smiles from Cold Mountains*. San Francisco: 1999: 47–55, by permission of San Francisco Zen Center.

"Will You Sit with Me?" by Bonnie Myotai Treace. Reprinted from *Mountain Record: The Zen Practitioner's Journal*, vol. XVIII, no. 4, Summer 2000: 11–15, by permission of Dharma Communications, Inc.

"Yangshan's Mind and Environment," by Geoffrey Shugen Arnold. Reprinted from *Mountain Record: The Zen Practitioner's Journal*, vol. XVIII, no. 4, Summer 2000: 16–21, by permission of Dharma Communications, Inc. Citation of "Case 32" is from ZMM internal translation.

"The Foundations of Mindfulness (Satipatthana Sutta)" Originally translated by Bhikkhu Nanamoli; edited and revised by Bhikkhu Bodhi. Reprinted from *The Middle Length Discourses of the Buddha (Majjhima Nikaya)*. Boston: Wisdom Publications, 1995: 145–55.

About Wisdom Publications

Wisdom Publications is the leading publisher of classic and contemporary Buddhist books and practical works on mindfulness. To learn more about us or to explore our other books, please visit our website at wisdomexperience.org or contact us at the address below.

> Wisdom Publications
> 199 Elm Street
> Somerville, MA 02144 USA

We are a 501(c)(3) organization, and donations in support of our mission are tax deductible.

Wisdom Publications is affiliated with the Foundation for the Preservation of the Mahayana Tradition (FPMT).